Exploring the Mystery of Marriage through Adam's Prime Rib

So, You Wanted To Get Married…

Sister, You've Got Mail!!!

Woman,

taken from the rib of Man's side:

The Immune System
Of Marriage

Please read as letters
from the heart of a mom to her daughter
(or from a big sister to her kid sister)
about lessons that just must be learned!

PREFACE

Woman's role in society is ever evolving at lightning speed, bringing fervent opinions on just who she is and dividing people into ugly factions. The subject of who woman is remains too controversial to handle without using an authority that is unchanging and consistent. So, however we discuss such a topic, our foundation must come from an authority beyond human experience and wisdom or social customs. The only such absolute authority is the Creator of all living things. Could anyone better explain the why questions of the differences between male and female and give the specific purposes of each? God's Word is the authority from which all answers must come.

The greatest need in a married Christian woman's life is to know the reality of Christ in her daily living, in relationship with her husband, and with her children. It is not in us as women, but only by Christ living in us, that these relationships may be satisfying to us and honoring to God. Therefore these studies first emphasize the importance of Christ, our Creator and Redeemer, as the center of life, His very life in us, and His Lordship over us in every facet of our lives - convenient, comfortable, or not.

These "lessons in letters" are intended to stir up personal searching of the Scriptures, with all references bearing up under the final authority of God's Word. Where opinions or speculations occur they are pointed out as such. It will pay dividends if you enter this study with an awesome respect for the human body that God so marvelously put together to accommodate the soul that He has placed within it. *"I will praise Thee for I am fearfully and wonderfully made: marvelous are Thy works; and that my soul knoweth right well."* Psalm 139:14.

There is no attempt to adequately cover in these following pages all God has to say about the subject of marriage and woman's high calling. Hopefully the following unusual analogy will (1) lay a strong foundation of encouragement to women who believe they were created by God for a specific purpose, joyfully accepting His role for them; (2) that they, in turn, can reach out to other women who are confused by the voices of humanism and equal rights; and (3) that together we will offer a strong defense to those who are lost in this world of perversion – each one reaching one.

To

Wayne, the Love of my life who has
crowned me his queen,
my beautiful daughters,
my precious daughters-in-law,
the many women over the past 20 years
who have attended classes on Sunday
evenings and helped me work out the
specifics of this study,
Sandra Daniels – the epitome of
submission to God & husband,
and to
the one to whom God has directed
this book for her good
and His glory
this work is prayerfully dedicated

HOW THESE LETTERS CAME TO BE

Some years ago I put together a Bible study to share at an upcoming women's retreat. I had just read an article about the immune system and it was so fascinating that I kept going back to reread it. Things began to click in my mind and before long I was running scripture references, totally absorbed in a captivating study that set me on my face in awe.

After our ladies' retreat, I expanded that 45-minute study and taught it several times as a 13-week class with the women of our church before laying it aside to work on something else. During that time my two oldest daughters sat under those lessons, learning and watching Mom work it out at home. My third and last daughter was too young at the time to benefit from the Bible study presented to adult women. Then I was too busy being school teacher and mom to her and 5 little brothers. Time waits for no one and passes too quickly. Susie was soon absorbed in college and work and then a young man and marriage... gone. But there was so much yet to tell her. Her schooling was not complete. Marriage is wonderful, frightening, maddening, glorious, and overwhelming! She had no idea what she had just gotten into. "Lord, she has so much to face and the world is pulling her in all the wrong ways," I prayed. The Lord replied, "letters!" So I began incorporating the lessons into letters, knowing she was an avid reader, hoping she would catch a glimpse of the glory God has waiting for her in the days ahead if she would only stick with the script He has written for her: letters of love, concern, anticipation and excitement; letters of wonder at the awesomeness of our Creator and this body with which He has gifted us; letters of challenge and hopefully conviction.

The letters were a joy to write but also terribly hard. I was tested in my own marriage. Could I walk what I talked? Times of testing and growth are difficult but glorious! Though we will never "attain perfection" this side of heaven, as we experience this walk of faith, we must never stop learning and growing in our relationship with Christ, learning God's will and ways. His thoughts are not our thoughts, nor are our ways His ways. Yet what joy and exhilaration to know the God of the universe wants to personally grow us up to be conformed to His ways and the image of His dear Son! Keep studying His magnificent Word and live the proof of what He teaches you, even when heartbreaks come and you don't understand the whys. He is just refining you, removing the dross, exercising your faith to make it stronger. I hope you will join me in this adventure of faith, married or not. Watch out for the adversary. He will do his best to discourage you and keep you from completing these letters. Read it to the end!

The following pages include the first and last of my letters to my own Susie – so you can get a glimpse of her introduction to education beyond the classroom and sense her questioning doubts. Just enjoy or ignore the personal references and apply them where you can. All of these letters are dedicated to you, wherever you may be in your walk with (or without) the Lord and marital status. I do hope you enjoy reading the "letters" as much as I have in writing and revising them for you, glorying anew in our God and Savior, learning new lessons and being reminded of forgotten truths. Just open up your heart and let the Son shine in.

Enjoying the adventure, C.K.

WOMAN:

THE IMMUNE SYSTEM OF MARRIAGE

TABLE OF CONTENTS

A WARNING BEFORE YOU PROCEED...

Beware of Satan's tactics to stir up a root of bitterness that defiles many (Hebrews 12:15). Every good thing attempted for the glory of God brings close surveillance of the enemy looking for an entrance to do his mischief. It is for the good health and vitality of our marriages that we must intimately know ourselves, our husbands, our Savior, and the enemy we are battling. Don't proceed any further if you are not prepared to experience some tough soul searching and trials that will purify both you and your marriage. If you are ready, take your battle stations; proceed with this study and the promises of God.

These letters make for a great around-the-table Bible study for a group of women. Read awhile and talk for a while. Look up Scriptures and discuss the comparisons made. Evaluate individually and as a group of wives. "Prove all things; hold fast that which is good." 1 Thessalonians 5:21.

This study is meant to bring to light very personal things that we often overlook and sometimes even deny exist. We all as women have a tendency to want to share personal things from our lives that bolster sympathy from others for our particular circumstances – even at the peril of lowering others' opinions of our spouses. As the Spirit reveals things to your heart about yourself, your husband, and your marriage, please share only those things that will bring both encouragement to others and glory to God.

We have a formidable foe seeking to destroy our marriages. Enough can't be said for the dangers lurking behind every page you turn as you study and attempt to put in practice what you learn. Satan will rise up to stop you, but stand your ground. Jesus has already won the war. These battles can be victorious and strengthen us as we stay within the perimeters of God's Word. Remember at all times Ephesians 5:33 as a command from God, "...and the wife see that she reverence (respect, stand in awe of) her husband." The wife represents the Church as the bride of Christ. We are compelled to bring honor to our husbands. Once you understand your purpose and critical importance in your marriage, you can then fulfill your ministry of making and keeping it healthy, functioning to the glory of God.

If your personal marriage needs no help (is that even possible in today's onslaught against it?), maybe you are being called to help your sisters fulfill their ministry. Happy reading... you will understand better what I'm trying to say after you read the letters.

Personal Note: *There is someone out there in this vast world with whom I desperately want to share these lessons of life, and I don't know who or where she is. It is for her that I write this Welcome Letter...*

WELCOME LETTER

*P*lease put your name on the line below, physically or mentally, and consider this as a personal letter to you. I regret that I do not yet know your name.

Grace to you, dear _____,

Greetings and welcome to my explorations into the mystery marriage. You may not know me nor I you, yet; but I hope to soon become a good friend, for you have become very dear to me. I've carried a burden for you and your happiness for a long time. Would you believe I have lost sleep, concerned for your well-being and not knowing how to contact you? That sounds preposterous, I know, but my heart aches to share some valuable secrets with you, mysteries I wish Mom or Grandma or someone, anyone, would have unveiled for me. Oh, the days of despair and confusion that could have been spared if only I had known!

Let me introduce myself. My name is Carolyn. I had almost completed my 14th year of life when I surrendered my heart to Jesus. What an adventure He has taken me on!

As I began my junior year in high school, my true love moved away after our summer romance. It was on our third date that he asked, "Some day, somewhere, somehow, will you marry me?" and we pledged ourselves to one another. My heart was devastated when his parents carried him a hundred miles away. Back in the 60's, long distance phone conversations were cost prohibitive, but postage was only a nickel for a letter. Every morning on the way to school I dropped off a letter to him and usually found mail from him in the box. By afternoon I had read his note and composed a response, so it was back to the P.O. again. Sometimes there were 2 or 3 letters a day – quick notes of love or thinking of you. Sometimes there were none because school and work were so demanding. Often a very long letter would arrive as details of life were added, and responses to previous letters brought new dreams, and plans, and a deeper understanding of one another. Letters have been dear to me for a very long time – thus, the format of this book before you.

At 17 I married that good-looking 18-year-old that made me feel alive and adored - until we said: "I do". We knew nothing! Of course, we were in love: he made me feel good; I made him feel good. That's not enough when you add in-laws and then pregnancy. It was disastrous, but God's grace found us and the journey with God turned our lives around. Although being "Christian" and "going to Church" was very helpful to our two-year-old marriage and set us on the right path of life, finding God's purpose was difficult because it was so contrary to culture. However, after forty years in the ministry in His Churches and 9 children later, I think I can safely say, by God's grace, this marriage worked. I can hardly wait for my 50th high school reunion to say "I told you he really loved me!" Not many teenage marriages last. Not many marriages last no matter the age. Too many don't even bother with marriage. Do you find it strange that in today's world few men and women see the need to commit themselves in matrimony while man to man and woman to woman are clamoring in the streets and demanding to be married?

Am I just old-fashioned or has something gone terribly wrong? It makes no sense. Do people today not know why they were born male or female? Or can I even say that in the 21st century? Can we freely discuss our questions? I have my opinions, as do you. You will read most of mine here but I would like to hear yours as well, as friend to friend, shaping and sharpening one another (Proverbs 27:17) to be better tools for Christ's sake. You will find my email address at the back of this book: in the P.S. of the Post Script "Do You Believe in Miracles?" Please feel free to tell me your thoughts and questions. Read the letters; jot down notes, questions, or comments; and then let me know how you are progressing in your own journey. I really would like to know. I have prayed for you for such a long time...

It would be so helpful if I already knew you and where you were in your walk through life. Maybe we can meet someday, somewhere, somehow, if not on earth, then hopefully on the other side in heaven.

As you begin reading, some of the letters are short - two or three can be read quickly. Others are lengthy and will take time to read and think about the subject matter. Look up Scriptures and write your own thoughts in response to what you're thinking and feeling.

So why have I been seeking you? Am I not content and busy enough with my own family, you ask? Sure, but when one finds answers that transform lives, there is an urgency to share it. What these letters declare is as valuable to a marriage as the cure for cancer would be to the body. As surely as my discovery of a Savior who loved me and paid the price for my sin overwhelmed my teenage soul and sent me home to share the salvation news with my little brother and my friends, so my discovery of the mystery of marriage has sent me seeking you. I hope I am not too late! If you don't need what I have found, you must know someone who does. Enjoy the read and pass it on to a friend in need.

I am old enough to be the mother of almost anyone reading this (or at least a big sister), so let me call you my daughter in spirit, or granddaughter, or little sister, and allow me to fulfill my Titus 2:3-5 commission as an aged woman.

Anticipating answers to prayer,
CK (momma #2 or grandmomma)

P.S. I was never one to fight, but it seems women want to get into battle: beginning with their own moms, then with society for the right to join the Boy Scouts, fraternities, West Point... Women are willing to fight for equal rights in the workplace, in politics, on the battlefield, and even the right to kill their own babies. It seems we are as willing to fight as men are...??? But that's good if we get in the right battle.

Satan has led women to horrific, unimaginable places in the attempt to keep her off the only battlefield where she is Commander-in-Chief with eternal consequences. You were indeed made for fighting! There is a war, and evil seeks to reign. You enlisted when you chose to love that man of yours. As your marriage vows were being made you were being given your official assignment. Have you gone to battle for him yet? Not with him – for him! This war will be vicious; beware!

There is no safe place in this world... Those who seek to kill us or reign over our lives in terror are a real part of life. There's no place to hide from that fact. Live boldly in confidence of who you are and Whose you are. If you are not yet boldly confident, or just need some reinforcement, please read on; and welcome to the Mystery...

Yours in Christ and for His glory,
C.K.

The Mystery of Marriage through Adam's Prime Rib

ONE MORE WORD BEFORE YOU BEGIN THESE LETTERS:

Within these pages, you will find a lot of loving advice from a front-liner who has gone before and engaged the enemy first hand. There is safety in counsel. I can help you see where the enemy is lurking, warn you before you are ambushed, and prepare you for battle. Hopefully, you will find consolation and remedies for wounds already inflicted in your heart and marriage.

There is also a lot of opinion written here. Please don't leave me until you hear me out. Though I don't say in so many words that a woman's place is in the home, and she shouldn't have a job to support the family (unless she is left as the sole provider), that is my opinion, based on the study of God's Word. It reflects throughout these letters. If God has gifted you to teach, or run a business or university, or design rockets, or excel in the medical profession, or ... that's between you and your Maker. However, I can state with bold confidence that if you are a wife, God will not lead you to do anything that will sacrifice your marriage or take precedence over that high and holy calling of being a full-time wife, especially if you have added motherhood to your life. As you read the letters, you will see the weighty importance of this profound vocation. You have an adversary whose sole purpose is to deceive you and antagonize you until you surrender. You have much power, precious potential, and riches beyond measure that he wants to steal and destroy. And he doesn't want you to read this any more than for me to put it down on paper. It's been a really, really long haul... The first and last letters are still basically those I wrote to my own Susanna – hope you can relate and enjoy. The rest are revised with you in mind and heart.

Please stay with me to the end!
C.K.

Welcome to the Mystery of Marriage

*M*y dear Daughter {and new Friend},

What's this? A letter from Mom?!? Why on earth is your mother writing to you with cell phones in our pockets and cars to transport us to our respective homes? Besides, letter writing went out years ago – that is so yesteryear in the computer and social media age. Well, let me try to explain...

Here you are all grown up and married. The "I do"s are now history and the day after day routine of living together has become reality. What were your plans for married life? We both know it wasn't to live like Mom and Dad did it. You have something different in mind because you are different; the world is different. Did you even have a plan when you agreed to marry this guy who spent all that money feeding and pursuing you? Did he win your heart? Was it just time to leave an old home and begin your own?

So many questions from a curious mom who watched you grow up so quickly. Were you really almost 20? I don't think I had enough time to enjoy you properly with five younger brothers demanding so much attention. Now you are gone and I see so little of you, yet I have so much more to tell you – about me, about you, about your husband and being his wife, about God... Though you know how to be pretty, sometimes it isn't going to be enough to please your husband. You do relate well with people, but sometimes you can be a real booger-bear. And, though you and your beloved love each other, there will be times that what you understand of love isn't going to be enough. You also have to admit that you actually intend to do some things differently from what Mom and Dad did. I'm not sure where my time went and how I could leave so much unsaid before we sent you off as a bride. But while I still have my breath and mind I will try to make the most of what time and experience God has allotted me. There are some things I just must tell you – gold nuggets and precious jewels I have discovered in mining my own marriage! So "letters" will be my method to begin.

Your love for travel, exploring new places, and reading should help as we begin this journey. {hoping you, my new reader, like exploring new reading material as well} I know you like a good mystery, whether you are on the edge of your seat in front of the big screen or curled up in your favorite chair under your purple afghan reading your latest novel (I'm so proud of your crocheting efforts). And when you have experienced a really good mystery with a great twist, you're quick to recommend it. It's fascinating to see how a great author makes the story unfold, interlocking the pieces together, neatly meshing the plot and the personalities of the characters. Mysteries are puzzling, intriguing, exciting, sometimes even frightening, and other times inspiring. But the best part is when the mystery is resolved, explained, disentangled. Remember being the victim of a book or movie that left you dangling? Sure you do – the time when your daddy taped that Sean Connery murder mystery off the TV and didn't get the ending. (O, the horrors of the old VCR days!) Your frustrated disappointment resulted in a fairly loud screech when the tape ran out. Did you ever thank him for renting the movie to relieve your exasperation?

Well, I want you to read with me the most intriguing, exciting, exceptional mystery ever written and discover that you are one of the main characters.

This story has it all – good and lovely; wicked and ugly; a mysterious plot; a diabolical contriving of annoyances, injuries, and evil; an incredible twist – and we are living it. Please promise to open your Bible and read with me as we focus in on the most mysterious storyline in the universe! What drama! What characters! What mystique! Recall the definition of "plot" from your high school literature class: careful foresight in planning complex sequence of events inside a story which affect other events. We will see that come to life. It is all in the marriage relationship!

[Okay! Before we can begin in earnest, you have to believe you were created! There was no big bang, and there I stood with a baby in my arms. There was a father with the gift of life in his loins that loved a woman with an egg waiting to receive that life. That life-filled egg implanted itself (through no talent of its own) in the mother's womb and began to develop into the beautiful little girl that was born on the 5th of June. I am pretty certain you must surely believe that story. Your birth was planned and prayed for, with the intentional purpose of bringing joy and delight to your parents and siblings. And you did (most of the time)! Yet I sometimes question your belief that the Father of heaven by His Holy Spirit created you with the purpose of bringing Himself joy and delight. You well remember Daddy's displeasure and Momma's grief when you were being a rebellious little toot wanting your own way. We knew your way would be painful in the long run and disruptive to the entire household. Wasn't life so much easier when you fell in step with your parents' expectations and deferred to their will? Obeying Dad's words paid great dividends! Now translate that to the Heavenly Father who has a plan for your life and infinitely knows you and all your tomorrows. The only way to fall in step with His expectations is to listen to His Word. There are great rewards when you revere and defer to His Word!!! He loves you... If we don't get that thought pattern established here and now, it will be senseless to proceed any further, except out of curiosity - although that would suffice me for now. Let's continue as you humor me...]

Mystery is used 26 times in the New Testament by Paul and the Lord Himself, and they weren't speaking of fiction! Each time it refers to something hidden or secret which is naturally unknown to human reason and is only made known by the revelation of God - a spiritual truth hidden in an external resemblance or similitude, and concealed unless some explanation be given. Just a few quick examples of these "holy" mysteries: the mystery of': the Kingdom of God, the gospel, Christ, Christ in you, the Church, the resurrection, faith, godliness, His will ... It would make an interesting study! But we are going to focus on the mystery of marriage and its similitude to the human body and to the Church. Such eternal truths are hidden in the bond of marriage! We must discover them! and quickly!

You know what is going on in society today. It's all around you with people at work and some of your friends. They like to talk about the jerk they married and how much better off they'd be without the baggage. Too many women are in that frustrated state and disappointed with what the Author of Life is doing with their particular character, through no fault of the Author. They just didn't stick with the story long enough to get to the rewarding part. Of course, to keep them from following the fascinating script so specifically laid out in the Bible, the devil always provides preoccupations or alternate sources of information, resulting in nothing but confusion, leaving them in a state of bitterness, dismay, agitation, perplexity, and turmoil. God is not the author of confusion but of peace. He desires to show Himself to us and in doing so, sets our personal relationships in beautiful harmony – free from fears, agitations, and moral conflicts.

It's my heart's desire that you know God's peace and perfect will, assured that you are fulfilling the role for which you were created. You, as a woman, have been designed according to a plan ordained by your Creator – fashioned in your own unique role. God has presented us with a tremendous allegory to live out. The character that woman is called upon to portray is so awesome, so exquisite, so honorable and excellent that any alternate role that the world could offer would be... why, in comparison, it would be like forgoing the starring role in the all-time, universal classic of all classics and settling instead for a two-bit part in some cheap, dime store novel that Satan himself contrived. Now I'm letting my age show with words like two-bit and dime store. We'll talk about those days another time. But it does make me wonder how anyone could choose the part in a trashy novel over the starring role of a masterpiece. What an opportunity!

You are the star! Join me for a few minutes as each letter comes. These are things I just must tell you. And I want more than for you to just read my letters, though I will pour out my heart to you in love and share what I have learned through personal experience. I want you to pick up the Book of books written by the God of love and accept the challenge of your life! Yes, a greater challenge than getting through chemistry, college algebra or even that of planning your wedding. God has chosen you to a great calling to demonstrate to the world God's great love and provision. Discover the fascinating character description of the role for which you, as woman, have been created. You have in your power the ability to make or break your man, providing spiritual immunity against the destructive forces of evil or forsaking, disgracing, and humiliating him unto the death of your marriage and possibly his eternal soul. Just watch the awesome mystery unfold. Will you accept the call from your Creator? Lay off the fluff stuff for a while and get serious about living!

Begin with Psalm 119:18 "**Open Thou mine eyes, that I may behold** (look intently upon with respect and pleasure) **wondrous things out of Thy law.**" Then go to Ephesians 5:22-33. Read it and think about it until I can get another letter off to you.

Love and expecting the best,
Momma (momma #2)

Hidden in Plain Sight

*G*reetings Dear Heart,

I hope my first letter to Susie let you catch a glimpse of my regret in failing to intentionally prepare her for marriage and the urgency to let her in on some important secrets for success. Even a good marriage can be better and a plain marriage can become glorious. God has all we need to know written down for us, but it is concealed to those who don't care. You surely must care or you would not be with me right now. I'm in hopes you will be curious enough to do some searching – both the Scriptures and your own heart.

Susie hadn't yet received my first letter when she showed up recommending her latest suspense mystery movie for us to watch. You surely have recommended a movie or had one recommended to you that was an absolute must watch – one of those high suspense, diabolical conspiracies with, of course, a twist in the plot. I must admit I like a good movie. I enjoy being introduced to the characters, getting to know them, seeing how they react and think. It's entertaining to follow the clues, speculate who the bad guy really is, and what the outcome will be. Movies are so much quicker than books. Yet I have **never** seen a movie do justice to a book that I've read (especially when it's Biblical). Hollywood always thinks it can improve on the script. Imagine that! So, we're off movies and back to the Book.

There is nothing like a good book, unless, of course, it is real life. We are going to read real life together!

Why do people read books? ... to learn; to escape out of mundane, routine, or even tragic lives; to vicariously visit exotic places, encounter new people in diverse circumstances, making friends and identifying foes; to discover subconscious things about themselves in a non-confrontational way... or to satisfy curiosity, to understand a skill... Do you read books or just quick snippets on the internet? Everything is so fast-paced today, like we know we are running out of time, yet there is so much to do and see and places to go – right now! I hope you are or will be one who takes time out to sit, relax, and read. Both Susie and her oldest sister are readers. The latter really enjoys Agatha Christie and Alfred Hitchcock mysteries, both books and movies.

My mom was a wonder at foretelling the outcome of a mystery show. Alfred Hitchcock once had a TV series with his unique mysteries shown every week. My mom drove the family crazy with her power to put the clues together. Ten minutes into the program she would tell us the ending and "who did it". The rest of our time watching was spent hoping she was wrong and looking for clues ourselves. I think a lot of her gift came from the volume of novels she read at night. She was really good at finding the author's clues, and played a private game between herself and the creator of her latest novel. But when it came to living, she didn't play her game so well with The Author of Life. There are obvious clues found in the Book of Life but she tried reading the Bible the same way she read through her paperback novels. The Author's clues are there, but must be sought after diligently. They are hidden in plain sight, read over, and missed by the casual or quick reader. Mom focused on preconceived notions, missed the clues, and her two marriages reflected it.

Hidden in plain sight means the physical words are written (or spoken) for anyone to read (or hear), but only those desiring spiritual truth can see (or hear) them. They are hidden to all others. Jesus repeatedly spoke, "He that hath ears to hear, let him hear." Many missed what He had to say. Open your ears and eyes and discover the clues to truth and life! Anything you can see physically will soon be gone: ruined, burned up, or dead. Only those spiritual things seen by faith will last – forever!

So much to be said about marriage and so many books written over the years! This is not one of those books. This is a book to explore and unveil the mystery of marriage by carefully following the storyline of the Author's Book, chocked full of clues for the enquiring mind and heart. God is a rewarder to those who diligently seek Him!

My kids' favorite Birthday Game was finding clues to the Present. The givers had as much fun writing the clues and hiding them as the receiver had finding them, each one leading to another, knowing he was getting closer to the Birthday Gift. Great anticipation and excitement made the search worthwhile and brought joy to both the giver and the receiver. You, too, can find great joy and excitement in following the clues hidden in plain sight. The prize is worth finding!

We will delve more deeply into finding the clues (mysteries of the Lord) in coming letters. There are two twists in our story, the first being you, which we will deal with right away. The second twist will come after you have a good grasp of our storyline, setting, characters and arch enemy. I must wait a bit for Psalm 25:14, but promises only get better when you wait on them... For now, let's get a quick synopsis of our present "mystery": Man awakes to his manhood in a world where he has the power to rule his personal domain. Yet something is lacking. Man finds Woman prepared just for him and feels immediate completion. Together they live joyfully and lovingly in the work set before them to carry out the Author's intended message. Life is good! But an enemy lurks close by, hating the joy and love the couple is experiencing together. Engulfed in contempt he has a plan to steal, kill, and destroy the happiness found and sets his plan into action toward an innocent, unsuspecting family whose only crime was following the Author's script...

Our Author has allowed each of us the liberty to make choices that will affect the outcome of our stories. If we determine to agree with the storyline He has already purposed, the flow of the story will be awesome, bountiful, complete, delightful, eternal, fascinating... If, however, we get defiant, adding our own contrary alterations, things get gruesome and very sad.

Did you read Ephesians 5? What were your thoughts? We will get more into the mystery part (v. 32) later; just stick with me. Most women can't get past the submission thing and the husband as her head in verses 22 and 23. "Not me, not to him, no way!" But there is a reason to it all - a script written to be studied and lived out for a successful life, not only here on earth but in preparation to live for all eternity. We, of course, need to start at the beginning. That would be Genesis, the text for our next letter.

Seeking answers with you,
CK (momma #2)

Let's Meet the Main Characters

*D*ear Adventuress,

Before we begin our adventure, it would be good to introduce the characters. Please keep in mind that although Adam and Eve were real people in a real conflict, they are also types for us as we read. You and your husband are the real main characters and your marriage is the setting of this story. The plot is the conflict of good and evil – your relationship with God and His subsequent blessing on your life, versus Satan's conspiracy to destroy that relationship and devastate your life, body, and soul while annihilating your marriage. That is not fiction! What we are talking about is more real than the blood running through your veins!

It's really hard to introduce the characters in our story without having some idea of the Mind behind the story, God, the Creator and Author of this great scheme of life, who brought into existence time, the universe, all living creatures, and man. ***"In the beginning, God created...And God said, 'Let us make man in Our image, after Our likeness: and let them have dominion'...So God created man in His image...And God saw everything that He had made, and, behold, it was very good."*** Genesis 1:1-31. We really don't have the time or space to go into the questions of "Why?" We just must accept that, in keeping with His character, whatever God does, He has a plan and purpose in doing it. Did He need companionship because He was lonely? Surely all of this was for more than overcoming boredom! Did He simply need someone to take care of the earth and animals He had just spoken into existence? What was His purpose in forming this first human flesh - Adam?

Why does any creator create? To communicate who he is, what is in his heart and mind. Regardless of the work – a painting, a sculpture, a symphony, a book, a poem, a house, a family – the creation reveals something within the creator that draws honor, respect, and recognition. Albeit, there are some very bad books, works of art, music, and even inventions that do not bring honor or respect but disgust because the character of that creator was vile. Our Creator is holy and awesome! The Creation we read of in Genesis draws reverence from the created beings and the hosts of Heaven to recognize God's glory. Psalm 19:1 tells us that *"the heavens declare the glory of God; and the firmament shows His handiwork."* Now let's move on to our first introduction...

Man: All of God's creation proclaims His splendor and excellence, but man is the crowning glory of His creation! Paul reminds us in 1 Corinthians 11:7 that man is in the image and glory of God. God says through Isaiah, *"I have created him for My glory, I have formed him; yea, I have made him."* Man was created to reflect the excellence and perfection of the divine nature, the splendor, the brilliance, the majesty of our Creator. Psalm 8:5 says *"For You have made man a little lower than the angels, and You have crowned him with glory and honor. You have made him to have dominion over the works of Your hands; You have put all things under his feet, all sheep and oxen – even the beasts of the field, the birds of the air, and the fish of the sea..." "The Lord God took the man and put him in the garden of Eden to tend and keep it."* Genesis 2:15.

Having dominion over all of creation is the result of bearing God's image. Man is to be God's visible representative, ruling creation as God would rule it. Man was given incredible dignity far beyond the animals (no brute cave-man here!) - endowed with reason and an intelligence that could name every living creature (which by naming them gives the implication of his lordship over them). Man had imagination, creativity (limited somewhat to materials at hand), power, responsibility, and freedom of choice. Wouldn't you like to know what our hero looked like? It is enough that you know your husband's appearance since he is the hero in your story, created in God's image. What did you say? He doesn't act the part? Have you ever thought to appreciate him as the glory of God? We most certainly would agree that man has done a poor job of reflecting the splendor of his Creator... nor has he done a top rate job in the dominion aspect. But that doesn't nullify man's purpose. It just makes it harder to recognize. (just wait until we get to woman's purpose and her malfunction!) Of course, he fails; he is only human flesh. But he is still a great revealer of the truth of God as Almighty, Creator, Covenant Maker, Father, and Refuge of Strength. I hope the Heavenly Father soon gives you the opportunity to respect your beloved as the glory of God. It is awesome and life changing!

But, 2:18 says, ***"And the Lord God said, It is not good*** *(in the best welfare)* ***that man should be alone; I will make a help meet for him."*** Introducing our second character...

Woman: After each act of creation from day one through day six, God said it was good. But after the breath of life was breathed into the nostrils of man and he became a living soul, God said it is not good, not in the best welfare, that man should be alone. After Adam had looked over his new world and named the animals, it was time to complete God's plan. So the Lord made woman. Man needed a wife. Let's first look at the word "make."

Created (Hebrew bara') and make ('asah) are alternately used in these first two chapters of Genesis. The first expresses the idea of creating something out of nothing, while the second deals more with refinement of the created object. In other words, when God said *"I will make"* it emphasized more of a labor in skillfully planning out and fashioning His creation of woman out of something (Adam's rib), still creating but forming her with an entirely different scope and purpose than of man's. ("Make" is the same word used in Genesis 6 of the ark Noah built for the salvation of his family during earth's destruction by the flood. Don't you expect Noah built it exactly according to the specific plans the Lord gave him? It meant life to his family!) God had a specific plan, a special design in mind when He made woman, because He knew exactly what man needed to be fulfilled and complete. And when He had finished His designing of man and woman, He said, ***"indeed, it was very good."***

Eve was also fashioned in the image of God – the same as man but oh, so different!: at one with him in dominion – he over the earth, she over the home; he, the source of life, she, the giver of life; he, never superior, she, never inferior but both equal in perfection as the work of God to reveal Himself and His world of order and meticulous precision.

God allowed man to name His newest work when He presented her to man. Adam responded with: "...she shall be called woman ('ishshah) because she was taken out of man (ish)." Don't you imagine his jaw dropped at what he saw! Nothing he had named that day looked anything like what stood before him now. She was the opposite of him. His eyes took in her form, similar to his own, but wow! His bearded face, broad shoulders, muscled biceps, chest, and abdomen sitting above his narrow hips and supported by legs like pillars of marble contrasted soundly to the delicacy of her smooth face, slender neck, and shoulders topping a figure of softness – rounded breasts, smaller waist, wide hips - standing on legs trembling in weakness as she stood before her Creator and her spouse. Naming her Eve (mother of all living) means he thought he fully understood her obvious purpose. But this lovely lady would be much more than a way to procreate.

Was she pretty? Would God do less than beautiful? Still, her looks were not of primary importance. She was to be his helper, one who would encourage Adam and with whom he could share his thoughts and aspirations. Her job was not cooking or mending; they were in the Garden, for goodness sake, with delectable food at their fingertips and no need of clothing! Her purpose went much deeper than of the duties any maid could fulfill. This bride was to complete her man, not compete with him, complementing his vocation in the garden, not replacing him. (Can't you hear it now – "For crying out loud, get out of the way and let me do it; you can't possibly prune these poor little trees right, Adam!") No, God gave this woman the awesome adventure of being the glory of man (1 Corinthians 11:7), reflecting his splendor and brilliance, as surely as man was to be the glory of God. Though woman was created totally opposite of man – as the weaker vessel, tender and delicate, with emotions that run on a roller coaster – she was, nonetheless, to share the powerful job description that God Himself fulfills as a help to man. (Boy, does that wipe out the foul-mouthed, muscled up, man-humiliating super heroine portrayed in today's novels and movies!) She was to be God's instrument in her husband's life that would keep him healthy and strong - like your immune system does for you. For indeed, there was an enemy lurking close by. Introducing our third character...

Satan: The chief enemy in our saga is, of course, the Accuser. His host of fallen angels accompanies him. Let me take a quote from the book The Maleficent Maestro by M. J. Ross (my eldest daughter) where she is describing this foe: "*Lucifer, the anointed cherub, the morning star. He surrounded, protected, and defended the throne of God. He was a prince among the angels, outshining them all. Perfect in wisdom and adorned with every precious stone...created a most skillful musician.*" Yet when pride was found in his heart, he exalted himself above the Creator and desired His throne. He was thus abased and cast down to await eternal destruction. Satan is set to destroy God's plan. He is the opposite of all the good that God is. He has a lie for every truth of God; he is the father of all lies.

Whatever his reason – hatred, jealousy, evil nature – Satan wants to destroy God's ultimate crowning creation, man. Though highly intelligent, ruling invisible principalities, and called the "god" of this world, Satan has no power to create. He is like a virus that cannot reproduce itself. He must do his evil deeds through those things that God created for good (the serpent in the Garden). And it gives him great delight to use those that God calls very good to do his stealing, killing and destroying. It is no problem for him to appear as an angel of light either (2 Corinthians 11:14, 15). You have to really be careful with whom you carry on a conversation! Advice too late for Eve! Doomed to eternal death, Satan hates the living and is seeking to devour and destroy his prey - mankind.

There is a fourth character, Jesus, our Redeemer, the Word of God Himself come to us in human form. As the Word of God, expressing the thoughts and plans of God, He was actually the source of our creation (Colossians 1:15, 16). Scripture tells us He is the Author and Finisher of our faith, the Beginning and the End! He not only formed man from the dust of the earth and breathed life into his lungs, He lovingly gave him a free will, reflecting the image of God Himself!

The Mystery of Marriage through Adam's Prime Rib

Yes, man has fallen short of the glory of God. Man was given the power to make choices and he chose wrongly, bringing decay to all of God's glorious work and death to all of mankind. This, however, was just the first blow of the battle.

We know the rest of the story – the Word becoming flesh – a little baby growing up as perfect man with perfect blood. Coming to fulfill what Adam failed to do, Jesus is the 2nd Adam. Our Redeemer overcame the enemy by sacrificing His own blood, blotting out the certificate of debt against man (all our sin of disobedience and failure to measure up to God's intended standard), nailing it to His cross, spoiling principalities and powers, making a spectacle of them openly, triumphing over them (Colossians 2)!!! He gives man and woman the opportunity to begin again as a new creation – man, the glory of God; woman, the glory of man, the help perfectly fit for him. We must, however, know our role or we will, in ignorant willingness, let Satan repeat his dastardly deed again and again. Of course, because of his defeat, the enemy cannot take Christ's redemptive work from those who have experienced His saving grace, but that roaring lion can sure steal our joy, destroy our witness, and kill our obedience and even our physical lives.

It is high time to set aside the fluff stuff of childhood, self-centeredness and silliness, and get serious about truth – the realities of life and death and eternity looming before us! You were not given life to fritter away your time in self-pursuits and become a spoiled brat...

You, my dear woman, have the staring role in this adventure, but you must read the script! You must learn your character and know her so well that you know what she should think and how she should react in the events of life. It is challenging. It is revolutionary. It is imperative! It is one awesome story!

There is a call on your life from God Almighty. He has chosen you! I will repeat my question from the last letter: Will you accept the call from your Creator and Author of life?

Love and on a mission,
CK (momma #2)

By the way, it's good to note: God's imagination is infinite. No two people are alike. We all have different fingerprints and DNA. So is each story unique! However different our Author has created us, we can be assured that, as the God of Truth, He will not violate His principles of truth in preparing our adventure through life. Follow that truth. He wants only the best for us, desiring our presence with Him throughout eternity.

LETTER 4

The Twist is at the Beginning

*G*ood Day my Sister,

Wish I knew what you are thinking... hoping that last letter was not too "old story" and elementary for you... just laying some groundwork for our study, hoping your curiosity will keep you reading and looking up Scriptures. Hang in here with me as we go through each letter. This should be fun reading for a good while. Some letters will seem tedious - looking up Scriptures and making lists – but we are putting down a foundation upon which to build some pretty fascinating lessons. When it gets hard I hope to have you hooked. It will get hard! It was for me as well as Susie as I wrote to her. As much as I would like to think there is an "arrival" (perfection attained), new lessons are constant in my own marriage. And the more I discover the more excited I become because the God of the universe cares enough to show me more! Please make this journey with me; let's enjoy and learn together.

Now that the characters have been briefly introduced, we want to get right into the storyline. We have an awesome creation and a beautiful garden. We have a man and a woman in all purity and innocence. We have a God who graciously walks in the garden to have sweet fellowship with His crowning creation. We have the image of God planted within man that includes free will. Man can choose to obey his Lord or not. God knows no limits in extending His love to mankind and His methods of expressing that love. But He desires that love to be reciprocated only by the choice of man, not from necessity or fear;

thus we have been given free choice. Satan enters the scene with such a case of vindictiveness toward God, embittering this once beautiful angel to the point that he has made it his sole purpose to destroy God's most excellent creation. Satan is an extremely intelligent being, more devious than the most underhanded con artist history ever produced, the most skillful in deception. He observed awhile, sizing up the man and the woman for the most vulnerable place of attack, weighing out the best mode of destruction.

Was the episode of the serpent and Eve Satan's first encounter with mankind? Could he have made previous attempts that were thwarted by man's innocence and love for his Creator? How long did Satan need to observe these two before he found the weak link? I don't think Adam and Eve sinned the first week, year, or even decade in the Garden. In fact, I personally think Eve had children before the Fall; childbirth without pain! Wow! After all, it was pain in childbirth that was part of the curse, not having children! (Where did Cain get his wife?) But the Bible only tells us what we need to know. Some things are just fun to speculate, as long as we remember it is our speculation. However, we do know to whom Satan directed his fatal attack. Woman! He could see what she was to man, his help, his aid, surrounding him with protection. Does that sound strange? Look again at Genesis 2:18. *"And God said, It is not good that man should be alone; I will make him an help meet for him."*

Okay! There is our first twist in the plot. That word help in Hebrew is "ezer" and it means aid. Webster's defines *aid* as one who promotes or helps in something done; a help or assistant that advances toward an objective. A *help* is defined as one who furnishes with relief, as from pain, disease, or distress; one who changes for the better, making more pleasant, bringing remedy, rescuing, preventing harm. "Ezer" is the same word God uses for Himself! It will assist our understanding to look at the meaning of the root word from which the noun "ezer" comes: "azar" a verb meaning to surround for protection.

Look up 1 Samuel 7. We find the Israelites gathered at Mizpah, fasting before the Lord and repenting of their sin of idolatry. When the enemy heard that God's people were gathered at one place, they took advantage of the opportunity to strike in hopes of destroying a multitude. (Isn't that just like the devil to attack while we are repenting and trying to get our lives right with God?) They cried out to the Lord and He not only heard their cry, but in verse 10 we read He thundered with a great thunder and discomfited the enemy. The word *thundered* means violently agitated, specifically to crash, and the word *great thunder* means a loud voice or sound. God made some really scary noises that day and it *discomfited* the bad guys. *Discomfited* means to harass, agitate, trouble, confound, to put to flight, to undo, to utterly destroy! In other words, God was Israel's help – their ezer. In fact, we see in verse 12 that Samuel set up a stone of remembrance and called it Ebenezer, which means stone of help. He wanted a memorial so the people would remember from whence their help came. No, God did not "do it all" for them. After the Lord put the enemy to flight, Israel pursued the enemy and drove them out of the country. We'll see the significance of that later.

The same word ezer is used again in Psalm 33:20, ***"Our soul waits for the Lord: He is our help and our shield."*** Also Psalm 70,115,121,124,146, Deuteronomy 33, Exodus 18... You get the idea? I don't think that the Lord referring to Himself as a helper was in any way demeaning to Him. Nor is woman lessened or inferior because she is designed to be man's helper. We seek God's help today just as King David did 3000 years ago when he wrote in Psalm 38:22, ***"Make haste to help me, O Lord, my salvation."*** Have you been in the enemy's sights, surrounded, outnumbered, panicked and afraid? God wants to fight for you! He creates opportunities for us to learn to trust Him as our Help!

The feminist movement and today's transgender culture have done much to change our way of viewing women. The old caricatures of a "housewife" that were presented to me as a young woman were intentionally repulsive. She was either: living in a tattered robe, uncombed hair, propped up on the couch with a bag of cookies or chips watching TV with a snotty kid or two fighting around her feet; or she was always at the neighbor's house drinking coffee, and catching up on the latest gossip. That's what the world offered me as a young bride who wanted to be a stay-at-home wife and mom - totally worthless to society with no job and totally "unproductive". I suppose my determination to falsify that world-view had a lot to do with the direction my life took.

That ugly depiction has gone by the wayside, but the replacement is even more repulsive: this modern woman who efficiently wins every battle whether in court or a war zone, while humiliating every man who crosses her path, and also whips the thug who unfortunately chose to rob this muscled-up, martial arts master with superhuman capabilities. Come off it, please. Why do men subject themselves to ridicule and debasement by accepting acting roles opposite these goddesses? No, when God planned for us to be our husbands' protection, it wasn't to be with muscles or superior intelligence. Though an expert marksman, it's not her place to protect Dad and the kids from an intruder in the home, or a trucker gone crazy with road rage, or ... let your imagination run with that and you can have a good laugh. Yet it is woman's solemn privilege and responsibility to protect her husband with all of her being. Without her, both he and their marriage are open prey to Satan's devices, just as surely as any one of us who has a malfunctioning immune system becomes susceptible to diseases plaguing the world.

Psalm 20:1, 2 is a prayer of King David's: *"**May the Lord answer you in the day of trouble** (a narrow, tight place; an opponent)...**may He send help** (aid, protection) **from the sanctuary** (a most holy consecrated, dedicated thing) **and strengthen** (support, comfort, establish, hold up, refresh, strengthen) **you from Zion** (the dwelling of God)."* What a job description for a wife! What an answer to prayer for the husband! When the adversary gets man in a tight place, may God send the aid man needs from a wife who is consecrated, dedicated to his protection, bringing him the support and comfort that will hold him up and re-fresh him, providing strength from the very throne of heaven. It kind of gives you a whole new perspective on being a wife, huh? Some might think I'm taking too much liberty with the word sanctuary by applying it to woman, but 1 Corin-thians 6:19 states that our body is the temple of the Holy Spirit who is in us, and I'd say that makes us sanctuaries. It just becomes a matter of our being conse-crated for the Lord, dedicated to doing His good pleasure.

*"**Our help is in the name of the Lord.**"* Psalm 124:8, and that is how we are to minister to our husbands - coming as help from the Lord. Jesus promised us in John 14:13-14, *"**Whatever you ask in My name, that will I do that the Fa-ther may be glorified in the Son. If you ask anything in My name, I will do it.**"* What a promise! *"**Unless the Lord had been my help, my soul would have soon settled in silence.**"* Psalm 94:17. I surely could not have been any kind of help to my children's daddy if the Lord had not been my help. Marriage is too hard! Can you tell that God led me to the Psalms during some troubling times? Want an additional little tidbit? That word "help" that the Lord uses for Himself is a feminine word! Chew on that awhile.

One last verse from Psalm is chapter 60, verse 11 - *"**Give us help** (aid, pro-tection) **from trouble** (a narrow, tight place; an opponent) **for vain** (empty,* worthless) *is the help* (rescue, deliverance) *of man."* This is a request for aid from the God who created and knows us best because the social, philosophical, psychological, emotional, financial help that humans offer will only disappoint the hope of those in need; it has no lasting value. Think of some examples of do-gooders: putting a suit on a homeless, hungry alcoholic, or giving a lazy man a new house with full cupboards. Think of your own scenarios... Certainly, it will fill his belly for a day or get him out of the weather and that is right and good to do. However, worldly help cannot address the heart issues that put him in his downward spiral. Until God gets involved, man's help is worthless. Our help is in God. And God has ordained man's help to be his wife. Wow! I am so anxious to get into the analogy part of comparing woman to our body's immune system, but I really want to try to lay this out in order because the Lord is a very precise, systematic God. Stay with me, Sis.

Unless you are a seasoned Christian, you most likely haven't had many occasions to encounter the devil in a personal way. However, speaking as both a wife and a parent, my husband and I have had some hand to hand combat with some of his demons in our marriage and over our children, especially two or three of them. Nothing would delight Satan more than to scoop you up wherever you are right now and flush your life, testimony, and future down the toilet of worldliness, apathy and humanism. He attacks so subtly at times and then with outright boldness at other times. He really wanted you during your teen years. Don't expect him to give up just because you are "grown-up" or "in" the Church. The devil is seeking someone to devour and he would just as soon it be you because chances are excellent he would get your husband in the deal. Be on guard!!

Yours in love and obligation,
Momma #2 (CK)

Bone of My Bones, Flesh of My Flesh

They Two Shall Be One Flesh.
This is a Great Mystery

ear Precious Daughter,

I wish I knew your name...whether you were a prospective bride, a new bride, or a seasoned wife. May I give you a new name for the purpose of addressing you here in these letters? I always liked the daughter's nickname in the old TV show "Father Knows Best" – Princess. She was her daddy's little princess. I suppose I just always wanted to be someone's "princess" and lo, and behold, one day a young man captured my heart and, years later, as we grew and matured together, he made me his queen. It took many years for me to learn to treat him as a king, but once I did, I became his queen and I have really enjoyed the role as we rule our little kingdom together under God's grace.

So, whether you are a princess by age or position or simply because you have not yet been crowned, until you take your position as Queen, you are a Princess-in-training. I can't even ask your approval, but I shall call you Princess for now, please and thank you (and forgive and bear with me if you have already been a biblically correct Queen for years)...

Have you already taken the plunge into marriage? If so, how long ago were those marriage vows? How are you feeling about it all right now? Love, honor, cherish, and obey (did you include that obey thing in your vows?), in sickness as in health, in poverty as in wealth … such high and lofty words joining you together as one. Are your thoughts one? Your goals? Your likes and dislikes? Does being single a little longer ever seem like a good idea? Too late after the vows and honeymoon. You and yours are forever united as one, with all your hang-ups and differences. But how does God do that, make us one flesh?

Having discussed the help aspect of Genesis 2:18, now look at the next words – *"meet for him"*. That is one Hebrew phrase and it means a part opposite, a counterpart. So we are to be that which fits exactly (the opposite of him), to complement him (not to replace him), to complete him (not to compete with him). I know women who believe God blew it when He made man so He fixed the mistakes when He made woman. And they aren't kidding! They have no concept of two totally separate beings coming together with opposite personalities and combining their own unique areas of strength to support one another's weaknesses, providing two halves that make one complete whole creature.

What does it mean to be one flesh? How can two different people become one? Well, let me ask how all the cells in our body - from the ears to the eyes, from the hair follicles to the toenails, from the heart muscles to the skin – all so completely diverse, visually and functionally, reproducing themselves uniquely, come together to operate in exquisite unity? If you ever *really* study the human body, you have to step back in wonder and amazement at the miracle of our creation! But even more amazing, how do millions of people become one with the Lord (John 17:20-23)? How can we, as Christians, who are so diverse in personalities, habits, vocations, opinions, etc., come together and function as one body? Look up some references: 1 Corinthians 12:12-27; Romans 12:4-5; Ephesians 5:30-32. More than 30 times the Church is likened to the body. Just like our body is made up of a vast variety of cells, none of which individually resembles the body, so the Church is composed of some really unusual, varied people, none of whom resemble the Lord. But God brings us all together to make one body. In like manner, a husband and wife come from totally dissimilar makeups, raised by different parents with unique pasts and personalities and various idiosyncrasies, strengths, limitations, advantages and disadvantages. You put them together and by God's miraculous grace He combines these two lives into one whole unit, not to be put asunder by man. He delights in diversity. Just look at nature! An artist wouldn't create a picture all in shades of blues. The beauty of the finished piece comes from contrasting colors that stand out from one another but blend delightfully into one picture, gaining richness and intensity from diversity.

So what do we do when this diversity causes disagreements??? Learn to accept the disagreements as opportunities: **for you**, to practice and perfect your submission skills (which Satan would pervert into feelings of being used and abused); **for him**, to hone in and mature his "having dominion" assignment from his Creator (which Satan would twist into a role of bully and dictator). We must guard against the devil's perversions and twisting of Truth, and rather be a living parable to the world - a picture of the Church submitting in love to her Lord and Savior as Christ rules her with tender, loving authority to the glory of God!

You can always count on differences in thoughts and behaviors because man and woman are just made up differently! True, we cannot put all men and all women into two categories and declare that is masculinity and this is femininity. But there are some basic nuts and bolts that make definite gears work in man, and there are some common threads woven into the hearts of women. God just made us that way. He intended for opposites to attract (and I'm not talking about Democrats and Republicans, atheist and Christian). The Bible says, "Can two walk together, except they be agreed?" Unity of heart, mind, soul, and strength is essential in the marriage covenant - knowing you have needs that only the other one can fulfill.

Bear with me as I rant for a minute. Multitudes of women reject and even recoil at the prospect of being "cared" for. I've seen my husband open the door for some of those women and you would have thought he had slapped them instead of being a gentleman. I believe my husband represents manhood well. He "needs" to minister to his wife, do for her, provide protection for her, and treat her as the weaker vessel (1 Peter 3:7) that she is: "I'll get it." "Let me do that for you." "Have a good time, but call me if you're late so I won't think you've been mugged, or worse!" There were times I wanted to scream and ask if he thought he married an invalid or the village idiot, but if I had, I would have just confirmed it. It is so foreign to this present society that people refuse to even entertain the thought that men and women have separate roles and duties. Children's TV programs began to "program" kids back in the 60-70s that women can do anything a man can do, never taking into account that they were created for different purposes.

God put into man's being a mandatory requirement for manhood: protect woman, keep her safe, out of harm's way. I allow this duty within him to be fulfilled when I accept his coddling; and I really do need him to protect me - from violation, from the pressures of life, from the vile things lurking in the darkness. He will "take the bullet" for me to keep me safe. Women on the battlefield in today's military is insanity and dangerous for our men!

A woman needs his arms wrapped around her, assuring her of his love and acceptance, caring for her as his own flesh. She needs the security of a home, no matter how modest that home might be, and she needs shelves to put her stuff! If her man can't build or buy those shelves, he should encourage her to use whatever ingenuity she has to supply them (a Proverbs 31 lady)! When discouraged or stressed out, relief is resting in his strength and approval, having her emotional, physical, and spiritual needs nurtured – being told she's beautiful when the devil is calling her ugly; being reminded how vital she is to his successes when worthlessness overwhelms her. She desperately needs what he does for her. And most importantly, he needs to know that she needs him.

God has also put within your husband an irresistible compulsion to need you! - to share the good times and the bad. When a man is discouraged or stressed out, he needs a wife to believe in him and his dreams and follow his vision. He needs her to praise and appreciate him, reaffirm her love and loyalty no matter what the circumstances; he longs for her presence. He desires her physical attention and admiration; he needs to enjoy her body, freely given in the fulfillment of their marital vows. At times of confusion or doubt or disappointments, he needs her to trust him unreservedly as he sorts through the pressures. Man was created in God's image and given dominion over His Creation, to rule it well with power and authority delegated from God Himself. It is in him to be a "fixer" of wrongs, to "rule" well. As God's delegate, a man needs his wife's respect, adoration, and deference to his will, not because he is good or even worthy, but because God made man to reveal Himself. Sometimes man's "solutions" to a problem miss the mark, but I still must trust my husband because that trust is a reflection and proof of my trust in God (Abraham & Sarah are a good example; God's grace covered Abram's fear, selfishness, and stupidity; and protected Sarah from harm - Genesis 12:10-20; I Peter 3:6).

Man is notorious for failing to ask for directions. After all, he is in charge; he's the man. Woman, on the other hand, may get from A to B faster because she's woman. Rather than challenging his wisdom or ability (giving Satan opportunity to create dissention), allow him the freedom to make that "wrong" turn. It may be God's way of keeping you off Accident Avenue, Calamity Court, or Disastrous Drive. Or the Father may be turning him aside to teach him to ask for direction! Only God has the right to humble man. Woman must never tread on that forbidden ground. She was not created to instruct man! God gives her children to teach!

God, in His infinite wisdom, knew man was not complete without woman. But is she fulfilling God's design for her? Just what is it He wants from her? Ironically, it is to be man's help, his protection! So many multitudes are missing out on the joy of knowing and being that for which they were created. I found that when I am pleasing to my husband, obedient and submissive, the Lord nods His head and tells me I am pleasing to Him, I have obeyed Him and submitted myself unto Him. The precept is contrary to our nature and upbringing. Women of the world claim that our Christian God has regulated women as doormats for husbands, or that the Bible teaches we are "second class" men. They haven't read the script! So they set out to prove their strength, intelligence, or whatever else they can do to compare themselves to men. There is no comparison!

Moving on from verse 18, look now at verses 22-23 of Genesis 2. **"And the rib, which the LORD God had taken from man, made He a woman, and brought her unto the man. And Adam said, This is now bone of my bones, and flesh of my flesh: she shall be called woman, because she was taken out of man."** Adam's prime rib! God took a bone, one of a pair, one of the lesser bones of the body yet its function indispensable in protecting the vital organs.

"Bone of my bones": the strongest, most durable part of the body, that which gives strength to stand, the part of the anatomy that produces life-giving blood. God took that bone of man and gave strength and life to this new creature. Woman is now what gives man his vitality. Leviticus 17:14 tells us the life of all flesh is the blood. The bones produce what nourishes the body – the red blood cells that carry life-giving oxygen and nutrients to its organs, cleansing and carrying off waste and impurities, and the white blood cells that fight diseases. Without it, there is no life.

"Flesh of my flesh": the soft substance which is spread over the bones containing blood vessels and nerves; implies flesh with all its qualities and appetites, its fleshly appetites and passions; also used of the nearest of kin. The wife is the closest one to man physically, emotionally, spiritually, feeling the same things as he, desiring the same, enjoying the same, sensing the same things that are a part of him. Momma may think she knows her boy inside and out, but nobody knows him as a wife knows him when they have become one flesh as God intended.

"Therefore shall a man leave his father and his mother, and shall cleave unto his wife: and they twain (2) **shall be one flesh** (move into the identity, intention, purpose of one whole person)." There just is no better description to show the bonding, the closeness, that God expects to take place in the marital union. The sexual union that consummates your vows physically is but a shadow of your spiritual union. *Cleave* means to fasten to, to cling or be adhered to like glue, conforming to the shape. My kids had no problem understanding this concept when their daddy preached this passage. They saw him do enough building over the years to know that when you glue two pieces of wood together, they adhere well. He always put nails in too, but with as much ripping apart as he has unfortunately had to do, they saw nails come right out, but the wood still adhered. It splintered the wood to separate the pieces after they were glued. Irreparable damage was done. That is just what people do to themselves when they try to separate through divorce. They will never be the same; the deep scars will always be there. In Matthew 19, Jesus reinforced the mystery of oneness, the joining of two as one, when He said, **"They are no more two, but one flesh. What therefore God has joined together** (divinely paired or yoked as a team)**, let not man put asunder** (place room between, create a chasm /marked division /separation)."

Too many people enter marriage like a partnership and retain the "mine" and "yours" mentality, never understanding the "ours" concept. In their minds, divorce is no more than dissolving a partnership that is no longer convenient. They can't understand why they are so miserable and in such pain emotionally. We've seen so much of that pain in people's lives over the years. There is nothing more grievous than their ignorance of God's design for them, or worse, their rejection of that design.

Again back to Ephesians, chapter 5 and verses 22-33, we are shown one of the great mysteries of the Bible through the analogy of marriage, giving the wife instruction in submission and commanding the husband to love his wife as Christ does the Church, **"...members of His body, of His flesh, and of His bones... This is a great mystery..."** verses 30-32. What an honor to be compared to the Church! What a mystery that stretches the imagination – the oneness of Jesus and His Church and that of man and his wife! That concept is foreign to our thinking so we just don't think about it (another well-used tool of Satan).

This has been such a feeble attempt to picture the two becoming one; stay with me and it will become obvious as we proceed through these letters. Marriage, as God ordained it, makes two become one. Volumes could be written, but we don't have time today...

Bear with me again, please, as I keep slipping into my "teacher" mode, relying heavily upon definitions from dictionaries to clarify understanding, using Webster's Dictionary as well as Greek and Hebrew dictionaries. The definitions helped me so much; I hope they do the same for you. For example... One more Psalm to dissect: 119:73 – **"Thy hands have made me** (toiled, labored to refine me) **and fashioned me** (established me, fixed me steadfastly, brought me into an existence that can not be denied, contradicted, or refused as fact)**: give me understanding** (the ability to separate mentally; superior knowledge, insight, discernment) **that I might learn** (study to learn, be taught, trained / be able to teach, give expert instruction) **Thy commandments** (precepts, laws, terms of the contract, particular conditions of God's covenant, clear-cut directives)**."** Until we as women can get out of denial, quit living in contradiction, and stop refusing to accept God's design for us, then the rest of what God has to say to us will mean absolutely nothing. God has ordained the woman to be the help behind the scene, laboring in love, as He so fashioned us, to meet the particular conditions, the clear-cut directives, that He wants us to learn and be trained in and even to teach others. It is a job that only she can do. There is no substitute for the woman; nothing else can fill the need in man's life. Your husband needs a helper, NOT because he is weak or impotent, but because every king needs a queen to rule by his side! Are you up to the challenge?

Jesus, our Master Teacher, taught by parables and analogies. He, as our Creator, has always taught us through His creation. Those analogies teach unseen spiritual principles through the visible, physical world (clues hidden in plain sight!). God's ways are eternal, unchanging and the only authority that society cannot alter with each changing of the wind. That is why it is imperative that we unlock the mysteries that God has recorded in His Book. It is only for those willing to search out those mysteries (hidden to the uncaring) that God opens the eyes so we may see and the ears so we may hear the wondrous things He has for His own. Volumes could be written and never could justice be done to the mysteries God has unveiled for those with spiritual eyes, such marvelous things that the angels long to look into (I Peter 1:12). Remember Psalm 119:18 and the word "behold" – to look intently, with respect and pleasure. That is what we want to do as we look in His Word and He teaches us through the wondrous analogy of the immune system born in the bone marrow of man to that of woman born from the rib of Adam's side.

With love and great hope,
CK (momma #2)

Wondrously Made

ear Princess,

This is going to be a short one. If you are a get-up-and-goer, I am going to suggest you sit-down-and-stay for a little while. The word meditation and its benefits will have to be scrutinized closely for you to want it to fit into your lifestyle, but that's what this letter is about. I want you to spend some time reading and rereading and maybe even rereading again Psalm 139. Yes, the whole chapter. Think on it, and think again. Give the Spirit of the Lord some time to impress your heart and mind with just how awesome your personal creation is, and, even more impressive, that Almighty God wants to have fellowship with little ol' you!

As you meditate on this Psalm it should fill you with awe, so you sin not; with courage, so you fear not; with delight, so you grieve not. It is written as though David and God were the only two in the universe. Read it as though you were writing it yourself...

Verses 1-6 speak of God's omniscience – He knows everything about me and understands – my thoughts, my husband, my circumstances! - the *downsittings* of life: times of weariness, depression, failure, shortcoming, and inconsistency, when I am far short of my best; the *uprisings:* the strongest, happiest, holiest moments, when I am at my best. God knows all. He cannot be surprised. He is intimately acquainted with my person, character, and nature! **"... such knowledge is too wonderful for me; it is high, I cannot attain it."**

Verses 7-12 tell of His omnipresence – He is everywhere at all times, never leaving me, regardless how dark it may be, always leading me. Nothing can separate me from those eyes of love and fire. This thought is terrible to those who are not at peace with Him, but delightful to those who love. No matter how dark my night of sorrow, to Him **"... the darkness and the light are both alike."**

Verses 13-16 proclaim God's omnificence – His unlimited creative abilities are marvelous and awesome... **"... fearfully** (awesomely) **and wonderfully made** (set apart differently) **...curiously wrought** (skillfully embroidered in variegated colors!)**..."** He fashioned my days like a potter molding them into a pattern before I was even born. Wow!

And last, but surely not least, verses 17-24 reveal God's omnipotence – He is almighty with unlimited power and influence to make His precious thoughts of me come true in my life so I may bring glory to Him... **"Search me, O God, and know my heart... and lead me in the way everlasting."** The more one meditates on the precious thoughts of God, the more freedom from evil one desires, whether enslavement shows itself in the ways of evil men or in the inward evil of my own heart. Cry out for God to lead in *the way,* eternal principles that guide ever upward from the lowlands of this world.

Our mind has no means to measure the Infinite. Do we then question Him? No! We adore! Try as I might, these Truths are too lofty for my mind. We cannot fully comprehend His power, His wisdom, or His holiness. We can only bow and worship, and trust the marvelous, clear-cut exhibition of His capable care!

You are so wonderfully made, unique and set apart from all others, put together by your Creator using both your father and mother and all of their strengths and weaknesses, skillfully embroidered in variegated colors just as He wanted you to be! Wow! Just for a change, instead of a novel next time you get an urge to read, pick up Fearfully & Wonderfully Made or In His Image by Dr. Paul Brand and Philip Yancey. Either one will bless your shoes off and put you on the holy ground of appreciation for the wonder of the human body with which our heavenly Father gifted us. But wait until you finish your letters from me, please.

The fact is, you were born to bring good pleasure to and fulfill the joy of the God Who created you. Give Psalm 139 a try and see if you don't have a really good time with the Lord. He wants so much to spend some special time with just you and Him. He's waiting for you...

Loving your creation,
Momma 2 (CK)

Your Worth to Your Husband

*M*y Darling Princess,

Did I catch you by surprise with that last short letter? This one will make up for it. Please allow me a little more time as I attempt to put into words the wonderful nuggets I've found. I don't want to just tell you what I have learned; I want you to read it and learn it from the Lord as well. I'm pretty sure you remember a number of things Mom was determined to ingrain in your habits and character. But, unfortunately, lessons Mom tries to pass on, you can take or leave. However, something supernatural happens when the Spirit of God Almighty teaches you. That's exciting! and glorious! and life changing!!! For whatever reason, if you have not dug in and searched the Word on your own, He will teach you - through parents and pastors, teachers and friends, if they are using His Word. He will even use circumstances because He wants to ready you for Heaven by changing you into the image of our dear Savior (Romans 8:29; 2 Corinthians 3:18-"... changed into the same image" [likeness]...).

Speaking of changing, you are no different from any other married woman throughout history; you married your husband fully intending to make some changes in him once you got him home. Honey, nobody, but nobody on earth, especially his wife, can change him. Only the Lord can do that! The more you try to reform, remake, improve, modify, alter, restructure, or transform your husband, the more obstinate and set in the mold he will become. It is in conforming to the image of Christ through the power of the Holy Spirit that a man changes for the better (2 Corinthians 3:18 again). So decide now to take your plotting hands off of God's creation, sit back in a submissive "yes, Lord," attitude, and enjoy watching the metamorphous take place. Only God can change you. Only God can change him. For the good of your marriage, you need to learn and accept that fact sooner rather than later.

And now the time has come for the analogy. The correlation between the physical and spiritual worlds is awesome! I do so hope you can see the parallel of our role as wives with that of the immune system. We will compare the two using the knowledge that science and medicine have offered and the scripture that God has provided as specific instruction to us as women. I mean not to take any glory from the working of our Lord through this analogy, but rather to help you understand the magnificent role He has shared with woman, the crown on man (Proverbs 12:4), His final work of creation. We can do nothing of ourselves. God is our help - for ourselves, for our husbands, and for our marriages. But He has chosen to use the woman to be one of the major vessels in which He brings His supernatural help.

First, let's look at a couple of verses in Proverbs and zero in on the word virtuous. *"Who can find a virtuous wife: for her worth is far above rubies."* 31:10. She is priceless, precious, and rare. Her value is far more than riches can afford. Now, look at 12:4. *"A virtuous woman* (a wife that is a force, valiant, full of virtue, a strength, an army, a great force, a mighty host) *is the crown* (a royal crown, from a root word meaning encircle, surround for protection) *of her husband, but she who causes shame* (disappointment of opinion, hope or expectation, causing public disgrace and confusion, humiliation and shattered emotions, utter defeat, disillusionment and broken spirit) *is like rottenness* (progressive decay) *in his bones* (strength, substance, life)*."* Okay, you can go back and read that again. It took me a while to look up all those words in my Hebrew dictionary so it would do you well to spend some time soaking up the implications put on you as a wife. Make it your goal to be a crown for your husband. Bring him honor and glory because God has ordained that as your job. I have seen some good men publicly disgraced, humiliated, and utterly defeated by a woman who was like something rotten growing in his bones. It's truly a sad sight! Pay particular attention to that definition of virtuous: a great force, valiant, full of virtue, strength, power, able, an army, a mighty host, wealth. That is exactly what you must be in your husband's life if you are to be a woman whose worth is far above rubies. God made you to be a valiant army, a mighty host, a great force!

Remember that last short letter on Psalm 139? Well, we are about to delve into a study on that awesomely fashioned body that God skillfully embroidered in variegated colors and set apart *differently*. The analogy is fascinating...

In spite of the world's beauty and splendor, it is teeming with vile, ugly things that threaten to annihilate us. Mankind is under constant assault from innumerable, invisible enemies. To survive this onslaught the human body depends upon an unbelievably complex, well-organized force, a valiant, internal army that battles those enemies. This mighty host kills germs that attack the body. It cleans the lungs when anything foreign intrudes so the breath of life can be maximized, providing life-giving oxygen to every cell. These bodyguards cleanse the bloodstream from noxious waste so the blood may do its vital job of distributing food to each cell and carrying away waste. They even seek out and destroy traitorous rebel cancer cells that would turn against their own body. This well-organized army is your immune system.

Battles are being fought within our bodies daily. Our enemies are unseen by the naked eye, some so small that scientists say over 200 million would fit on the period at the end of this sentence. It's a good thing that these things are microscopic or we would succumb to some very serious compulsive behaviors. If we could see our enemy we probably could not sleep. But usually we never even notice the battles being fought within us. We have a whole army of specialized cells that silently defeat these vicious, unseen enemies.

Sometimes, however, our immune system is caught in a weakened condition (no sleep, not eating right) and we easily develop colds, or worse. Sometimes these warriors of ours mistake a food, pollen, house dust, or animal dander as deadly foes, and they take up arms against these harmless invaders, making us miserable for no good reason. There are also times when our body's marvelous defenses miss consuming those mutating, self-feeding cells gone renegade in their allegiance to the body and cancer reigns. But, for every one successful strike against our health, thousands of attempts are thwarted. We rest securely, eating, working, sleeping, trusting the silent, invisible surveillance of our immune system, born in our bone marrow, to do exactly what it was created to do.

Okay, now we are going to compare that human body to your marriage – the husband representing the external protection and the wife the internal. Remember the marriage is the union of two now become one flesh. This union with your husband is also under constant assault from innumerable, invisible enemies. (Read Ephesians 6:12 to get the list of our alarming foes. Your marriage has also been given a remarkably complex, hopefully, well-organized army of defense, a "virtuous wife", to battle those spiritual invaders. You are there to keep the spiritual lungs cleaned up so the Spirit, the Breath of Life, can be maximized, providing life-giving direction to every aspect of your marriage that together, as one, you might walk in the Spirit (Galatians 5:16-17). Your ministry must cleanse the bloodstream of your marriage from contaminants of worldly traditions and philosophies (Colossians 2:8-10; 2 Timothy 2:16) that would cheat your marriage of the holiness provided by the blood of Jesus which does the job of cleansing from sin and waste, and providing nourishment that will keep the "body" pure and righteous (Colossians 2:6-7; Hebrews 13:20-21; Romans 5:9). You provide the vitality to walk in newness of life (Romans 6:4-7), freeing your marriage from destructive thoughts and actions of the "old man" (apart from Christ's salvation) that create guilt, stress, depression, etc.; (Colossians 3:5-10; 1 John 3:20). Those things are cancers that can consume your husband and destroy his growth in the Lord. You, my Dear, must be that well-organized army, a mighty host, full of virtue, his wealth, a Proverbs 12:4 woman, to keep him and your marriage healthy. Woman is the immune system of this "one flesh", born in the marrow of that rib taken from Adam's side.

Unseen battles are being fought within a marriage daily, the enemies invisible to the eye, most so subtle and cunning that we are totally unaware of the magnitude of the spiritual wickedness that surrounds us (Psalm 40:12), [don't forget to read these scriptures, Sis]. It is a very good thing that this evil is unseen, considering every incident in the Bible when men encountered a holy angel from God they were terrified and fell on their faces. What would the reaction be to an evil being? If we could see our real enemy we probably couldn't sleep at night, or we would succumb to some very serious compulsive behaviors. In spite of this, there should be little notice of the battles that a wife silently wages using a meek and quiet spirit, fear, submission, and a chaste life, the resources that God has placed at your disposal to rout out the unseen enemy (1 Peter 3:1-4). (We will delve into that "meek and quiet" spirit a little later! Don't tune me out...)

Sometimes, unfortunately, you are caught spiritually unprepared to deal with the attack and both you and your husband feel the brutal effect of the enemy. And sometimes you will mistake harmless intrusions in your marriage as if they were evils to be fought, reacting unreasonably by attacking them, creating an irritation that he can hardly bear. You become like a bad case of hay fever or poison ivy, or worse. There are times, too, that your husband will begin a self-inflicted pattern of destruction through undue stress, feelings of inadequacies, or unconfessed sin, defeating the growth of the new man and strengthening the old nature, and it may escape even the vigilant heart of his wife. But for every successful penetration of the enemy, thousands of attempts of Satan and his demons should be repelled. Your husband (and marriage) should rest securely, trusting the silent, unseen vigilantes of this immune system, you! Proverbs 31:11 "**The heart of her husband safely trusts her** (to be confident in, so as to be secure and without fear)."

Keep in mind as you read these words of "instruction" that this is your goal as a wife. There is no way you are going to accomplish all of this by next week. But if you don't know your inherent purpose, you will never achieve it. These letters can be picked up and read again, and again, and again. I found that each time I taught the class I learned something new about myself, about my husband, and about how to do my "job" as his help - meet for him. Just recognizing your role and putting a goal before you is the first step to succeeding.

This letter is going to be too long. I thought about making it 2 or 3 letters but I want you to read this ugly stuff all at once. So please take the extra time today...

Identifying the Enemy

Have you caught a glimpse yet of what I am trying to show you? I don't mean to give you a biology lesson. My Susie didn't like science in school any better than I did when I was in high school. But as an adult I have come to be totally amazed at the scientific world; we only get deeper from here. You see, those things in the unseen physical world have a counterpart in the unseen spiritual world. Just stay with me as we look at the enemy.

First, we will deal with the enemies without. Nature flourishes with protozoa, bacteria, and viruses stalking us in countless forms. And Satan has a spiritual counterpart for every one of those physical foes. These are all coming at man outside of himself to bring harm inside.

You probably won't care for this next section, but read it anyway. (oops, I sounded like Susie's mom) In a teaspoonful of pond water, there are a million or more living creatures, each so tiny that it can be seen only through a microscope. Protozoa are the simplest animals known, more than 15,000 different types, some of them parasites that plague man. Protozoa are a major threat in underdeveloped countries where water is contaminated and the people do not know the danger lurking there or do not have the knowledge or capabilities to do something about it. There are a number of deadly protozoa usually present in our bodies but they are kept in check by our marvelous immune system, unless it has been weakened, maybe by malnutrition or perhaps by another disease. Pneumocystis carinii (just read over these words; pronunciation is not essential to our purpose) causes lethal pneumonia, a leading cause of death in AIDS victims because of their immune deficiency. Another protozoan is Plasmodium falciparum, which causes malaria. A mosquito carries the germ and infects even the healthiest of humans through its bite. This germ divides and multiplies destroying red blood cells and causing repeated attacks of chills and fever and, many times, death. Millions of people in the tropics die every year of malaria, one every 30 seconds just in Africa alone, and there is little hope of a cure, only treatment of the symptoms.

Now let's take that thought into Satan's realm of influence. Protozoa compares with the ugly evil that is out there in the world preying on mankind, especially the weak. It is a major threat to lives that are un-evangelized, those who are drinking from the cesspools of this world in total ignorance of the danger lurking behind immorality, drinking and drugs, wickedness and pride. They have no knowledge or capability of how to clean up the sludge from which they are drinking. Those evils are lurking everywhere, wanting to influence Christians as well, but they should be kept in check by the grace of God working in our lives through our immune system. You must allow God to use you to be that force of a mighty host in your husband's life to keep him free from all that filth. But when you are spiritually and emotionally malnourished or Satan has already gained entrance into your marriage and has it in a sick and weakened condition, then you cannot come to the rescue. That evil will gain ground and begin to multiply and divide until it destroys the influence of the blood of Christ in your marriage, leaving it chilled, feverish, and, yes, facing possible death. Millions of Christians are caught up in despicable evils right along with the lost world. Their joy of salvation is gone, their fellowship with the God of heaven is broken, and their testimony is destroyed beyond repair. Satan has victory and he has no right to it. We have all the capabilities to overcome the protozoa of evil when we have Christ. You and your husband must keep yourselves pure and clean and use the intelligence with which God has gifted you to avoid those cesspools.

Let's look now at our second foe, bacteria, single-celled organisms that come in varying sizes and shapes. Bacteria gain access to our bodies through the air we breathe, the food and liquids we consume, or an opening in the skin. There they lie in wait for favorable conditions in which to grow. Bacteria get nourishment by digesting our blood, muscle, or other body tissues. Their waste finds its way into the bloodstream and causes diseases such as tuberculosis, pneumonia, leprosy, gonorrhea, and syphilis.

Remember your biology book calling the skin an organ? It truly is an amazing thing: huge, durable, resilient, strong, yet tender, covering the entire body in a continuous flow to protect everything within our bodies. There are still some major holes in the body (eyes, nose, mouth, private parts) that would allow access, but God has provided some preemptive guards with mucus, tears and saliva. Both tears and saliva have intrinsic antibacterial attributes, which help destroy many germs entering those breaches in our skin. There is even evidence now that the skin actually destroys certain types of germs on contact. Streptococci and staphylococci are ever present on our skin and yet with no ill effects; but they are seeking access into our bodies. When entrance is gained and resistance has been lowered the results are a sore throat or bronchial-pneumonia.

Our skin is the most effective barrier to invasion by most bacteria. Yet wounds do occur and a break in the skin allows bacteria entrance to the body. Often it is willful sexual appetites that lend an open invitation to venereal disease. When a cut, or even a bruise, has wounded the skin, staph will create boils or worse. A single bacterium can grow and divide into two new cells in less than half an hour, 16 million new bacteria in 24 hours, billions in 48 hours. Our immune system has its work cut out for it!

There is also a bacterium that grows in improperly preserved foods, producing a potent toxin that when ingested causes botulism. The bacterium can only grow in an oxygen-free atmosphere (for example, in canned or preserved food). Symptoms of poisoning, which appear 1 to 6 hours after ingestion, include disturbances in vision, speech, and swallowing. Botulism ultimately results in death from respiratory paralysis and suffocation. The mortality rate for botulism is really high. That thought kept me from attempting to can our vegetables out of the garden for years. One batch of bad tomatoes thirty years ago and I gave it up until the Y2K scare. Then we decided it was time for us to overcome and we haven't had anything go bad yet. It is a scary thought, though, that you don't even have to swallow the bacterium, just the toxin that it has produced in the food. Yet it only takes 5 minutes of boiling at 212 degrees to destroy that dreadful and fatal toxin.

It is the toxin produced by various bacteria that causes the diseases of diphtheria, tetanus, and scarlet fever, all of which are more potent than that of poisonous snake venom. That's why children are given a small dose of the possibly fatal disease through a vaccine so they can build immunity to it before it can create its toxin. (We'll pick up on vaccines later; please don't dismiss me.)

Now think spiritual again... Just as it is impossible to keep bacteria out of the body, so it is to keep free of its spiritual counterpart - temptations. (Just a note here: when asked "if the woman is the immune system, what's the man?" I Corinthians 11:3-15 is more than we have time and space to develop here, but know that it tells us the husband is the wife's "covering." Accept that and let's move forward.) Just as our physical skin is huge, durable, strong, tender, covering the entire body in a continuous flow to protect everything within, so it describes the man's responsibility of first protector in this marriage. Yet, individually, each of us must have that protection from sin and it only comes in the form of our personal relationship with God through Christ. And just as skin is the most effective barrier to bacteria, so our amazing, personal, on-going relationship with the Father is our best protection against an attack from the devil. This durably strong and tender personal fellowship with God creates a huge, continuous, protective covering over our vital spiritual organs and will destroy certain types of temptation on contact! And just as saliva fights bacteria, when we get a taste of some temptations, the spiritual digestive power that God has given us can destroy them and we can spit them out before they do their damage. And don't short-change the cleansing power of spiritual tears in defeating entrance of the enemy. Genuine godly sorrow is a powerful asset in our lives. Are you praying for your marriage's first line of defense?

Bacteria are opportunist germs because they wait for favorable conditions in which to grow. In like manner, Satan has his demons ever present, waiting for an opportunity in which to grow, regularly testing our spiritual health. When our fellowship with God is unbroken, temptations have no ill effects on us. But when that relationship is wounded or *even bruised* access is allowed. When we are walking in the flesh, we are weakened and the enemy springs into action. How do you respond to criticism? If you respond wisely, the agents back away; if you react in anger, the agents know you are weak and spring into action. How do you react when your plans are altered? If you can pleasantly defer and accept the change as an appointment from the Lord, the demons can do nothing; if you react with a stomp of defiance, well, they know they are in for a good time. Do you keep those fleshly appetites and feelings under control? Temperance keeps some pretty dreadful temptations at bay; if you allow feelings to dominate your thinking you have given entrance to an enemy as debilitating as a venereal disease with far reaching tentacles. How self-centered or selfless we are will be tested by the powers that be. Remember, the devil was confident enough in his abilities to thrust his power of temptation on our Lord, tempting Him in every area in which we are tempted. Sis, you and your husband are a piece of cake to Satan. And just like bacterium, every single temptation succumbed to multiplies within the heart in manifold proportions, diseasing the spirit, body, marriage, and testimony in a matter of moments and days. We have an awesome responsibility to watch and pray that we enter not into temptation (Matthew 26:41).

Remember, too, sometimes we don't even have to ingest the temptation, just feed on those things around us in which those temptations have produced toxic waste. Just as botulism grows in an oxygen-free atmosphere, there are those temptations that grow in an atmosphere that is void of the Spirit. There are some people that would never yield to adultery but they think nothing of feeding their minds and emotions on adulterous movies and books and even friends. The poison will soon invade their own marriage. It will affect their vision on how they view things; soon their speech will lose its clarity and become foul; they will swallow what the devil puts out, but choke on the Word of God. It then paralyzes their ability to breathe in the Breath of God and results in the death and destruction of another marriage. The mortality rate is high. It's like that botulism in those jars of tomatoes. Some things you just must throw out for your own spiritual well being. And since that botulism toxin can be destroyed in boiling temperatures, you can expect God to turn up the temperature in certain areas of your life that you have allowed that toxin to grow. Be encouraged; the heat, before ingestion, destroys the poison.

Before we leave this yucky subject, let me also put in a good word here for certain bacteria. It is important to keep in mind that just as some bacteria are beneficial to our body, absolutely necessary for digesting our food and protecting us from potential invaders, so, too, some testing is necessary that we may also digest spiritual food and discern good from evil. And for some things, it is profitable to get a small dose of those possibly fatal temptations so you can build immunity to it before it can create its toxin – like a spiritual vaccine. The Lord will allow the devil to tempt us in areas in which He is confident we will overcome. Job came out on the other side of his ordeal knowing God more fully, and an even greater servant than before, doubly blessed. Some temptations will make us even stronger and keep away fungus that wants to take up residence in our lives. I absolutely have to be critically ill to take an antibiotic because it not only kills off whatever bacteria is making me sick but also the good bacteria that keeps in check that awful yeast that can drive a woman insane.

So stay in the Word and be proficient in it when Satan comes at you with his various temptations. Trust God and use them for your good. And watch out for those opportunity-seeking intruders the next time something goes haywire or criticism comes or whatever the weak link is in your marriage. The demons are lined up just waiting for a chance to get in and do their dirty work.

This letter is too long but I just mustn't quit until we cover all three enemies. The last nasty thing I'm going to bring up is the virus. They say it is the simplest and most devious, entering the body deceptively. It contains instructions for making identical copies of itself but lacks the ability to reproduce. A virus slips into a weak cell, cancels the DNA of that cell issuing its own instructions, robs the cell of its nutrients, and establishes its own virus factory. It will eventually rupture the cell and cause thousands of viral clones to invade nearby cells. If a cell is strong, it can reject the virus; if it is weak it allows entrance. And once in the bloodstream, even after the virus has been conquered by our immune system, it can have far reaching effects. The mumps not only swells the glands in the throat, it can cause sterility when a boy grows up. The measles not only causes a rash and fever, it causes birth defects in an unborn child if an expectant mother is exposed. Chickenpox is just a harmless childhood disease unless you have experienced the revival of the virus in your mature years as agonizing shingles. I personally have been plagued over the years with my fever blisters coming up every time I lose sleep or get an infection. The sad part about that is once I have the herpes simplex-1 virus in my body it is there for life, lying dormant, waiting for an opportunity to strike again; and I have passed it on to some of my children, who have passed it on to their children. How sad.

Some viruses also have the ability to mutate, resulting in the constant epidemics of the different influenza that attack every year. Even after we have the antibodies for one type of virus present in our bloodstream, when the new virus attacks, our body must go through the process of making new antibodies to overcome this new virus.

Then we have the hepatitis virus, the rabies virus, the yellow fever virus... it's a vicious unseen world out there assailing us at every turn. But our Creator has equipped us with an immune system that is truly amazing and wonderful. Did you know that as your T cells mature in the thymus gland (we'll get into T cells before too long), each learns to recognize the antigens of the hundreds of millions of different shapes of viruses, fungal infections, bacteria, and even our own malignant cells? We have T cells trained to recognize even artificial antigens created in a laboratory! Are we wonderfully made or what?!

Now let's transpose that into the spiritual realm. False doctrine is the simplest and most devious work Satan does as he enters into a life in deception, a wolf in sheep's clothing, doctrines that sound good, even godly, but kill, steal, and destroy. False doctrines are unable to reproduce just like angels (demons) do not procreate (Matthew 22:30). They must beguile a host. If the life it tries to indoctrinate is strong, that person can reject the doctrine; if the life is weak, entrance is allowed. Once inside it robs that person of the needed nutrients to live for Christ and issues its own instructions for the production of Satan's lie, causing the victim to become a factory of deceit, affecting everything within contact. It happens in churches relentlessly, the disaster of a false teaching being propagated by some enlightened church member. It always tears up and breaks apart a fellowship of believers. Someone has been infected by the lie proposed to him, making him doubt the truth experienced; he now believes it and spreads the infection of deceit. It can happen to anyone at any time when our defenses are down. And it has such far-reaching results, sometimes lasting through a lifetime and even affecting future generations. Many times the lie brings disaster into the lives of innocent victims who are born with spiritual birth defects, handicapped in fulfilling the purpose for which they were created. Some of the deceit seems trivial, nothing to make a to-do about. "It doesn't matter what kind of music one listens to - that's just a personal preference." "Women have as much right to pastor a church as any man." Those can be dealt with and overcome. But some doctrine is overwhelming and consuming, almost always resulting in death. "It's healthy for a marriage when a spouse has a harmless affair." "It's my body and I can do what I want with it – use it as a canvas for artwork or choose if I want to be a man or woman today." There is a vicious unseen world out there assaulting marriages as well as the Church. But God has provided an amazing immune system. She must be functioning correctly, having received some massive training by her Creator on just how to react to each deception. Once an attack has been conquered there should be immunity built up to that particular temptation. Unfortunately, there are some lying doctrines that mutate just enough that we don't recognize them and must go through the cycle again.

We will deal more thoroughly with the AIDS virus later, but I must introduce it now as it is killing thousands daily. It is such a deadly virus because it attacks the immune system, specifically the helper T cell, the commander in chief of the immune system, that first part of the defense system that alerts all other defenders. The AIDS virus enters the body; then, when some other infection triggers the immune system to activate, infected T cells divide, not with their own DNA but with that of the virus. One by one, thousands of HIV clones emerge to infect nearby T cells and the body loses the very sentinels that should be alerting the rest of the army. The enemy runs free. With no protection, even the slightest infection or illness brings further destruction. Death is sure.

Satan sized up Adam and Eve looking for the most vulnerable place of attack. He could see what Eve was to her husband - his help, his surrounding protection. That was the twist in the beginning. So it was to Eve, the woman, the weaker vessel, that Satan went with his deception. We know the rest of the story. She was deceived, she doubted God, she believed the lie, and spread her infectious doctrine of liberation to her husband. Death followed. The lie goes on. Satan's deceitful entry into woman's heart and man's soul is continuing at full speed through the influence of the "virus" of the false doctrines of feminism, humanism, equal rights... The equal rights movement is not new. It began when Satan demanded to be equal with and rise above God; and continued when he tempted Eve, saying she could be as God. One of our greatest problems is the desire to "know more and be more than ...!" Why should we submit to man if indeed we are equal to, or, as some suppose, superior to man? The only place woman and man find equal ground is at the foot of the cross in need of repentance and mercy, and then, once forgiven, we stand equally as joint heirs with Christ. Who could want more!

Once the virus of deception enters a woman's heart, she loses her ability to recognize the enemy. That leaves the deception there to spread, slowly but surely throughout her being, until there is no concern for the well-being of her husband or her marriage, no alert is sent to prepare for spiritual battle, leaving him and their marriage defenseless: no prayer, no power, no protection, no love, no needs met. Woman's positive influence has been eradicated, replaced with a virus spiraling out of control. The enemy runs free with the smallest temptation or evil or false doctrine meaning certain destruction to their marriage. It means a slow, sure death to him; but first to her. That is a heartbreaking fact that gives the accuser great joy. We'll deal more with AIDS further into the study; just forewarning you.

I have so inadequately expressed the evil of the principalities, powers, rulers of this present darkness, and spiritual wickedness against which we wrestle. I do hope I have given you some food for thought. Protect your heart, my Dear. Your worth is far above rubies to your husband. Remember the words of the Lord when He said **"Watch and pray, lest you enter into temptation. The spirit indeed is willing, but the flesh is weak."** (Matthew 26:41) Until another day...

Yours in microbiology and love,
CK (mom 2)

Your Husband's Worth to You

*P*eace and Grace Princess,

Things happen in a marriage that ought not to be, but are natural and even expected in today's society. Fussing with each other in play before marriage somehow loses its playfulness after you say, "I do." Hurtful things said in "jest" can cast doubt over your love, loyalty, and acceptance of one another. Marriage is such a delicate thing and needs to be handled with gloves of abundant kindness and great patience. You are still in the process of discovering yourselves and where you fit into the scheme of life, not to mention trying to figure out each other. And that, my dear, will take a lifetime!

I hate not knowing if you've already taken the plunge into marriage or are just in the hoping and planning stage... Have you yet celebrated an anniversary or are you an old-hand at this marriage thing? Have you had time to make your mom a grandmother? Coming from a big family, my Susie swore she was never having kids. But a year into her "I do" she found herself expecting and those resolute words went right out the window! Once the initial shock and four months of nausea and weight loss were over, I saw a glimmer of excitement and anticipation in her eyes, especially when she felt the baby poke her with a foot or elbow. It is fascinating to have a life growing inside of you, watching your own body change to accommodate the life of this developing child! What precious memories stir in my heart! Any mother is excited for her daughter to experience what she has - apart from the pain of childbirth and the excruciating agony awarded for your labor of sacrifice and love as your little darling grows too big for his britches and treads all over your heart. As a mother of adult children, I can also testify of the joyous benefits and bountiful blessings that are poured out when that little bundle of joy becomes full-grown! But that is another subject to be addressed in another day. I bring up pregnancy to give you an illustration to help you grasp what I am about to say about the tremendous value one life has on another.

The illustration falls short because Mom is not dependent on the baby. However, as surely as that baby in the womb is vitally dependent on Mom for nourishment and existence physically - separate from you, yet one with you - so, too, is the relationship you and your husband must have - two separate people, yet essentially one in dependence. You should be unable to live without each other until the Lord separates you in death. Right now you are a wife; he is a husband. Whatever other roles you have in life - mommy and daddy, employee, siblings, daughter and son – the roles of husband and wife must take preeminence. We last talked about your worth to your husband, introducing you as his immune system, protecting him from all the yucky stuff out there in the world. Now we are going to look at his worth to you.

(If your husband is not a believer, keep reading... You may very well be the key to his salvation, which we will get to shortly! I am assuming you are a believer or you most likely would not have reached this letter. If not, there is no better time than right now to accept the work done on the cross by the Savior, and give yourself wholly to His plan of salvation. How well or poorly either of you has followed Jesus in the past has little bearing for this moment. If you open your heart to Him and receive His Spirit's leadership right now, you are in for a revolutionizing journey with Jesus. These Scriptures will all apply to you and your marriage if you will accept the challenge to follow Him. Wow! What a life changer!)

Let's pick up on Ephesians 5 again. **"Husbands, love your wives, even as Christ also loved the church and gave Himself for her, that He might sanctify and cleanse her with the washing of water by the Word, that He might present her to Himself a glorious church, not having spot or wrinkle or any such thing, but**

The Mystery of Marriage through Adam's Prime Rib

that she should be holy and without blemish. So husbands ought to love their wives as their own bodies; he who loves his wife loves himself. For no one ever hated his own flesh, but nourishes and cherishes it, just as the Lord does the church. For we are members of His body, of His flesh and of His bones. For this cause shall a man leave his father and mother and be joined to his wife, and the two shall become one flesh. This is a great mystery, but I speak concerning Christ and the church. Nevertheless let each one of you in particular so love his own wife as himself, and let the wife see that she reverence her husband."

Think just a minute on what Christ has done for us as His church, His Bride. He surrendered His all for us, providing us with life, setting us apart for the most holy purpose of our existence - that of service to and fellowship with Him. He loved us so unconditionally, so sacrificially, that He took every spot, wrinkle, and blemish upon Himself that He might present us as glorious.

He has called us His own body, nourishing and cherishing us as His own flesh and bones. He, of course, is the great example for husbands that they may know how to properly love their wives. As a Christian, I am totally dependent upon my Lord to cleanse me and keep me clean, to give me strength and keep me strong, to give me victory over sin and death and enable me to resist the devil. He is my life. Without Him, I have no purpose in living, no power to exist on my own, lifeless, worthless. With Him, I am His Bride, of which there is no higher calling. As I abide in Him He gives me life. He has done all that is necessary to keep me healthy that I might serve Him faithfully.

Not only does His sacrificial love profit us with eternal salvation, but Christ Himself also benefits in that He obtains the Church as a pure, chaste Bride, untainted, without moral flaw, prepared to rule and reign with Him in His Kingdom. So also, the husband who loves his wife as his own body, nourishing and cherishing her, not only blesses his wife but will himself also benefit as she adores and serves him in love and gratitude ruling in the home and marriage with him, by his side. This is all a fantastic mystery yet God has allowed us the privilege of understanding His mysteries. God has concealed secrets that He might reward and honor us when we search them out (Proverbs 25:2). Hebrews 11:6 tells us He rewards those who diligently seek Him. That is my purpose in these letters: to help you diligently seek God and His purpose for you. It is to His glory and grace that He has given us the human body to help us search out His marvelous mysteries and understand them more fully.

So, let's look at the human body. The health of a person's immune system is by nature dependent upon that person. God has created that incredible system within us to attack and destroy germs that come at us, but it can only do that when we take care of our bodies physically. Cleanliness, proper nourishment, adequate exercise and sufficient rest are all mandatory for good health. When proper care is denied in any of those areas the body suffers. Filth breeds disease. Junk food starves the body of essential minerals and nutrients. Laziness creates inactivity that devastates our physique and health. Poor sleep habits drain our vitality. Neglect in caring for the body that God has entrusted to us puts us in serious physical danger. This is an enemy of the flesh that must be fought and it comes from within us. This is no germ attacking from without but only our own negligent and ignorant behavior.

In addition to neglect, we have to deal with bad habits and a self-indulgent lifestyle. Tobacco, alcohol, drugs, promiscuous sex, excessive behavior in any area, will destroy the body's ability to keep itself healthy. There is a lot of pressure to indulge in some foul vices as the world dangles its temptations. Why the world idolizes a bronzed body is bizarre, because too much sun lowers the ability of the immune system to fight – you can just expect a cold after a bad burn. Then there are such seemingly little things in which we indulge: too many sweets; too much junk food is bad for your stomach and heart; too much pop leaches calcium from your body. Too much of anything is not good (even good food)!

We also have to deal with another enemy that keeps a constant war going on inside of our own bodies. There are mutinous cells within us that grow and try to take more territory than is rightfully theirs. We call them cancer and quake at the mere mention of it. We all have cancerous cells rebelling against the rest of the body, yet they are attacked and kept in check by our marvelous immune system. Unfortunately, our self-imposed lifestyles (smoking, drinking, poor diet, stress, too much sun, exposure to chemicals, etc.) inhibit the immune system's ability to destroy those cells, resulting in our own destruction.

Okay, now let's pick up on my baby talk at the beginning of this letter. For just a moment, picture yourself as that little baby inside a mother's womb, totally helpless and dependent, yet capable of bringing so much delight, pleasure and satisfaction, but only if "mom" maintains your health and growth by maintaining her own health. Your life and potential are totally in her hands! Now let's look at your "oneness" in marriage spiritually, your husband as the body and you as the immune system. Though your job is to keep him healthy, your ability is vitally dependent upon your husband. God has created this "virtuous" wife to be a priceless help for her mate, but she can only do that efficiently when he takes proper care of himself spiritually. Cleanliness, proper nourishment, adequate exercise and sufficient rest are all mandatory for good spiritual health. When proper care is denied in any of these areas he suffers and so do you, the immune system.

Remember the old adage "cleanliness is next to godliness"? Though the phrase is not scripture, God does want His children clean! Uncleanness breeds spiritual disease. He must maintain a clean relationship with the Lord and allow Jesus to wash his feet just as the Lord washed Peter's. We get dirty in this world even after we are washed in the blood for salvation; we must be washed in the Word, too.

Junk food that he feeds into his mind and spirit will starve him of vital teachings that enable him to grow in the Lord. He must have proper nourishment coming from the Word of God, from preaching and teaching and his own personal Bible study. Most of that junk food comes into our lives because we won't take the time for a "proper" meal.

Spiritual laziness is one reason for poor spiritual nutrition, but it also engenders inactivity in his service to God that devastates his spiritual muscles. To work the works of God he needs only to read John 6:28-29. Jesus told the Jews that they must believe in Him to do the works of God. To believe in Jesus enough to adjust his life to live by the words of the Savior is the hardest labor he can do, but each exercise of believing builds his spiritual muscle and strengthens his ability to endure. (No pain, no gain!)

The rest that his spirit requires comes from depending on the faithfulness of God. A lack of active faith robs him of that spiritual rest, without which he will be drained of the vitality needed to continue in the Christian life. He will develop an attitude of unbelief, lacking confidence in the power of Christ, and become unbelievably irritable and just plain run down. Neglect in caring for the new man that God has entrusted to him puts both of you in serious spiritual danger. Again, there is no satanic force attacking from without, only negligent behavior from within.

In addition to neglect, he has to deal with bad habits and a self-indulgent lifestyle. Even though your husband may not personally indulge in tobacco, alcohol, drugs, promiscuous sex, or excessive behavior in the sense of the world, there are still bad habits he can allow to creep into his life that will destroy his ability to keep him and you spiritually healthy. You may find yourself harping a hundred times over about too much of something that he is doing. He may expose himself to too much of this world's shine and glitter, creating much the same effects as too many ultraviolet rays from the sun. Expect a serious temptation or even acceptance of one of Satan's lies after a bad burn from the world. Too much of the sweet, fleeting pleasures of this world will rot his desire to live for Christ. In fact, dependence on anything other than the Spirit of God will take his heart and soul and make him out to be a fool just as surely as liquor exposes a drunk to be a fool. Too much of the bubbly, seemingly harmless, fizzies that the world offers for cheap entertainment or amusement will leach your spirit of the good doctrine that has enabled you to stand strong in the Lord. Amusement has an interesting connotation: "muse" means to meditate, be immersed in focused thought, which is very good for us as Christians in a hostile world; "a" means not. So amusement means an activity in which there is no focused thought. Now that is where the devil would like to lure us and keep us locked up. The world says indulge now because there is no tomorrow. But we know there is an eternity of tomorrows. Too much of anything but Jesus is not good, and since you can't get too much Jesus, just indulge in Him. The dividends are incredible!

You also have to deal with the constant war between the spirit and the flesh going on within. Look up Romans 7 and pick up at verse 14 and go through 24. Now, if you just read that in the King James Version you are probably scratching your head and wondering just exactly what it said. Put real simply, Paul was telling us that when he wanted to do right he found he could not do it, and the very thing he hated, he would do. There is no good thing in our flesh. When we find something good to do, we find we have no power to do it. In our spirits we delight in the law of God, but **"I see another law in my members, warring against the law of my mind, and bringing me into captivity to the law of sin which is in my members. O wretched man that I am! Who shall deliver me from the body of this death?"** (verses 23 & 24). That sounds like a very frustrated man, does it not? He is in the middle of a great war going on inside of him. There is within us the old nature that does not want to die but wants to reclaim ground that does not belong to it. Go through and count the "I"s and "me"s in those 11 verses of chapter 7. I came up with 36! There seems to be a "me" problem in this section of the Scriptures, but we see it resolved in chapter 8. Count the word Spirit in the first 17 verses. I found 15. Now add to that the words God, Christ Jesus, and the Son. When we understand the problem lies within the strength of the flesh and the solution is in the strength of the Spirit, it ends a lot of frustration and stress. Those mutinous cells that grow within our old nature are cancerous. If not kept in constant check by a vigilant immune system they can grow out of control and consume a marriage. Unfortunately, the bad habits, wrong attitudes, poor spiritual diet, a stubborn and rebellious heart, indulgences of the "too much"es, and over exposure to the ways of the world self-impose a lifestyle much like smoking, drinking, poor diet, stress, too much sun, exposure to chemicals, etc. Those things inhibit the wife's ability to combat old nature cells, leaving their marriage unable to deny the flesh, resulting in the destruction of his testimony, his walk with God, his spiritual growth, even the life of his new nature. That reminds me of the old saying, "I am my own worst enemy"? Another battle needlessly lost. (Lest you become one sided in your thoughts, beware of your own mutinous attitudes... "it's that man I married; he doesn't appreciate me; I deserve better; he's a bully; I can run away to...")

There is so much responsibility resting on the man. He must conform his life to that of the Savior's example in Ephesians 5, nourishing and cherishing, that he might protect you and enable you to rule and reign with him! Romans 12:1-2 is appropriate here. **"I beseech you therefore, brethren, by the mercies of God, that you present your bodies a living sacrifice, holy, acceptable to God, which is your reasonable service. And do not be conformed to this world, but be transformed by the renewing of your mind, that you may prove what is that good and acceptable and perfect will of God."** Of course, we know God's will is that every husband be saved, a man of God, growing in the knowledge of our Lord and Savior, strengthened with all might, being a good provider and husband and daddy, living with his wife in understanding, giving her honor that his prayers be not hindered. We know His will is that your marriage succeed – more than succeed, excel, because it is an example to the world of Jesus and His Bride. He carries a heavy load if he is to keep you healthy and functioning as God intended. He is worth a whole lot to you, Sis. As a married woman, you are indeed dependent upon him just as surely as an unborn child is dependent upon that mother. Guard him well!

Love and anticipating the miraculous,
CK (Mom 2)

P. S. I must add a quote from a great preacher of the 20th century, F. B. Meyer:
"We must serve. It is our nature. Our Lord said we would serve God or mammon...
We either yield ourselves servants of righteousness, or of iniquity... (Know ye not,
that to whom ye yield yourselves servants to obey, his servants ye are to whom ye
obey; whether of sin unto death, or of obedience unto righteousness? Romans 6:16)

"It is a solemn thought: if we are not serving God with joyfulness and gladness of
heart, we are serving things which are our worst enemies. A man has no worse foe
than himself when he lives to serve his own whims and desires. These habits, and
appetites, and fashions are luxurious and pleasant just now; but their silken cords
will become iron bands.

"On the other hand, if we would be secure from the service which hurts us, let us
give ourselves to the Lord to serve Him with joyfulness and gladness. He will put
gladness into your heart; joy is the fruit of His Spirit... When you are in a healthy
state, joyfulness and gladness rise spontaneously in the soul, as music from song-
birds. When the sacrifice begins, then will the song of the Lord begin...

"The heart finds the well-spring of perennial blessedness when it has yielded
itself absolutely and unconditionally to the Lord Jesus Christ. If He is Alpha and
Omega; if our faith, however feebly, looks up to Him; if we press on to know Him,
... if we count all things but loss for the excellency of His knowledge - we may
possess ourselves in peace amid the mysteries of life, and we shall have learned
the blessed secret of serving the Lord with joyfulness and with gladness of heart."
(Wasn't he an eloquent writer?!)

First Things First

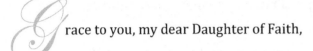race to you, my dear Daughter of Faith,

You will need grace for this letter, and a pencil, too. The last letter referred to some very practical health issues. A whole lot of that is just common sense, something that people are not likely to exhibit very often. The medical field has proven our first line of defense against illness is cleanliness, nutrition, exercise, and rest. In comparing those physical principles to the spiritual realm we may pursue spiritual health. See why I say that by actually looking at the Scriptures for yourself. Remember, what I say can be taken as a grain of salt; what God says is tried and true, convicting and convincing and life-changing. So get your Bible and a pencil and spend some time with me.

What has been said about your husband's responsibility to keep himself clean, well fed, exercised and rested is certainly true. But personally speaking, what is good for the gander is good for the goose, too. I know that's backward but it is sometimes practical to work that way. So as we go through these Scriptures on the necessity of these four facets of defense, I want you to apply them to yourself as well. Since you cannot preach to your darling husband (1 Peter 3:1), you are not allowed to go stick these verses under his nose and say, "Okay, buddy, read these and do them." My, oh, my, wouldn't that set well! No, you read them, apply them to yourself, and pray them for your husband. Let God do the rest. That is a terrific exercise of faith in itself.

Proverbs 16:7 says, **"When a man's ways please the LORD, He makes even his enemies to be at peace with him."** That is a powerful statement, especially when applied to the subject at hand and knowing our enemies. I hope you can identify with the following examples as readily as Susie did while watching us raise her younger brothers. Does it please the parent when the child comes to the table to eat with dirty hands or meanders through the house in muddy shoes? Does it please the parent when the child is caught sneaking snacks fifteen minutes before a dinner is served (having taken an hour to prepare), only to have that child turn up his nose and say he isn't hungry? How about a couch potato child that refuses to follow through with assigned tasks? How pleasing is it when that two year-old refuses to take a much needed nap or that ten-year-old stays up an hour after he was put to bed for the third time? I could go on, but you get the idea. Are the parents just plain mean to demand so much? Or could it be love for the child, their desire for his health and best interest in his character as he learns obedience? There's nothing like being the mean old mom! There are disasters waiting when a child defies his parents. There are benefits for the child when he pleases Mom and Dad; and there are tremendous benefits when our ways please the Father.

Philippians 2:12 exhorts us to work out our own salvation with fear and trembling. Now you know we cannot work for our salvation; that is a gift of God by His grace. He knows we would boast about how good we are (Ephesians 2:8-10). No, that "work out" has a very interesting concept. It means to work to full completion, to accomplish all, to finish fully. It was used in Greek times in the sense of working out a mine, getting all the ore out of it that was possible, or working a field, getting the best harvest one could get by toiling in the field to make it produce well. Our ore, our produce, our goal is to become Christ-like, conformed to His image (Romans 8:29). That is an overwhelming goal but one which we are to strive towards, getting everything valuable out of our "mine" and the best

The Mystery of Marriage through Adam's Prime Rib

harvest possible out of our "field". Our lives have tremendous potential! "There's gold in them thar hills." But you have to get the dirt and rocks moved to find it.

Go back to Philippians 2 and read verse 13. The word "work" is a totally different Greek word here, and it means to prove oneself strong and efficient, to make oneself felt by energetic working. God is the One working in this verse. He is the Energy of the Universe! In fact, that word in the Greek is where we get our English word energy. It is God who works in you both to will (He not only desires a matter to be done but presses on to see that it is accomplished) and to do for His good pleasure ("to do" is the same Greek word as this "work"). He tells us to work out our salvation and then tells us that He is the One doing it all. Yet He still puts us to work and our part is essential to living this Christian life. It is not accomplished by imitating what we think Jesus would do in a certain situation; it is Christ living in you, allowing Him to do what is right and pleasing! Read John 8: 29. Just as the Father was in Christ, Jesus is in us enabling us to be pleasing to the Father. We are to work out, while God works in. He will not force anyone to live pleasing to Him, but He is the One who enables us to do just that. As we work out that salvation with godly fear and trembling, there comes a wholesome, serious caution in walking the Christian life. And that allows God to work in you.

One word of caution: that second word "work" (energy, proving oneself strong) is also found in Romans 7 speaking of the flesh and in Ephesians 2 speaking of the devil. Those are enemies that also prove themselves strong. Just keep the goal of pleasing God ever before you and remember that He is the One who enables you.

Have you ever wondered why Jesus healed so many people physically? That is not what He came to earth to do. He came to declare the Kingdom of God, to reveal God to man, to call out those who would come to Him for eternal salvation, to die in my place that I might be forgiven, to conquer death that I might live in eternity. Why did He give sight to the blind, heal the lepers, remove fevers, enable the crippled to walk again, and even raise the dead? Certainly His great compassion for His creations was a driving force, but the healings were also a teaching tool as surely as His parables. They could understand the spiritual realm as Jesus worked through the physical. At least those who were truly seeking Him could. Disease does to the physical body what sin does to the spirit. If He can set us free from the power of sin, (Matthew 9:6) what is the power of a little germ, or crooked bones, or blinded eyes? They all gave Him opportunity to preach the glories of God and declare who He is, the Light of the world, the Bread of Life, the Resurrection and the Life, the Creator and Sustainer of Life.

So, if we are going to peer into the spiritual realm and our goal is to be pleasing children to God, we must now zero in on that first line of defense. In our analogy of your marriage, with the body being your husband and the wife being the immune system, this first line of defense is his responsibility, so keep him in mind. But for right now, in this letter, we are going to refer to your own spiritual readiness as well. So keep both of you in mind...

We must first and foremost tend to our cleanliness. Being clean physically is vital to the prevention of disease, so naturally being spiritually clean is essential to the prevention of the malady that sin brings. To begin we are going to deal with acknowledging the need to be clean. Again I refer to little children. How many times must one tell them to wash their hands before they eat and they respond with "I don't need to"? They honestly did not see the dirt on themselves or they thought they weren't dirty enough to engage in such a serious task as that of seeking out soap and water. Why, they weren't near as dirty as the other boys fishing. Yuck! If one does not see the need, it is hard to convince him. There are many who do not see the need for salvation. "Hey, the old boy down the street is a lot worse than I am. Go save him." No, one has to confess, agree with God, that he or she is dirty, sin has left its mark, and a Savior is needed. Now get out your Bible and follow through with me.

Psalm 51 is one of David's most beautiful prayers of repentance. In verse 2 he asks God to wash him thoroughly from his *iniquity* and cleanse him from his *sin.* In Psalm 41:4 he asks for mercy and healing as he confesses his *sin* against the Lord. In Psalm 32:5 he acknowledges his *sin*, does not hide his *iniquity*, and confesses his *transgressions.* Let's do some identifying. *Sin* is missing the mark, coming short of God's glory, but not necessarily willfully; we are born with the sin nature. *Iniquity* is perversity, a moral evil, a depraved action. *Transgression* is a revolt, rebellion, faithlessness, defection against lawful authority. Whether I have been marred by sin out of stupidity or ignorance, or through a purposeful evil deed, or open rebellion against the authority that my Creator rightfully has over me, I must admit it and agree with God that it is "sin". That is the first step to salvation, without which we cannot appropriate the blood of Christ to wash us. Once we acknowledge our sin, God purges us through the blood (cleanses, frees from filth). Read Hebrews 9:13, 14, and 22. Only God can wash someone in blood to remove a scarlet stain and make it white as snow. (Use your concordance and find that Scripture on your own.) Matthew 26:28 tells us His blood was shed for the remission (forgiveness releasing from the power) of sins (missing the true goal and scope of life, resulting in guilt). Read Revelation 7:14, too. And in **the kindness and love of God our Savior... according to His mercy He saved us, by the washing** (bathing) **of regeneration** (being born again) **and renewing** (making different than in the past) **of the Holy Spirit"** Titus 3:5. God does it all, cleans us up and sets us aright through the blood of Jesus and renews us by His Spirit. All we have to do is confess (agree with God).

So if God "does it all" where is man's responsibility in this cleaning process? Look up 2 Corinthians 7:1. There's the command to cleanse ourselves from all filthiness of the flesh and spirit. That is the same word for purge in Hebrews 9. Go back three verses and find out what promises Paul is talking about. (I know, I'm working backward again.) We are the temple of the living God (I Corinthians 3:16-17; 6:19-20) and He likes a clean temple! (Read Leviticus to get a picture of His requirements.) Almighty God has called us to be his sons and daughters and to be separate from the unclean things of this world. Yet living in this world our temple gets dirty, just as surely as your house gets dirty when you live in it. My husband had this fantasy of coming home at some point in his life and seeing a "Home and Garden" living room, kitchen and bedrooms. With kids?! By me? Some women may be able but not me. My house gets so dirty, so quickly. Nevertheless, it must be cleaned up, and if not done daily, it becomes very depressing and overwhelming. It's no one's fault, though all are guilty; it's just in the living as traffic comes and goes. (Though sometimes there is guilt involved...)

God is able to clean us up even when we don't know just what is wrong. Read Psalm 19:12. He can understand our errors when we can't because He knows the truth even when we lie to ourselves. The Word bathes us as pure water, sanctifying us for His purposes. Look up and jot down something beside each of the following verses to help you remember what they say:

- *Ephesians 5:26*
- *Hebrews 10:22*
- *John 17:17*

Now read all of Psalm 51 with an attitude of a truly repentant sinner before the Almighty God... There you are! All cleaned up and ready for defense.

On we go to nourishment. Proper nourishment feeds the body the essential nutrients it demands for proper growth and good health. My dear Grandpa Williams used to ask my new husband every time he saw him those first few years we were married, "Son, are you reading your Bible?" "Well, not lately, Grandpa." "Did you eat today?" "Well, sure I did." "If you care enough for your body to feed it, care enough for your soul to feed it the Word of God." "Okay, Grandpa." But did he? No. Did it show? Yes. Spiritually we looked like refugees from a concentration camp. We couldn't see it, but Grandpa could. Your spirit must be nourished even more so than your body. The enemy is so much more devastating in the spiritual realm.

Psalm 119:103 says, **"How sweet are Thy words unto my taste! Yea, sweeter than honey to my mouth!"** I took particular pleasure to see my girls take an interest in cooking and trying different foods. Offer a child a balanced meal or cookies and ice cream and 99 out of 100 will choose the latter. We all have a sweet tooth that likes the indulgence of comfort foods. Just look at the waistlines across the country! Spiritually, we are the same way. We like to indulge on the feel-good doctrines of salvation from hell and the love of God. But those doctrines are for the newborn. They are the milk of the Word that 1 Peter 2:2 tells us about, which we must have as we begin our new life. Read 1 Corinthians 3:1-3. Here Paul is admonishing the people of Corinth because he could not speak to them as spiritual folks; they were still babes in Christ wanting only the sweet milk so easy to swallow and digest. He had much to teach them about living the Christian life, but they could not receive the solid food he was trying to feed them. The writer of Hebrews had the same problem when addressing the Hebrews, "God's Chosen People", who had been entrusted with God's Word down through the centuries.

They should have been teachers themselves, yet they had need of someone to teach them the principles of God. They still needed milk when they should have been sinking their teeth into the meat of the Word. That solid food belongs to the mature, those who by reason have exercised their senses to discern that which is good and evil. (By the way, that is chapter 5:12-14.) And the mature find even the meat is sweet, sweeter than honey, more to be desired than fine gold, giving great reward. So grow up in your taste for spiritual food. Desire those things that will keep you strong and healthy and up to the task of keeping the enemy at bay.

The Lord is always a good source to quote. Jesus told us in Matthew 4:4 that we are to live by every word that proceeds out of the mouth of God, not by bread alone. What does He say in John 6:48-51? Boy, did they choke on those words. Just a few verses down, many of His followers said this is a hard saying; who can receive it? And they left Him! But without the Bread of Life there is no life. Of course, He is the Water of Life, too. Just ask the woman at the well in John 4. Man can live without food for forty days without disastrous results, but only three days without water and he is critically flirting with death. We could go on about the importance of water in our diet here, but suffice it to be said, that our diet must contain both proper food and water. Read the invitation God gives to us in Isaiah 55:1-2. Isn't that beautiful? At no cost, we are invited to come, buy, listen, eat and let our souls delight in abundance. Now, here is a string of verses of instruction, doctrines, food for the inner man, from Proverbs. I want you to look them up and, again, jot down beside them something to help you remember just what they say and maybe what it means to you:

- *Proverbs 1:1-7*
- *2:1-9*
- *3:1-4*
- *...7:1-5*

The dot, dot, dot before chapter 7 means all those verses in between. Proverbs is chock-full with words of wisdom from the Lord on how to live pleasing to Him. How can one pick out just a few? Besides, a Proverb a day keeps the devil away. Let me conclude those from Proverbs with 13:13-14. **"He who despises** (makes light of, shows disrespect toward) **the Word shall be destroyed, but he who fears the commandment shall be rewarded. The law of the wise is a fountain of life, to turn one away from the snares of death."** The Word of God is powerful (Hebrews 4:12) and as Psalm 17:4 says, **"By the Word of Your lips, I have kept away from the paths of the destroyer."** We are enabled to battle the enemy by the strength gained through that spiritual nourishment. The longest chapter in the entire Bible, Psalm 119, deals exclusively with praise for the Word of God given to us that disciplines us and keeps us healthy and away from the destroyer's path to death. We are what we eat!

Okay, now that you are both clean and well fed, let's curl up and sleep. Oh, no you don't! Only a baby can get away with that. Well, you can see from our society, and the extra flab hanging over, that there appears to be an epidemic of well fed, curled-up sleepers, void of any exercise. But that's not how it's supposed to be. It is now that we should be ready for exercise, and, like I told my boys wanting to lift dead weights, the best exercise is work. Physical exercise not only keeps the body trim and well-toned, but also stimulates the brain to release chemicals called endorphins and enkephalins. These are natural painkillers which reduce anxiety, create a sense of well-being, and affect macrophages and T-cells with increased levels of chemicals to strengthen our defenses against germs and disease. That's pretty impressive to me. The Lord thought of everything when He designed this body.

Proverbs 3:7 says, **"Be not wise in thine own eyes: fear the Lord, and depart from evil. It shall be health to thy navel, and marrow to thy bones."**

That is a good first exercise. Put aside the thought that you know it all already; self-wisdom and over-confidence are false weights. Pick up the proper respect and healthy fear of the Lord, and while carrying that on your shoulders, depart from evil. It really is hard work. Evil abounds on every side and we have to turn from it. It is hard to just turn off a movie. You know you would not be watching it if Jesus were your guest for the evening. But He is! Sometimes motivation is the key to exercise. Rewards motivate well; so does embarrassment!

Let's look up some more Scripture. 1 Timothy 4:7-8 has always been a great encouragement to lazy people because it says bodily exercise profits little (somewhat; puny in duration or value.) So why exercise? Because it does profit our bodies; we can see the benefit to our muscles and weight and we know it even strengthens our bones, not to mention the immune system, but only for the duration of this life. That does seem mighty puny when compared to spiritual exercise. Exercising oneself unto godliness is profitable for everything, promising life for the here and now and for eternity. Promised life - the expression of all of the highest and best which Christ is and gives to us! It is hard work to exercise unto godliness, to keep yourself morally pure that you might worship God well.

Remember in the last letter, that I said the hardest labor a Christian can do is to believe? Faith is believing what God says with no evidence, without seeing proof. Jesus told Thomas that because he had seen, he believed; but blessed are those who have not seen and yet believe. Hebrews 11:6 tells us without faith it is impossible to please Him. Saving faith is only the beginning. Our faith must be exercised if we are to be strong in the Lord. What sad words Jesus spoke to Peter when He said, **"O you of little faith, why did you doubt?"** It is in exercise, striving for the goal, that the conscience becomes clear toward God and man (Acts 24:16.) In Proverbs 4:20-22 we are commanded to give attention (prick up the ears and listen) to His words, incline the ear, keep them in eye-sight and in the midst of the heart, for they are life and health. Whatever is in the midst of your heart controls your life, so whatever God says, we just must believe and act on. James tells us faith without works is dead. We do because we believe. 1 John 3:7 & 10 both speak of doing righteousness or not doing righteousness. That means to practice righteous acts that we may prove we belong to Him. Practice makes perfect. How many times have you heard that over the years! If you never try, you never do. Practice, practice, practice. How I hated practicing the piano! And who wishes she could play the piano today but can't? Training is never really pleasant but without disciplined training, perfection is never in sight. Hebrews 12:11 is one my children heard a lot over the years of childhood. The fruit of righteousness (conformity to God's will - in purpose, thought and action, resulting in right living and right relationship with God), the very character of our Lord Jesus being built into our spiritual muscles, is the result of the training, exercise!

We are given a lot of direction in exercising our bodies. Walking is something anyone can do; running is a little more challenging. We are also given direction in exercising our faith. Look up these Scriptures on walking:

- *2 Corinthians 5:7*
- *John 12:35*
- *1 John 1:7*
- *Romans 6:4*
- *Romans 13:13*
- *Colossians 2:6-7*
- *Ephesians 4:1*
- *Ephesians 4:17*
- *Ephesians 5:2 & 8*
- *Isaiah 30:21*

And then there is Genesis 5:24 where we read that Enoch walked with God and was no more because God just took him on to heaven. I'd say walking is about as beneficial as it gets. (My favorite walks were when exploring new places with my grown children!)

Isaiah 40:31 speaks about walking and running. Running is more intense and requires a definite determination. Hebrews 12:1-2 tells us to lay aside every weight and sin that slows us down and run with endurance the race that is set before us, with Jesus as our example, the author and finisher of our faith. In Philippians 3:12-14 Paul confessed that he had not yet attained unto the goal, but pressed on, forgetting those things that are in the past and reaching for those things ahead, the goal before him, the upward call of God. In 1 Corinthians 9:24-27, Paul encourages us to run the race and gives the key to winning the prize – discipline/self-control. Then in 2 Timothy 4:7, he declares that he has fought the good fight, he has finished the race, and kept the faith. His life of disciplined training in exercising his spirit stands before us as one that strove successfully and lived by the faith of Jesus (Galatians 2:20 – meditate on that one for a good while). Not only are you then well pleasing to the Father, but the spiritual benefits are even greater than those gained through physical exercise.

After much exercise of our faith comes the building-up process of our spiritual muscles. This spiritual process is not without pain, just as surely as the process hurts when increasing the strength and stamina of our physical muscles, but there is a point of exertion in which spiritual painkillers and comfort kick in. Imagine the benefits of spiritual "endorphins & enkephalins" kicking in, reducing anxiety, creating a sense of well-being, and strengthening our immune defenses against evil and Satanic attacks. Check out the following Scriptures:

- *Acts 9:29-31*
- *Romans 15:1-4*
- *2 Corinthians 1:3-4*

When our faith has been exercised, our anxiety is reduced:

- *Psalm 3:5-6*
- *Philippians 4:6*
- *1 Peter 3:6*

Exercised faith brings a sense of well being that settles over our spirits:

- *1 John 3:18-20*
- *Romans 8:15*
- *Ephesians 3:17-21*
- *Matthew 6:32-34*

And most importantly there is an increased strength of your husband's immune system (which is you):

- *Proverbs 12:4*
- *Proverbs 31:10-12*
- *Ephesians 3:14-16*

And that is just skimming the surface! Someday I would like to take the time to do this section justice. But I am not disciplined enough in the way I use my time. Something to work on... (I am overly anxious to get to the second line of defense, the immune system.)

The last area of this first line of defense is rest. Rest is demanded if one is to be in health. When proper rest and sleep are denied, the body is affected by fatigue, which will result in irritability, confusion, lack of eye focus, even susceptibility to viral attacks. Compare that to one's spiritual life. Do you know anyone who is irritable? Check out his rest in the Lord. The things of this world pull at us and keep us in confusion when we are not at rest in Him. You will find you cannot focus your eyes on the things of the Lord, and heaven is so out of sight that we forget there is an eternity to live with Him. Resting in Him clears our minds and brings life all back into focus.

There is nothing like lying down after a long, industrious day, letting my head sink into the pillow and feeling all my tired muscles begin to relax. I can just feel myself becoming at one with the bed that is holding me up, sort of melting into the comfort of the covers around me. There is no struggle to hold myself up, no anxiety about falling off or through - just sweet release of all those tired, aching muscles. That's how sweet it is when I can rest in the Lord. And without that rest shall we mention how susceptible we are to the attacks the devil is blasting our way. If we have not found rest in the Lord, our lives and our marriages are left defenseless against those fiery darts that Satan will hurl at us. He is just waiting for the opportunity to deceive and destroy.

I'm going to leave you with the following verses to look up and ponder. They all deal with rest, and rest comes in trusting.

- *Psalm 37:7*
- *Psalm 4:8*
- *Psalm 127:2*
- *Psalm 16:8-9*

- *Isaiah 30:15*
- *Hebrews 4:3, 10-11*
- *Matthew 11:28-30*

Rest! sweet, sweet rest that comes from the Lord. I want to be a believer - the kind that totally rests on the truth of God's Word and His faithfulness to perform. Father, don't ever let me doubt You.

This has been a very long letter and yet I have only skimmed the surface of what should have been said. But I am afraid, too, that I may have overwhelmed you with too much. God's Word is so rich and lush. I have given you only a sampling of what He says to us. And though this is addressed to you and for you that your own relationship will be clean and nourished, exercised and rested, don't lose sight of the analogy of the body. This could have been addressed so easily to the man, and with sons maybe I need to work on a letter to them (it's so hard to outgrow the macho man and the size of their biceps). But even with that first line of defense for the marriage so dependent upon the man to be clean before the Lord, well fed in the Word, walking by faith and trusting the Lord to do what only God can do, that still does not let you off the hook. The wife, too, must be spiritually attuned in every area or she cannot have the proper fellowship with the Lord that keeps her functioning in a miraculous way. In fact, the woman must have extra training as you will see shortly...

I'm trusting God will speak to your heart in a marvelous way as you apply these verses on our first line of defense to your own spiritual walk with the Lord. As you conduct yourself in a manner that makes your husband "behold" your behavior (sit up and take notice, do a double take), 1 Peter 3:1-2, you can then watch the blessed results in your own husband's relationship with God. It is then that you will reap the spiritual blessing of being set free to fully perform the task of being your husband's help meet. The closer he gets to God the better your relationship with one another and the healthier your marriage becomes. Stick in there. No one ever said it would be easy. But it is worth every ounce of effort you put forth. You keep your marriage healthy; God will make it holy!

Resting in His grace,
CK (Momma 2)

Let's Take Inventory

race to you again Princess,

Have you caught your breath yet after that last letter? Inhale deeply and let's sum it all up. It may not yet be the end of the year, but it is time for inventory. So, take out your pen and paper; a notebook would be terrific. We're going to do some identifying and classifying, and then you are going to take personal inventory of your own husband and marriage. (This won't be one of those "just spend a few minutes with me" letters.) Please don't let me overwhelm you. This will be the hardest letter to read and do, but persevere with me, please, and thank you!

Ephesians 6:11 tells us how to stand against the wiles of the devil. That word "wiles" informs us that Satan is a strategist, a schemer. He beguiles us: persuading by deception, giving false appearances. He surpasses all in his outwitting skills; cleverly enticing mankind with promises of pleasure or gain. He lures us: baiting a trap; using a decoy to attract and capture; bringing us into difficulties, danger, evil, even death; keeping us from our true course. He is playing for keeps while most of us are walking around in a fog or lollygagging about as if life were just a lark.

To better understand our enemy and the battle tactics he uses against us, look up the following verses and try to identify and categorize them. Worried about overwhelming you, I put a snippet of the verses' essence in parentheses. Which verses would correspond with the definition of evil, temptations, false doctrine, neglect, bad habits, pride, rebellion...? You may need to go back to letters seven (Your Worth to Your Husband) and eight (Your Husband's Worth to You) and refresh your memory. There is oh so much to battle against, from without and from within.

Let's go first to Ephesians 6:12 because you will especially need to remember this verse the next time you get really put out with your husband, or mother-in-law, or mom, or dad, or boss, or...you get the idea. **"For we wrestle not against flesh and blood, but against principalities and against powers, against the rulers of the darkness of this world, against spiritual wickedness in high places."** Unless we know who the enemy is, where he is, and what he can do, we are going to have a tough time trying to wrestle him and come out on top. A spiritual battle is going on in this world and in heavenly places, and we are in the big middle of it. The important thing to remember is that our battle is not with people, as much as we sometimes would like for it to be. It would be easy to see victory as we kick shins, pull hair, or get the final "ha"! No, our fight is against the devil as he maneuvers his spiritual demons seeking to control people and make them oppose the work of God. It is in an unseen realm!

Okay, here come the verses. This will be a little of that spiritual exercise I spoke of in the last letter. You'll have to schedule some time with the Lord to do this next project. Got your Bible? Identify the enemy – is it coming from within: self, the old nature, neglect, pride, rebellion...? or is it coming from without: evil, wickedness, temptations, deceptions... or perhaps both?!

I've identified the first three to get you started. This would be a good time to find a Bible study buddy! Good reading...

- *Genesis 3:6, 13 (forbidden fruit; beguiled by the serpent): came from without / "bacteria" of temptation ... also from within / desire for more than allowed, pleasing self over God*
- *1 Samuel 15:22-23 (Saul's disobedience): within / "cancers" of rebellion, pride, stubbornness*
- *Psalm 40:12 (innumerable evils): from without / "protozoa" evil in the world*
- *Proverbs 19:15 (slothfulness, idleness):*
- *Matthew 12:22; Mark 9:20-27; Luke 8:26-36 (possessed by a demon):*
- *Matthew 26:41 (weak flesh):*
- *John 10:10 (thief that steals, kills, and destroys):*
- *Acts 20:29-30 (grievous wolves speaking perverse things):*
- *Romans 1:18-22, 24-32 (ungodliness, unrighteousness, vain imaginations, foolish hearts, sexual immorality, reprobate mind, wickedness, covetousness, maliciousness; full of envy, murder, debate, deceit, malignity; whisperers, backbiters, haters of God, despiteful, proud, boasters, inventors of evil things, disobedient to parents, without understanding, covenant breakers, no natural love for family, implacable, unmerciful, having pleasure in those things worthy of death!):*
- *Romans 3:10-18 (deceitful speech, poisonous lips, cursing, bitter, swift to shed blood, destructive, miserable, no peace, no fear of God):*
- *Romans 7:21-23 (evil is present, law of sin):*
- *Romans 12:21 (evil):*
- *Romans 16:17-18 (causing divisions and offences, contrary doctrine, self servers, deceivers):*
- *1 Corinthians 5:1-2, 6 (sexual immorality, boasting):*
- *1 Corinthians 5:9-13 (companion to sexually impure, covetous, extortionists, idolaters):*

- *1 Corinthians 7:5 (lack of self restraint):*
- *1 Corinthians 15:33 (deception, evil companionship):*
- *2 Corinthians 2:10-11 (unforgiving):*
- *2 Corinthians 7:1 (filthiness of flesh and spirit):*
- *2 Corinthians 11:3-4; 13-15 (seduced by trickery, false apostles, deceitful workers, demons as angels of light):*
- *Galatians 5:16-17 (lust of the flesh):*
- *Ephesians 2:1-3 (trespasses, sins, desires of flesh and mind, children of wrath):*
- *Ephesians 4:14 (winds of doctrine, sleight of men, dunning craftiness, deception):*
- *Ephesians 5:15-16 (foolish, evil days):*
- *Ephesians 6:11, 16 (wiles of devil, fiery darts of the wicked):*
- *Colossians 3:5-10 (sexual and moral impurity, appetite for worldly goods, worthless lust for the forbidden, desiring what others have [idolatry], anger, wrath, malice, blasphemy, vile conversations, lies):*
- *1 Timothy 4:1-3 (seducing spirits, doctrines of devils, lies of hypocrisy, seared conscience):*
- *1 Timothy 6:9-10 (desire to be rich):*
- *Hebrews 2:3 (neglect so great salvation):*
- *Hebrews 3:12-13 (unbelief, hardened through deceitfulness of sin):*
- *James 1:13-15 (lust):*
- *James 1:19-22 (wrath, filthiness, abundance of wickedness, self-deception of sufficiency without doing):*
- *James 4:1-4 (over desire for self, friendship of world):*
- *James 4:16-17 (boastings, failure to do good):*
- *1 Peter 5:8 (the devil seeking to devour):*
- *2 Peter 2:1-3,7-8,9-10,12-19 (false teachers with damnable heresies, cov-*

etous, artificial [plastic] words; filthy living, vexation; lust of flesh and
immorality, presumptuous, arrogant, speaking evil; rioters, adulterers,
unable to cease from sin, those who promise liberty with swelling words
while servants of corruption):

- *1 John 2:15-16 (love of the world, lust of the flesh, lust of the eyes,*
  pride of life):
- *2 John 9-11 (not abiding in the doctrine of Christ):*
- *3 John 9-11 (loving preeminence, speaking against and rejecting*
  the brethren):

Okay, okay, I know I went overboard. But once you start looking for verses and running references, it just seems there is no end. I actually left out a lot! And I certainly did not do an exhaustive search on the subject. But more than adequate. The point is, we have a lot to deal with here in this battleground. The marriage relationship is one of Satan's hottest targets because he *hates* the family. Keep in mind, family is God's best tool to demonstrate His love to this lost world: the Father with His children and the intimacy between Christ and His Bride. We are a picture of that and the devil can't stand it! So he turns his wiles on us to steal, kill and destroy. And to top it all off, we have to deal with this inherited sin nature passed down from Adam!

Now I want you to turn your attention to your own dear spouse and marriage. (If you have not yet taken the plunge, this is critical training, so ask others or observe intently.) There are some evils in this "world" which must be resisted that correspond to the protozoa of this world. These things should be kept under control by the immune system (a virtuous wife under the control of the Spirit) unless weakened (spiritual malnutrition, exhaustion). These protozoa type evils should affect him only as a vexation of his spirit, with his wife as the silent strengthening force. Let me get you started with a few evils with which my own husband has had to resist.

Preachers have some pretty evil things come at them, too. Pornography and an adulterous woman are two that have been thrown at him repeatedly. He made successful efforts to remove smutty magazines from several communities (back before the internet days), but in order to do that he had to buy them, see them for himself, and show them to others in the community to prove it outraged public decency before the DA could do anything about it. Those pictures stay with you and have an effect on the mind. However, he has a clean lifestyle, a good diet on the Word, a strong faith, and a healthy relationship with his immune system (that's me), so these evils have had little effect except to vex his soul and spirit. Just imagine what could have happened during that ordeal with pornography had his wife been a problem to him.

Also, it is with good reason that he no longer counsels a woman by himself. A frustrated woman tends to become religiously infatuated, placing her affection on the "man of God," and soon can't think of any good thing about that sorry devil she married. Do you have any idea how many preachers have succumbed to that admiration and then adultery? And there are a lot of women just looking for a "good" man to conquer. May God help us! Then, too, there is the political corruption, crime, greed, cursing, homosexuality, the spirit of anti-Christ, none of which is going to become a threat to his life, just a vexation that he has to live amongst it all. He has to live in it but not be part of it. However, let me stress that these are no threat to him because he is strong and healthy with a functioning immune system. Even as a Christian, he becomes susceptible if there is a breakdown in his defense. And an attack could most certainly mean death!

Now your Darling has some evil he has to live amongst also. See if you can add to the list. Put names to the evil that surrounds him when he goes to work, when he tries to relax, when he associates with friends. He has to deal with all that somehow. Does he have to live with bigotry, ungodly music, corruption in the work place? Think about your marriage and the effect these things have on your life together. Name them.

Okay, now what temptations do your husband and marriage face that correspond with the description of bacteria? Is it daily, occasionally, at work, at home, at leisure, with friends or family or enemies? These are going to come from everyday, normal encounters, but his "skin" (close personal relationship with the Lord) should serve as a barrier to most of those. However, as "cuts" occur, those wounds that cut into his life or into the oneness of your marriage, you both become more susceptible. Once those temptations enter, one is drawn away, lust is conceived, bringing sin and sickness to the soul, and, yes, even death. The temptation yielded to, lives and grows in the very being of his life or the life of your marriage, digesting the worth of living, its waste causing a diseased life. It should be immediately recognized and attacked by his immune system, which should know him so well that she is alerted to the invading enemy immediately, calling out all forces in order to defeat it. We will get to the means of defeat in the next letter or two.

Just to get you started again, I will refer to the Love of my life once more. He will be the first to admit that he is prone to be a workaholic. And the devil will tell him that he is doing good, holy things for God. But wouldn't it be a delight to Satan to steal our own children out from under our noses because the preacher was compromising his duties as a father to do the work of the Lord? What kind of far-reaching results would that have on the "good" works performed? Your husband is facing all kinds of temptations, from women to success and power, from compromising with the world to self-righteous judgment against others. Again, you put names to the temptations he faces. It wouldn't hurt to ask him. How do these put your marriage at risk?

I'm sorry I don't know where I got this quote about temptation but it is worth repeating. "The bait of temptation is the false promise that we will get what we want by compromising God's principles." Does that take you back to Eve and her encounter with Satan? When bacteria weaken us, viruses have much quicker access to activation in our bodies. When a temptation is yielded to, be assured, Satan has one of his hissing lies waiting for access into our lives in order to destroy.

Are you ready for the "viruses"? What lying doctrines has Satan presented to your husband - like a wolf in sheep's clothing? These lies intend to make clones of false teachings replicating themselves in order to destroy. They cannot reproduce without a human host. The host then becomes a deception factory, propagating the lies of the devil, robbed of essential nutrients, and ultimately destroyed itself.

These falsehoods attack weakened areas unnoticed! They come at a moment of doubt or when one has questions about life, and they almost always sound smooth and flattering to the ego, just what one wants to hear to justify the answers to the doubts and questions. And even when the false doctrine is outwardly defeated, it sometimes remains dormant within the body, just waiting for another weak moment of doubting the truth.

Some of these lies are so subtle they are hardly recognizable as even important. Some are blatant, but they make so much sense to the flesh that they are hard to resist. Let me throw a few out to get you started thinking. "It's different in today's society than it was in Bible times." "My wife is better at decision making & leading the family." "An affair is good for a marriage." "Homosexuality is an alternate lifestyle." "Everybody cheats on something - taxes, wife, poker." "Hell is only here on earth." "God helps those that help themselves." "Tolerance is the key to peace on earth." "Everybody's working to get to the same place." "The Bible is just another religious book like the Koran." "Religion is a private matter." "My sin affects no one but me." "Quality time is better than quantity time." "It takes two incomes to survive today." "I don't need help from anyone." "Abortion is the woman's right." "The world is over populated now." How about universalism, works salvation, humanism, feminism, positive thinking, prosperity religion? What is it that could be lurking close by waiting for a "wound" in his relationship with the Lord, or lying dormant already within your husband, maybe passed on from his parents, waiting for a weak area to be manifested so it can spring to life? This one might be a good one to talk over with him, too. But first see if you can do some inventory on your own.

Has your marriage faced any of these lying philosophies? There are too many marriages today which claim to be Christian but have become factories of deceit, propagating lies of the devil, stealing the truth of God's Word out of the sacred institution of marriage, and destroying wherever and whatever those lies touch. Just look around you at the divorces abounding, couples living together outside the bond of marriage, marriages that are abusive and so contrary to God's plan. We must strive to present the marriage relationship as the example God intended it to be of Christ and His Church. Make it your goal to be on the alert for these heresies that will steal the heart of your marriage, or disease the beauty with which the bond of marriage provides you to be free and at peace with one another and with your Creator. You have a nasty, vicious enemy lurking.

Okay, this is the hard part. We want to identify some "not so good" things in hubby's life and still stay above the temptation that Satan will throw at you to "get down" on him. You must remember, we are listing these things so we can better understand what we are up against and how we can best serve him and keep him healthy and pleasing to the Father. What kind of neglect has your husband allowed in his life? What habits are wearing him down physically, emotionally, and spiritually? This is an area that we probably don't have to think real hard about. All those "bad" things in his life rise to the front of our minds quickly. Those are the idiosyncrasies and bad habits we intended to clean up and redo once he said, "I do." Plus, you have found several things that you did not know about until you were married awhile. (I had no idea my darling had to win at Monopoly or curse words would come out of his mouth towards his beloved bride after only one week of marriage. He wasn't always a preacher.) Check back to the last two letters to refresh your memory on this neglect and bad habits issue. While wearing your thinking cap, be alert for Satan's attack on you. And while you are working on "his" list, it would do you well to compile a list of your own neglect and bad habits. (Surely you don't have any!) Now list…

Not "so good things" about him:

Not "so good things" about me:

Didn't I leave enough room to write it all down? It might be a good idea to keep a small notebook for your lists. Just keep in mind - you are composing your prayer list in this letter. Will you have enough time to pray for all that you have come up with so far? Use your notebook to keep record of what God is doing in your lives.

We are now moving into a serious area of the spiritual realm that compares with that dreaded "c" word, cancer of the body. Are you aware of a war going on within your husband that is destroying his goals for himself or God's plan for him? What evidence is there of rebellion against that plan or attitudes that are tearing down his relationships with God, you, his family, his friends, his employer, etc. Has stress moved in, crowding out the peace of God? Are there jealousies or a bitterness that is putting down roots into his spirit that will defile both him and those around him? Unfortunately, as with cancer, the victim is totally unaware of the mutiny going on within until the damage has been done. I had a huge lump come up quickly on my breast not too long ago. The doctor was encouraged by the fact that it hurt; cancer doesn't hurt until it is too late. That is why it is so vital that the immune system be healthy, up-close and personal. Is it any wonder that God included in His laws for living that when a man took a wife he was to spend the first year with her without the demands of work or military duty – just time together to get to know each other and "cheer" her (to brighten up, make gleesome)! (Deuteronomy 24:5) God wants you to know your husband and be so much a part of him that you can recognize that cancer even before he knows it is growing. Your love can cover a multitude of sin. And you have to be aware of what a healthy marriage should be like before you can recognize a cancer growing within it. Do you have your pencil ready? Go...

Please don't be overwhelmed. It is a tremendous responsibility for a wife to bear. However, God has laid this burden of spiritual health of the marriage on both the man and the woman as a unit of one, dependent on one another (1 Corinthians 11:8-11). For a wife to effectively do her job as help meet for her man, he must know his standing before His Creator (Psalm 8:3-4; Isaiah 40:12-31) and exercise himself unto godliness (1 Timothy 4:7-9). But before a man can exercise properly, he must be healthy and free from attack – that's the woman's job. Yet for her to perform her job well, he must be well nourished (Hebrews 5:14, eating strong meat), feeding himself and strengthening his marriage and immune system on the Word of God, and he must be well rested, totally trusting in the Lord. Again the woman must see to it that he has time to be alone with God. But he won't take that time to be in God's Word until he has experienced cleansing (1 Corinthians 6:11; Revelation 1:5). Back to the woman as the help God has provided to bring him to obedience to God's Word simply by living a godly life in his presence (1 Peter 3:1-2). It is an unending circle of love and dependence upon one another that God intended from the beginning, a oneness in unity of life and purpose. You need him and he needs you.

Still, with this weighty listing of these wicked, evil things to overcome, remember the victories that have already been accomplished. Colossians 2:15 reminds us that Jesus spoiled those principalities and powers, making a public spectacle of them, triumphing over them, disarming them, nailing them to the cross. And in Hebrews 2:14 we are told that through His death, He has destroyed him that had the power of death, the devil. Psalm 41:11 assures us that we can know when we are well pleasing to the Lord; our enemies will not triumph over us. Philippians 1:28 admonishes us to be terrified in nothing by our adversaries. If you are not alert and prepared, then fear of Satan and his demons and our own backwardness at the thought of spiritual warfare will take you out of the battle before you even begin. **But "God has not given us the spirit of fear** (cowardice, timidity)**, but of power** (capability) **and of love** (doing best for others) **and of a sound mind** (self discipline, self control)." (2 Timothy 1:7). Philippians 4:13 assures us that we can do all things through Christ that strengthens us. Then there is that beautiful Scripture in Romans 8:37-39 – **"Nay, in all these things we are more than conquerors through Him that loved us. For I am persuaded that neither death, nor life, nor angels, nor principalities, nor powers, nor things present, nor things to come, nor height, nor depth, nor any other creature, shall be able to separate us from the love of God, which is in Christ Jesus our Lord."** I will close with this encouraging word from Psalm 44. **"Through Thee will we push down our enemies: through Thy name will we tread them under that rise up against us. For I will not trust in my bow, neither shall my sword save me. But Thou hast saved us from our enemies, and hast put them to shame that hated us. In God we boast all the day long, and praise Thy name forever."** Amen, and amen!

Fighting in the battle victoriously,
CK (Momma 2)

The Internal Defense Created by God's Design

My Dear Daughter of Faith,

And how are you this fine day? Doing well, making plans, and enjoying life, I presume. If it just didn't cost so much money! That can be a real hindrance to a fun marriage. Have you have already seen some pitfalls in that area? I must press on to get you through these letters on being a wife; I have new letters on motherhood that I want to share. But a wife you are and a wife you will remain even when you add the role of mom. So on with our topic.

I know that last letter was really time-consuming. It took me quite a while to put it together as it did you to work on it. I prayed it would not be discouraging. You have to admit it was a good review for everything up to this point. I hope you have come to realize how vital your role is in your hubby's life - physically, emotionally, and spiritually. God has given woman quite a task!

You will like this next verse. **"Whoso findeth a wife findeth a good thing, and obtains favor of the LORD."** Proverbs 18:22. Amen! Put that in your memory bank and pull it now and then to deposit on hubby when he is wondering why he chose marriage. Now open your heart and breathe in again this verse from Proverbs 12:4 that we looked at a few letters ago. **"A virtuous woman** (a wife that is a great force, an army, a mighty host, valiant, full of virtue, strength) **is a crown** (royal crown, encircling/surrounding for protection) **to her husband: but she that makes ashamed** (causes disappointment of opinion, hope, or expectation, causing public disgrace and confusion, humiliation and shattered emotions, utter defeat, disillusionment and broken spirit) **is as rottenness** (progressive decay) **in his bones** (strength, substance, life)." I guess the point is, God's Word declares it is good to take a wife, and when a man's wife is living as a great and mighty host, full of virtue, she encircles her husband with protection of all that he is in his manhood. But there are those that bring shame to their husbands, not only breaking their spirits and decaying the lives of these men, but also bringing cause for scoffing and blasphemy to the Word of God, which has declared marriage as a good thing.

Okay, we've *finally made it to the really neat stuff.* I am a little worried about sounding too much like a science textbook, but you really can't see the analogy without viewing the wonders of the human body that science has opened up for us. You can relax though because I am pretty elementary in the field of science. My "knowledge" won't be too hard to follow. In fact, I would be mortified if a real expert ever read what I am about to write, because my version of what goes on in the immune system is pretty simplistic and probably would give a physician a good chuckle. Just bear with me and pretend you're one of my kids in our schoolroom; I am not a professional teacher but I do what I can. These facts opened my eyes to the wonder of my creation, and I not only stand in awe of the human body but in double awe of my place in life as my husband's help. I hope it does the same for you, my friend.

Just a quick review... We have spent quite some time referring to the harmful things to which the human body is exposed. Those in the know call these disease-producing organisms pathogens. But God has endowed man with this remarkable defense system, beginning with the skin covering our body. This first line of defense against disease prevents pathogens from entering the body by forming a terrific, flexible, waterproof suit of armor preventing an invasion. (I could really go to seed on the wonders of the skin – keeping the inner tissues moist, preventing fluids from leaking, acting as a sensory detection system with millions of nerve endings that respond to touch, temperature, pressure and pain, and even a thermostatic control that cools an overheated body or conserves warmth when needed. The skin is remarkably wonderful! However, my purpose is headed elsewhere at the moment so you will have to do your own analogy comparing skin to the husband's duties. Hopefully, it would make you appreciate your hubby more and you could brag on him like a schoolgirl enamored with her true love's capabilities... but back to the issue at hand...) Those "holes" in our skin that let in food, smells, and light - and germs - are equipped to trap and dispose of, not only these ugly micro-organisms, but even simple irritants like dust. Even our tears are protecting us with powerful enzymes that attack the cell walls of bacteria. And, as extra defense, God has even graced us with some "good" micro-organisms to live in our intestines. These are beneficial to us and keep the "bad guys" in check. You know, kind of like the ladybugs in your garden help keep the bad bugs from taking over.

But, for those times when the bad guys do get past your first line of defense, God has established your immune system as your body's very own personal army against these harmful invaders. Wait until you see how this army works for you! We most certainly are fearfully and wonderfully made! (Psalm 139). Out of the 100,000,000,000,000 (that's 100 trillion) cells in your body, better than two in every 100 are there just to defend you (that's billions). They are the white blood cells that are born in the bone marrow. You have three distinct regiments of warriors: the phagocytes, and two kinds of lymphocytes – T-cells and B-cells. All share one common objective: to identify and destroy all substances that are not self, including traitorous cancer cells. That is the remarkable system we are going to examine to get a picture of our own ministry.

Keep in mind the verses in Genesis and Ephesians that declare man and woman are no longer two people when they marry but one. God has provided for this body of your marriage a first line of defense - the "structural" part that identifies with the man's responsibility, (which we have covered pretty thoroughly considering these letters are addressed to the woman's specific function). God then created a second line of defense, an immune system, born in the rib taken from Adam, fashioned to be the help man needed to battle the spiritual pathogens that come to attack and sicken and destroy. There should be constant vigilance going on in every marriage because there are constant dangers and hazards lurking about. Woman needs to know she is in a battle and being a warrior is a very real aspect of her life. She must learn to identify the enemy and learn her own varied resources to best counter attack and defeat that enemy that would undo her marriage.

Now follow with me as we do some comparisons. Physically, when pathogens get past your first line of defense, the *phagocytes* are the first defenders to arrive. These white blood cells leave the bloodstream and travel to the site of the infection. They isolate the invaders from the rest of the body by forming a barrier around the area. The phagocytes engulf and digest the pathogens. In the process, toxins from these invaders kill many of these white blood cells. Pus is the result of dead bacteria, white blood cells, and fluids that remain after the conflict. It's evidence of the job performed! These vigilant phagocytes are constantly scouring the body, alert to anything that seems out of place, and are willing to sacrifice themselves in the role of defense for the body. They silently perform their duties, consistently "cleaning house" of whatever foreign material or debris they find, even old worn out red blood cells. These little jewels literally eat anything suspicious - in the bloodstream, the tissues, or the lymphatic system, might it be a living microorganism or just particles of dust or some other pollutant that enters as we breathe - such as the nasty contaminants of cigarette smoke. Unfortunately, as with too much smoke in the lungs or non-digestibles, like asbestos, the phagocytes are sometimes overwhelmed and cannot keep up with their housecleaning, or are destroyed in the process of trying. However, in most cases of minor infections, these fantastic phagocytes solve the problem. If the pathogen succeeds in passing this barrier, a more complex process is called into action.

In like manner, a wife must be first to come to her husband's defense, always ready to provide her complete unswerving allegiance to his welfare. Titus 2:4 tells us the older women are to admonish the younger women to love their husbands. Now that seems kind of silly to a young woman who thinks she knows more about love than those old women could ever experience. (been there!) But the love spoken of in Titus means a settled good will towards a dear friend, a zealous, tender love of the heart, devoted, ardent, passionate sentiment, stretched out and eager. Sometimes a young wife does not have that "settled" good will towards her husband - zealous, passionate, and eager to do what is best for him. Without that, she will not be a good defense. She must also believe that she has been called by God to be her husband's aid (Genesis 2:18, 22; 2 Peter 1:10). That is a tremendous enabling force. Her strength comes from trusting in His power to perform her responsibilities. (Romans 4:20-21 – not wavering at the promise of God through unbelief but strengthened in faith being fully convinced that what God promised He is able to perform.) She must make Psalm 18 her battle cry. Verse 32 says, **"It is God who arms me with strength, and maketh my way** (course of life, mode of action) **perfect."** and verse 39, **"For You have armed me with strength for the battle; You have subdued under me those who rose up against me."** (The word "strength" in those two verses is the same word used in Proverbs 12:4 for "virtuous" wife!)

Just like the phagocyte, she must be alert to anything that seems out of place. That means she must know her husband, inside and out, his strengths and weaknesses, his virtues and faults, alert for any sign of attack in any area. (Review your lists made in your last letter.) Proverbs 31:27 reminds us to look well (lean forward to peer into the distance to observe, keep the watch) to the ways of our household (family, house, home). When an invasion comes, she must love every part of him enough to sacrifice her wants and rights for his good and the sake of the body of their marriage. 1 Corinthians 9:19 – though free, making myself a servant to all. 2 Timothy 2:10 – enduring all things for the sake of the elect, that they may obtain salvation. Galatians 5:13 – through love serve one another; 6:2 – bear one another's burdens. John 13:14-17 – Jesus gave up His right to be served in order to serve us. Philippians 2:3-4 – do nothing through strife or selfishness but in humility esteem others better than self. Remember, we are ambassadors for Jesus, standing in His stead, representing Him. **"A faithful ambassador brings health,** (is medicine, curative)" Proverbs 13:17.

She silently performs her duties, behind the scenes, with a meek and quiet spirit and a consistent lifestyle (1 Peter 3:1-4 – that is a whole instruction book in itself and we will delve deeply into that in a future letter). In her quietness she is ever watchful for intrusions that would be foreign in his walk with God, removing the debris that would hinder his spiritual health (dirt from this world, the contaminates of bad habits...) Romans 7:21-23 remind us that evil is ever present within us; even when we would delight in doing good, there is a war going on in our members bringing us into captivity. A good wife understands that and is patient with her husband as the Spirit is patient with each of us. However, it is dangerous to allow sins of the flesh to go unchecked and 2 Corinthians 12:20 warns us of the consequences of living carnal lives. Self-seeking and pride cause debates to arise (have you ever found you and your husband disputing or quarreling?), envyings (that is a zeal that grieves, not because another has it good, but that self does not have it and so makes war against the good it beholds in the other), wraths (outbursts of anger!), strifes (that is plain old selfishness, being self-willed), backbitings (ouch, it hurts when you start speaking about your spouse in a slanderous way, insulting the character of your mate), whisperings (don't you hate to walk into a room and everyone looks at you in silence and then turns to whisper something to someone with a side glance towards you?), swellings (here comes the inflated ego, the haughtiness that comes when you are down on someone else, thinking more highly of self), and finally, to cap it all off, tumults (a swelling, noisy uproar with confusion, agitation, and violent outbursts). Wow! How many marriages do you see in that wretched mold? Has yours had a taste of the uglies? When we see any of that working its way into our marriage we must consume it, destroy it completely, or it comes full cycle and destroys us. Don't worry about a little pus that develops from the fracas. It just shows the battle was done. Pour a little cleansing peroxide of devotion over the wound and go on.

You must also be aware of the pollutants of philosophies and vain deceits that plunder your marriage, taking it captive down into the elements of this world (Colossians 2:8). You must help deaden and subdue all of those ungodly desires and attitudes that pull the flesh so strongly (Colossians 3:5-6). Hebrews 3:12 sternly warns us to beware of an evil heart of unbelief. Satan wants to lead man away from God so he subtly challenges his trust in God, his obedience to Him, his confidence in what He says and does. In the Garden, it was Eve he used to do just that. Don't ever let Satan use you to defeat your husband! You have the power of the Spirit in your life that Eve did not (1 John 4:4). You must be grounded so you can be the encourager and reminder of God's goodness and blessings. Praise is such a good way to ward off the devil's attacks on our faith. As a woman of God you will help your discouraged husband to stand up straight again, restored, to follow peace and lead a life of holiness, observing and overseeing so that your marriage does not fail the grace God has extended it. In doing so, you help protect him from that poisonous root of bitterness that wants to grow over him and crowd into his relationship with God. That poison is a pollutant that stains and defiles not only him, but all who see him. (Hebrews 12:12-16) Remember the grace of God is not just His unmerited favor. It is His divine influence on the heart and the outward reflection in one's life. When we fail the grace of God, we come up on the short end, deficient of His divine influence, rejecting what only God can do for us. The result is a profane person, void of any relationship or affinity to God. Bitterness is probably the vilest pollutant Satan throws at us and we must be vigilant to remove it.

Do you love your husband that much? Are you willing to be so intimate with him that you can know him as no one else, better than he knows himself, recognizing those intrusions in his life that can make him ill? Are you willing to sacrifice of yourself for his good and the sake of your marriage? A sacrifice is something precious to you that you offer to God, surrendering one thing for the sake of another. We tend to place a high value on our self-will, our comfort, looks, success, ideals, pride... The sacrifices are usually trivial when counted against the eternal rewards. The service to him and to the Lord will far outweigh anything we must give up. And, yes, sometimes a man will get involved in something that you just cannot cover or consume in your love. There are women who have lived with the consequences of a habitual spiritual "smoker" and no amount of housecleaning on their part can remove the devastating effects on their marriages. A spiritual emphysema or cancer sets in and overcomes their labors of love. Intensive "oxygen" may need to be manually forced into the lungs of the marriage to prolong its life, or it may even require some drastic measures to save the marriage, either "surgically" or by "radiation therapy" through trained "physicians". But we think better things of you and your dear husband! God has a terrific plan for the two of you and it is time for you to buckle down and get to it.

Now before I move on to the lymphocytes (which is my favorite part), I want to mention that we have a specialized phagocyte, the *macrophage*. By the way, phage means one that eats and cyte means cell – phagocyte, a cell that eats. Now this macrophage is a big one – macro meaning large = a large cell that eats. These are the largest cells found in the blood. And they can swell up 5 to 10 times their original size when confronting microscopic invaders. They engulf and digest the enemy, but instead of being destroyed by their own digestive enzymes as other phagocytes, macrophages can empty the contents of their meal into surrounding tissue and continue the fight. And they can live for years. When fighting a particularly large or resilient invader, the macrophages can fuse into giant cells producing powerful chemicals that will break down and destroy the components of the enemy. While doing so, this wonder cell takes the invader's antigen, the distinct marking (fingerprint) unique to that particular substance, and displays it on itself for recognition by the Helper T-cells. The Helper T can then identify the enemy and alert the remainder of the army to attack. The macrophage produces the chemical lymphokine, raising the body temperature, which enhances the activity of all immune cells. But we will save that for the next letter...

The macrophage for years was regarded as just a big garbage collector. Researchers now believe it to be a critical agent in a vast communications complex, one that links not only the cells of the immune system, but also hormone-producing cells, nerve cells, brain cells. Macrophages respond to the chemical messengers created by brain cells, and are even able to produce many of those same chemicals. There seems to be talking back and forth between the brain and the immune system.

The links between the mind and body are astounding. When we are under stress, the body releases large amounts of a steroid called cortisol and adrenaline known as epinephrine, which raises the blood pressure. When macrophages encounter these, they can no longer respond normally to infection. Exercise, on the other hand, stimulates the brain to release chemicals called endorphins and enkephalins, both natural painkillers, reducing anxiety and creating a sense of well-being (who needs drugs, just exercise!) These chemicals that our own brain manufactures affect macrophages and T-cells with increased levels of interleukin-1 and interferon, strengthening our defenses. Why, even laughter has been proven to produce stress-reducing chemicals that actually promote health, with remarkable results in even serious illnesses, so much so that hospitals across the country are setting up centers with comics, funny movies, joke books, whatever will make one laugh out loud. Laughter lowers blood pressure, relaxes muscles, and combats depression. I just ran across this tidbit the other day: researchers showed healthy adults two movie scenes while monitoring artery function – one from a comedy, the other a battle scene from "Saving Private Ryan". After viewing the funny scene, the volunteers' blood vessels dilated by 22%; they constricted by 35% after the war sequence! Dilation allows the blood to flow with ease, taking the strain off the heart and arteries. Laughter triggers the release of nitric oxide, which relaxes the blood cells, and endorphins that repair blood vessels. Laughing increases disease-fighting antibodies while reducing the effects of that nasty cortisol and epinephrine that interfere with the body's ability to fight illness. Man should have taken Proverbs 17:22 literally years ago: **"A merry heart doeth good like a medicine: but a broken spirit dries the bones."** And Proverbs 16:24 **"Pleasant words are as honeycomb, sweet to the soul, and health to the bones."**

Now, are you ready to compare yourself to the macrophage? You are not just a big garbage collector (or laundry picker-upper)! When those really tough times come in your marriage, you are going to have to enlarge yourself for the task at hand and allow that powerful chemical to permeate through your life that will enable you to break down and destroy any enemy in your marriage. That chemical is love, the kind of fervent, stretched out, continual, intense love that wraps around to cover up a multitude of sins (offenses that come when missing the true goal and scope of life - 1 Peter 4:8). Proverbs 10:12 is a little more intense: **"Hatred stirs up strifes** (quarrels**), but love covers** (conceals, forgives, keeps secret) **all sins** (willful deviation from the path of righteousness, premeditated crossing the line of God's law, a rebellious act of rejecting God's authority)." Sure, there will be times your sweetheart misses the goal and offends both you and God. There will also be more times than you can count that he will rebel with willful, premeditated acts that will infuriate both you and his Creator (so do you!). But love is the answer. Love is the most powerful force we have going for us. It enables you to forgive and keep secret any wrong doing that has gone on in your marriage. The Song of Solomon tells us love is as strong as death (8:6). That is strong! Death never lets go of its victims no matter our tears. Become a victim of love, agape, the love that allows the one who is possessed by it to give the very best to the recipient of it, even to the hurt of the giver. Jesus gave us the example when He laid down His life for us.

And remember the macrophage can produce the same chemical as the brain! God allows us the privilege to have His same love in our lives so we may see the same miracles done in lives today! Wow! Chew on that thought for a while, Sis. This is powerful stuff we are talking about.

Take a couple of minutes to read the love chapter, 1 Corinthians 13. We are nothing without love. Our abilities, gifts, works are all worthless if they are administered without love. Love is patient; love is kind. There is no envy when you love, no bragging, no arrogance (gentleness). Love is not rude but self-controlled. Love does not seek self (meekness) and is never easily provoked (peace). There are no thoughts of evil when love is there. It is love that causes joy in truth, never injustice. Love covers all, believes all, expects good in all, endures all (goodness). Love never fails (faithfulness). The greatest of all is love. (In case you didn't recognize those underlined words, they come from Galatians 5:22-23 – the fruit of the Spirit.) And one final reference for love found in 1 John 4:7-11, "**Beloved, let us love one another: for love is of God; and every one that loves is born of God, and knows God. He that loves not knows not God; for God is love. In this was manifested the love of God toward us, because that God sent His only begotten Son into the world, that we might live through Him. Herein is love, not that we loved God, but that He loved us and sent His Son to be the propitiation for our sins. Beloved, if God so loved us, we ought also to love one another.**" Giving to His own hurt, that we might have life! That about sums it up! Love conquers sin and all. Don't we all need to work on our love life!

You must also have your communication system (prayer life) in full operation, sending questions to and receiving answers from the Lord that will enable you to react in knowledge of *what* to do and *when* for complete health of your husband and your marriage. Anything less is short-circuiting your entire ministry and purpose in being a wife. **"Pray without ceasing...And the very God of peace sanctify you wholly; and your whole spirit and soul and body be preserved blameless unto the coming of our Lord Jesus Christ."** (1 Thessalonians 5:17, 23) Can we really pray without ceasing? Just as surely as your cells constantly give and receive messages to and from your brain. Do your cells ever take time off or go on vacation or take a little R&R in Hawaii or maybe get so caught up in just living that they forget to communicate? Disaster results if that happens. Ditto in the marriage.

Now these next verses are for you to pray and earnestly desire for your mate, but I also pray this especially for you. **"Wherefore also we pray always for you, that our God would count you worthy of this calling, and fulfill all the good pleasure of His goodness, and the work of faith with power: that the name of our Lord Jesus Christ may be glorified in you and you in Him, according to the grace of our God and the Lord Jesus Christ."** (2 Thessalonians 1:11-12) Ephesians 6:18 exhorts us to pray always with all prayer and supplication in the Spirit, watching with all perseverance and supplication for all the saints. Be persistent in asking for benefits from the Lord for your marriage. He likes us to be persistent. Join in with Paul's prayer in Colossians 1:9-13 as he proclaimed he would not cease to pray for his readers (that's us, too) and desire that we might be filled with the knowledge of His will in all wisdom and spiritual understanding, walking worthy of the Lord, being fruitful in every good work, increased in the knowledge of God, strengthened with all might according to His glorious power into all patience towards people and circumstances, giving thanks to the Father who has delivered us from the power of darkness and translated us into the kingdom of His dear Son! Amen and wow again! What a prayer to pray for your husband!

Read those verses out of your Bible and put your husband's name in place of you and ye. Pray it from your heart.

Now, after you have made sufficient communication with the Lord He will give you wise counsel on each situation you come up against. That is where Proverbs 20:18 comes in. **"Every purpose is established by counsel: and with good advice make war."** The Lord sure isn't going to give you bad advice so prepare yourself for battle!

Do you feel a little battle weary already? You didn't know what your marriage vows were really all about did you? When you said, "I do!" at that same moment you were enlisting as a soldier in a war in which the enemy has the sole purpose of destroying your marriage. Your vow was 'til death parts you! So how does one go about doing all of this stuff to keep that vow? Can we really defeat the enemy before it can cripple us – or worse, declare victory? A really good verse to memorize is Psalm 61:8 – **"So will I sing praise unto Thy name forever, that I may daily perform my vows."** Yes, you do have to take up singing. That literally means "to make music accompanied by the voice in celebration." Singing praise to Him is how we perform (fulfill, complete, make good) our vows made to Him and before Him concerning our marriage. Furthermore, it is a day-by-day process. When we are not praising Him daily, we cannot perform daily. And we sing to His name always and for eternity, knowing that what we do, we do for Him. Colossians 3:17, **"And whatsoever you do in word or deed, do all in the name of the Lord Jesus, giving thanks to God the Father by Him." "Give unto the Lord the glory due unto his name; worship the Lord in the beauty of holiness...The Lord will give strength** (force, security, majesty) **to his people; the Lord will bless his people with peace** (health, security, tranquility, a satisfied condition, a harmonious state of soul and mind both externally and internally).” Psalm 29:2 & 11. That word peace means more than the absence of strife; it expresses completeness, harmony, and fulfillment. Now that is a much better condition in which to live than what we just went over in 2 Corinthians 12:20 with all that quarreling and envying, wrath and strife, backbiting and whispering, swellings and tumults! Give me peace! Amen and amen!

Now take a few minutes to read 2 Chronicles 20. Are you there? Good King Jehoshaphat was afraid of the enemy. He prayed. He set himself to seek the Lord. Take a good look at verse 12 **“…for we have no might against this great company that comes against us; neither know we what to do: but our eyes are upon Thee.”** That’s where we need to be – overwhelmed by the oncoming enemy and turning totally to the Lord for His deliverance. Now look at the last of verse 15 **“…Be not afraid nor dismayed by reason of this great multitude; for the battle is not yours, but God’s.”** If only I could remember that when the enemy attacks! Keep reading. They fall before the Lord, worshiping Him. What an absurd battle plan they proceed to engage! Jehoshaphat puts singers before the army, praising the beauty of holiness, singing praise to the Lord for His mercy endures forever. And what did the Lord do in response? Why just as the king had “set” himself to seek the Lord, the Lord “set” ambushes to defeat their enemies. He so confounded and confused them that they fought themselves and Israel had only to carry off the spoils of victory, so much of jewels and riches that it took three days to gather it all. They went home the same way they had come - singing praises to their God. Now turn your attention to verse 29. There is a wonderful reputation that follows a victory that God wins. I can look back on those victories that were won in my marriage through the power of the Lord and there was a good spoil of the enemy, benefits that enriched our lives. The devil was defeated in that area and knows not to raise his ugly head there again. But more attacks in new arenas still lurk even after all these years of marriage. Just think of all the great victories that the Lord has waiting for you! Are you up to the battle? You had better get ready so you are not found consorting with the enemy!

Sing, Girl, sing! Until another day, my sweet...

Enjoy your meal, Miss Macrophage,
Momma 2

P. S. Laugh a lot with hubby; it's healthy for your marriage...

LETTER 12

Let's Meet the Staff

*M*y Dear Princess,

Are you feeling like a princess today? (This is where I was in my letter writing to my Susie; she had just delivered her first baby and I chose to leave these first two paragraphs hoping you could relate [if not yet, soon.]) This whole motherhood thing changes life a lot, doesn't it? It's really good to get rid of that heavy burden you had to carry 24/7 but the noise factor has gone up a lot – not to mention the lack of sleep! Oh, the memories that flood my soul. Life's adventures are about to take you to a whole new playing field. I can tell you are already loving the journey. I've never seen a mother so camera-happy!

What effect has the arrival of a baby had on Daddy? We get to see a new dimension of our husbands when they become daddies. After a few months of fatherhood you may want to update those "lists"... There will be a lot more to pray for now and new areas of attack on your marriage. Did you know differences in raising and disciplining children rank up there in the top three reasons for divorce? Satan now has a whole new realm in which to work. Just thought you ought to be warned up front. Be on guard!

Let me see – we last spent time together here on those fabulous phagocytes and marvelous macrophages that serve us so well patrolling our insides, devouring anything foreign that makes it past our skin. One of the outstanding features of the macrophage is that as it "eats" the enemy, it takes the distinctive marking, the antigen, that only that particular pathogen (enemy) has, kind of like unique fingerprints, and displays it on itself for recognition by the Helper T-cells, thus beginning the battle. As the war proceeds, the macrophage produces a protein that activates those T-cells and stimulates the brain to raise the body temperature, which really gears up the immune system for combat. With those things in mind, let me proceed...

We are going to be a little silly now and I am going to call upon your creative imagination to help us "see" our army? I always loved watching my children play – as all mothers must. It brings such pleasure watching those little wheels in a child's brain spinning round and round, turning the most ordinary things into fantastic adventures. Can you remember? An imagination is a wonder to behold as one explores the universe in a cardboard box or turns mud pies into a banquet or the front room into Cinderella's ballroom (personally as a child, my house turned into NYC and Broadway) - but back to the task at hand. I want you to take a few minutes to visualize these fearfully important soldiers that make up our immune systems. If we could line them up in different uniforms it would be so helpful. A picture is worth a thousand words. You could get on the internet and find some fantastic images of everything we have gone over. That might be a good project for you, but for now let's just try to visualize in this silly way what they might look like. Bear with me; this is going to be a really simplified picture of our fantastically complicated immune system... Now wipe the lint of your practicality from your lenses of the microscope of imagination and let's inspect our soldiers.

Before us stands the first regiment of our soldiers, a strange looking lot for sure. Because they are on constant surveillance duty searching out anything foreign to "self" we see them in a more comfortable uniform than most. I'll let

you imagine what those comfort clothes look like, but put them on your phagocyte soldiers. And on each shirt is an image of a really big mouth reminding us
of their great calling: to eat the enemy. They have noticeably long arms pro-
truding from their shirts because, after all, reaching out to grab things to eat
would naturally call for long arms. Now amongst this great line of defense you
will notice some extremely large Goliath phagocytes. Yes, those are our macrophages, bold and brave and in-charge kind of guys. Because of their great
size their shirts have room above that big mouth for a chest pocket that carries
around their own communication system. Remember, they have to stay in constant contact with the brain to receive orders and pass them on to the rest of
the defense system. And we see on their backs chemical packs that have trigger controls at their fingertips to be released when the battle commences. Oh,
yes, one more thing about these giants. They have Velcro attached to their hel-
mets to display the antigen of the enemy they encounter. Got a good picture?
This first regiment is passing by and now the second one stands at attention
ready to be recognized.

I'm anxious to personally introduce you to each battalion of this next regiment but I want you to "see" them first. This group is known as the lymphocytes and there are five distinct divisions. The first to approach our review
stand is the Helper T-cells. These comrades might be compared to the picture
you conjure up when thinking of Gideon's army – no weapons, just a trumpet
in one hand and a jar in the other. However, they wear uniforms – crisp, pol-
ished and sporting stars on their shoulders. Don't let the name "Helper" allow
you think this soldier just lends a helping hand (remember our word "ezer").
They are the commanders of this army and without them there would be no
call to arms. That is why they carry a trumpet. And in the jar is a complex
chemistry lab that produces several different chemicals to be released at just

the right time by these highly trained experts in warfare. Oh, yes, this Helper T also wears special glasses which enable it to identify the one specific antigen in which it has been trained to identify. When this T encounters the Macrophage that has that particular antigen posted on its helmet, the T immediately springs into warfare mode and brings the trumpet to the lips. This is the first battalion of the T-cells.

The next division to approach is the Killer T-cells. This proud group of soldiers knows the value of their expertise to the survival of the body. They are comfortable in their combat uniforms with their weapons drawn. You may picture the weapon as a modern rifle, an M16 or the like, but I prefer to see it as a sword. Each Killer T has been specifically trained to do the job that only it can do and they all stand tall before us and ready to respond at first call. They, too, like the Helper Ts, have special glasses (goggles perhaps) that enable them to identify the one specific enemy they have been trained to destroy. There are more T-cells that we will see, but we must wait until this next division passes by if we are to review them in the order in which they are called into the battle.

We now see the B-cells approaching. Their dress is more of a working uniform that looks like a chemist's lab coat since they are the soldiers that staff their own individual biological arms factories. They work directly from their frontline bases, which are either the spleen or lymph nodes. Although they don't take part in the "hand to hand" combat, they are the ones that produce the weapons called antibodies. As dynamic as the Killer Ts are, without these faithful B-cells churning out their weapons, there would be no way to gain advantage over the invading enemy. They, too, carry their heads high, and rightfully so, for their crucial contribution to this warfare.

Now we see another battalion of T-cells passing our review. This regiment contains the Suppressor Ts, the peacemakers. Our image of these important soldiers must be dignified. They are wearing dress uniforms and have the honor of wearing all the medals of honor, decorations for bravery and commendations of victories won by their comrades. They, like the Helper Ts, carry no weapons, but a horn is carried in one hand and a briefcase in the other. They carry the authority to command all Ts and Bs to cease all activity. The Suppressor's instrument does not carry the sharp note of alarm and call to arms as the Helper T's, but a sweet, mellow tone of peace and tranquility that flows through the immune system's rank of soldiers causing them to halt the attack because the victory has been won. The briefcase carries the signed surrender of the enemy. Smiling success is written all over these soldiers.

The final battalion is made up of both T-cells and B-cells that have been created during the warfare. These are called Memory cells and I'm not sure how to describe them. They are decorated with special emblems that have resulted from the battle and consequential victory. Each battle this valiant immune system army fights produces new Memory cells that proudly display the latest emblem of victory. In addition to their badges of victory, they carry spyglasses that vigilantly scour every nook and cranny for an invasion by the specific foe just conquered. There is tremendous power in these cells that prevent that particular, conquered enemy from ever posing a threat to the body again. Most of these Memories will circulate through the body the rest of your life, providing complete immunity to another attack from the same enemy.

Okay, the soldier review is over. I wish I were an artist and could have drawn cute little pictures. But I hope this simplistic, sketchy description is usable for you to catch a glimpse of our immune system with a reference point to come back to. Now, with no further ado, let's move on to intimately get to know the rest of our fearfully and wonderfully made army.

All the cells of our immune system are born in the bone marrow, that soft tissue in the hollow center of the bones. (Suppose that's why God used a bone to create Eve?) Some of those cells are then directed to the thymus gland, which is kind of like a West Point for immune cells. These troops are known as T-cells (T for thymus). Here they receive their thymic education – learning self-tolerance, being programmed with self-markers so they can live peaceably with their own body, while being trained to recognize the enemies' antigens that have been collected and displayed on the body's cells. By the way, the body knows its 100 trillion cells by name, be it lung tissue, eye cones, or heart muscle, no matter how diverse, and these T-cells protect them all because they are "self". We will get more into the importance of that a bit later. As T-cells mature in the thymus gland, each learns to recognize one specific antigen of the hundreds of millions of different shapes of viruses, bacteria, and such other ugly stuff. As T-cells circulate through the body, they scan the surface of its cells looking for the presence of that particular foreign antigen for which they were trained to recognize. (Remember the glasses we have them wearing?) They also have been trained to recognize self-markers so they won't attack the body they have been programmed to serve. When mutations in the body's own cells occur, as with cancer, they recognize the mutant cell as foreign and proceed with the elimination process. It's because of this training that organ transplants are so difficult; the immune cells know these new cells do not belong to their body so they proceed with their plan of attack.

We have three distinct classes of T-cells. Our first to get to know is the Help-er T. Don't you like that title – Helper? That's what God called woman even before He fashioned her. Take a stroll back to that letter called The Twist is at the Beginning, your fourth letter, I think. Jog your memory with a quick review. I love the fact that the Almighty God, Creator of the Universe, uses the same word for Himself that He uses for woman! And here we find the commanders-in-chief of this remarkable immune system also called the Helper Ts. I don't know who so named these cells, but it was surely divinely inspired. As these travel through the body and receive the message from a macrophage, who has just had a delicious meal of an enemy intruder and now has its antigen displayed on himself, the Helper T, who has been trained to recognize that particular enemy, binds to that macrophage, like a lock fitting onto that unique antigen key, and thus becomes activated. That Helper T then begins to multiply and sends out the alert to the rest of the defense team that there has been an invasion. These commanders carry no weapons, but they do carry the key to communications by activating lymphokines, vital chemicals (interleukin-2, BCGF, BCDF, gamma interferon) – the stuff that calls to arms the Killer T-cells and the B-cells, as well as additional Helper Ts and macrophages. These also signal the Killer Ts and Bs to proliferate and function more efficiently. And the gamma interferon actually protects non-infected cells by interfering with the ability of the invading virus to enter healthy ones and enabling those cells to resist the viral attacks. The Helper Ts direct the cellular traffic and organize the plan of attack, coordinating the entire immune response, making it the mighty host that brings down strongholds.

Let's see how the wife's role corresponds to this Helper T. First, she is going to have to get some specialized training in learning the "antigens" of the enemy, those special markings which alert her that their marriage has been assaulted and invaded. Moms should be giving their daughters some vital training, but unfortunately most moms have failed to do so because they never learned themselves. There are some great books out there on marriage but one has to do a lot of wading through some bad advice to find the good. So why not just turn to the best in the beginning. The Bible is the infallible textbook to be used in this training. It is the answer key to all the questions. It is surefire, right-on, dependable truth, showing us what marriage should be, teaching us those self-markers that enable us to live peaceably (which is crucial to the success of two becoming one), as well as identifying the enemy and how attacks come. She must read the Textbook!

Although the whole theme of Psalm 119 is the beauty and truth of God's Word as the means of purity and spiritual growth, I would like to zero in on verses 97-100 ... **"O how I love Thy law** (God's instructions, not restrictions, to His people showing them His will)**! It is my meditation all the day. You, through Your commandments** (clear-cut directives) **have made me wiser than my enemies: for they are ever with me. I have more understanding** (more insight, skill, expertise because I know the reasons) **than all my teachers** (those educating me)**: for Thy testimonies** (witness, going over again) **are my meditation. I understand** (have superior knowledge, discernment) **more than the ancients** (aged)**, because I keep** (guard, protect, obey) **Thy precepts** (appointments, mandates, specific purpose designated to me)**."** Fall in love with the Textbook!

But reading alone is not going to equip her. She must have some very specialized teaching that can only come from the Teacher. Jesus called Himself Lord and Master in John 13:13, 14. The King James' translators used the word **Lord**, which means possessor, owner, *master* of all; and the word **Master**, which means *teacher*. As their Lord and Master, He was their Master and Teacher. Confusing, huh? As Jesus was preparing to go to the cross, leaving His disciples, He promised He would not leave them alone, orphans. He would send **"another Comforter"**, one of equal quality as Jesus; only He will abide with us forever as the **"Spirit of truth."** Comforter, *parakletos* in the Greek, is one who has been called to help, a *helper*! The word was used by the Hebrews to speak of a legal advisor or advocate who came forward to help on behalf of or as the representation of another. You know, I have always heard that the Spirit is *our* helper, *our* advocate with the Father, which He surely is. But He is also the Lord's advocate, undertaking Christ's office in the world while Jesus has gone to prepare us a place with the Father. He picks up the role as our Teacher in the absence of the Master/Teacher. Jesus said, **"If a man love Me, he will keep My words."** Of course we love Him, but how can we possibly know or remember all the things He taught? The Spirit, **"whom the Father will send in My name, He shall teach you all things, and bring all things to your remembrance, whatsoever I have said unto you."** (John 14:26) Do you realize the magnitude of that statement? Jesus has told us He will not leave us alone but another like Himself, the Comforter (the Helper), will stand in for Him, teaching us (instructing by word of mouth to shape the will of the pupil) all the things we need to know, bringing to remembrance (reminding quietly) everything Jesus taught. We have a Teacher to instruct us every step of the way. So, Wife, get the proper training. Spend time with the Teacher and let Him teach you all things. It is imperative to get an education (one better than West Point provides) before one tries to take command in the battle! (I guess we could call our Teacher our Thymus for this Helper T-cell aspect of our ministry.)

Who and what are the enemies we need to recognize? We have discussed this in previous letters but go to 1 Peter 5:8 for a frightening description of our adversary. You won't find a lion in any zoo that is like a wild lion on the prowl. My husband's trip to South Africa gave him a whole new appreciation of the roaring lion metaphor Peter used. And, of course, anyone having seen the movie "Ghosts in the Darkness" has vivid ideas of what a lion can do to his prey. We have gone over Ephesians 6:12 before, but reread it to remind yourself that it is not flesh and blood that we are dealing with but principalities, powers, rulers of this present darkness, spiritual wickedness – things not seen with the physical eye but the spirit. Women *must* learn to recognize the markings!

Let's take a minute to check out the two names most frequently used for this foe. Satan – the prince of the fallen angels, our opponent in this struggle to live godly lives. When Jesus said to dear Peter, His beloved friend and entrusted leader, "Get thee behind me, Satan," He was speaking to Peter's opposing of the divine plan of redemption by the suffering on the cross. When anyone, no matter how good and godly, opposes what God has planned, well, that one has just crossed over to the ranks of the great adversary. Of course, for Peter's own good Jesus rebuked him, as should all be rebuked who unwittingly fall into the same trap. How many times are we found speaking our own thoughts that oppose the plan of God, simply because we don't understand the storyline and what our characters have been created to do? Find the time to run some references on "Satan": I Chronicles 21:1; Job 1:9-11; 2:4-5; Zechariah 3:1-2; Matthew 16:23; Mark 1:13; Luke 22:3,31; Acts 5:3; 2 Thessalonians 2:9; Revelation 12:7-9 – and then there are my favorites - Romans 16:20 and Revelation 20:1-10. Halleluiah! and Amen!

Another word Jesus used for Satan is the devil, which means an accuser, a slanderer. He has accused both God and mankind. Jesus called Judas a devil in John 6:70 because He knew that under Satan's influence Judas would be Christ's accuser and betrayer. The word comes from two words, the preposition *dia* (through) and *bello* (to cast). According to Zodhiates Lexical Aid, the devil is "one who casts either himself or something else between two in order to separate them." And accusations and slander are the great separators. His attacks are daily occurrences – usually several times a day. Isn't that what he did in the Garden? He slandered God and separated Eve from her trust in her Creator; her relationship with Adam was severed through accusation (it was that woman You gave me). She was even separated from life itself. Death is separation. How many are the heartaches, broken relationships, dead friendships, severed ministries, devastated marriages because the devil, through accusations or slander, has separated two once united hearts. In John 8:44 Jesus called the devil a liar, a murderer, the father of lies. He has his own army scattered throughout the world and his battle tactics are sinister, wicked, and dirty. Watch out! He takes special delight in bludgeoning Christian marriages!

This dutiful wife must be trained to recognize the markers that reveal the enemy has gained access. 2 Corinthians 2:11 admonishes her not to be **ignorant** (not to know because of a lack of information or intelligence) of Satan's **devices** (thoughts, purposes, disposition) or she will give him leeway, of which he is quick to take advantage. The particular device Paul was speaking of in that passage was an unforgiving spirit. Satan really goes to seed on a heart that holds a grudge. Keep in mind, his only purpose is to **steal** (attack to take booty), **kill** (to rush upon to slaughter as a bloody sacrifice) and **destroy** (kill, whether temporary destruction or fully destroy for eternity). (John 10:10) Think on that a while for some hair-raising thoughts! There is also a warning in 2 Corinthians 11:13-15 to be aware that Satan and his ministers will **transform themselves** (disguise) as **apostles of Christ, angels of light, ministers of righteousness.** Just because it looks and sounds good does not make it so. That is the deceptive virus trying to sneak in unawares. She must know the truth so she doesn't fall for the counterfeit. Don't be ignorant!

Then there are those people who are being used by the enemy to **"cause divisions and offenses contrary to the doctrine which ye have learned"** (Romans 16:17-18). They must be **marked** (contemplated, given attention, literally spied out) because of the quality of their work: they **cause,** meaning the doing once and for all, producing and bringing forth something which, when produced, has an independent existence of its own. They become a virus factory, bringing to life deceit and false doctrine. Think back to how the virus works: it slips into a cell, cancels the DNA of that cell issuing its own instructions, robs the cell of its nutrients, and establishes its own virus factory, eventually rupturing the cell, causing thousands of viral clones to repeat the process, now reproduced with an independent existence of its own. The **divisions** (separations, incitements of disorder and rebellion) and **offenses** (literally the trigger in the trap on which the bait is placed and springs the trap when it is touched, causing the trap to close; the enticement that incites certain behavior which leads to ruin!) come from teachings that come along beside the doctrine taught in scripture but go beyond, swerving from the true point, coming short of truth – **contrary**. But it is done so deceitfully, using doctrine we know and trust as truth and putting a twist on it that intrigues and entices the hearer. Satan tried it on Jesus by quoting truth from the scripture but used wrongly to swerve from the true heart and meaning of the scripture. Don't think he won't use people to practice the same tactics against marriage and every other sacred principle God has given us. I can hear some past "friends" still in my memory: "You let him tell you what to do?"..."You've got too much to give the world to be stuck at home with kids." They wanted to offer me freedom, independence, control, authority - with feminism engrained in their lives. We are warned to absolutely shun, separate away, depart from such; they aren't serving Jesus, but their own belly through **good words** (plausible, reasonable speech) and **fair speeches** (elegance of language, expressing good wishes, praise, commendation to man). We just really like to

The Mystery of Marriage through Adam's Prime Rib

hear fair speeches, don't we? Beware! That is what Satan uses to **deceive the hearts of the simple** (seduce wholly the heart, thoughts, and feelings of the innocent or unsuspecting). Again, Eve has gone before us to demonstrate how the deceiver caught her in his trap. Guard your heart, your head, and your emotions! You simply must read 2 Timothy 3:1-7 for a warning to "silly women" – literally little wives, foolish, gullible, simple in their thinking, always learning but never able to come to the knowledge of the truth. Women are a playground for the vermin that creep into our houses with their corrupted minds. And while you are in the vicinity, look at 1 Timothy 6:3-5. Withdraw thyself!

But in addition to the Accuser and those he works through to deceive us, there is still another formidable enemy. Look at I John 2:16 – **"For all that is in the world, the lust of the flesh, and the lust of the eyes, and the pride of life, is not of the Father, but is of the world."** The prince of this world uses our own desires for this world to destroy us. Have you ever really given serious thought to what that word lust means? To **lust** is to long for something forbidden, the active desire that comes from the diseased condition of the soul. We long to indulge **the flesh**, those *outward*, physical, sensual pleasures of our bodies as opposed to the spirit. We are told in Galatians 5:16-26 to walk in the Spirit so we will not fulfill the lust of the flesh. **"For the flesh lusts against the Spirit and the Spirit against the flesh: and these are contrary the one to the other: so that you cannot do the things that you would."** What a battle is going on within us! Paul then lists the works of the flesh and the fruit of the Spirit; refresh your memory – reread those verses in chapter 5.

The second lust John spoke of is of the eyes. In addition to the flesh, we also long to indulge **the eyes**, to have the pleasures of our *inward* imaginations - that internal sense that relishes whatever is grand, new, or beautiful. It's hard to keep that forbidden desire in check when we go house hunting, huh? Or shopping in general! But Proverbs 27:20 and Ecclesiastes 1:8 and 4:8 all remind us that our eyes are never satisfied. We always want bigger and better, just a little bit more.

And just what is this third worldly enemy, **the pride of life**? When I looked up the word pride in my Greek dictionary it gave the definition of braggadocio. Well, I got the brag part, but I went to my Webster's anyway. It means empty boasting, an arrogant braggart, self-confidence. The next time someone plays "brag" on the Scrabble board, you could get your 50 bonus points by playing "gadocio" on it. Keep that in mind for future reference. Excuse me, back to the lesson at hand... So we have a braggart about **life**, *bios* – the Greek word that gives us the word biography. It is all the pomp in clothes, houses, profession, manner of living, which procures honor from mankind and gratifies pride and vanity and the desire of praise and applause – self-confidence in "doing it my way." Why else does one boast but to receive praise from others about self's life? It's not from the Father; it leads us astray to destruction. The very next verse tells us that the world is passing away and all those vain pursuits and delusive pleasures that go with it. It is only in the doing of God's will that we find eternity. And His will is not commands or demands. It is God's good pleasure and divine purpose, that when done, brings joy to both the Father and child. That's what brings everlasting satisfaction and eternal rewards - being found faithful in doing His will. Jesus said in John 8:29 that He always did those things that pleased the Father. That is our objective, which leaves lust and pride totally out of the picture. Jump back to where we were in Galatians 5 – verse 26 says **"Let us not be desirous of vain glory, provoking one another, envying one another."** Those are more markers of the enemy! Paul sums up the book of Galatians so powerfully when he states emphatically in 6:14 **"God forbid that I should glory, save in the cross of our Lord Jesus Christ, by Whom the**

The Mystery of Marriage through Adam's Prime Rib

world is crucified unto me and I unto the world." Then, of course, we have Galatians 2:20 and 5:24 to add to that verse as well as Romans 6:6. So don't succumb to the enemy's onslaught. God has given us the right and the power to say no. **"Greater is He that is in you, than he that is in the world."** 1 John 4:4. The more time you spend in the Word with your Teacher, the more markers you will recognize. Find the time, my Darling.

Now when this good wife has her "thymic" training well ingrained, she should be able to recognize the enemy and his tactics, that she might know from whence cometh the attack, as well as knowing self-markers, that she might live peaceably with herself and her spouse. By the way, those self-markers are vital! Just as the body knows its 100 trillion cells by name, regardless whether bone, lung tissue, or heart muscle, no matter how diverse, she must in like manner know her husband, no matter how diverse from herself. He is self and must be known and protected. We will look more into the importance of that a bit later. When she encounters the markings of an intrusion, she locks onto that "antigen" and then sends out an alarm to her defense mechanism which puts all of her spirituality on alert and in battle mode – not with her husband, but against the powers that have come against them and their marriage.

1 Corinthians 14:8 reminds us that the trumpet must give the call to arms or no one will prepare for the warfare, including herself. She must sound the sure alarm if her spirit is to prepare for battle – no wishy-washy, well is it, or isn't it, no hidden or vague sound but a loud and long alarm. Look at the promise in Numbers 10:9. Wow! **"And if you go to war in your land against the enemy that oppresses you, then you shall blow an alarm with the trumpets; and you shall be remembered before the LORD your God and you shall be saved from your enemies."** Do you suppose that command in Numbers was

why Gideon had his 300 men blowing trumpets as they began their battle with no weapons? You talk about faith that God is going to intervene for you! The same basic tactic was used with Joshua blowing horns and shouting as they circled Jericho. What is the purpose of blowing the trumpets? We don't need to wake up The Almighty. We don't even need to bring it to His attention that we are in trouble. He knows our thoughts from afar, our every word before we speak. Did you do your meditation on Psalm 139 way back there when we started all of this? He is omniscient! Why the trumpet alarm? It's a different sound than the blowing at feasts or memorials used to assemble the people for worship. This was a call of distress, fear, apprehension, trepidation – a time of acknowledgment that self-sufficiency was out the window and God's presence was priority and the only hope of survival. It was something totally physical that God commanded the people to do to summon spiritual help by faith. That's the kind of alert this good wife is going to issue. She must give the sound of alarm, a sound that pierces every nerve in the body and gets the adrenalin flowing, a sound that only her spirit and God hears, but a sound that moves into action both her resources and God's.

Keep in mind this alert is not a weapon but a calling for the defense mechanism to activate. There are no weapons at this point of the battle. It would do well to reread 1 Peter 3:1-4 – overcoming resistance to the Word of God without speaking a word. We are so terrible at keeping our mouths shut. The mouth can never, ever be used as a weapon. Our tongue only adds fuel to the enemy. God tells wives that we gain ground by a meek and quiet spirit manifesting itself in behavior that is calm and remains seated, under control and not demanding or jumping up in anxiety or fear or vexation or even authority. The best thing we have going for us at this stage is submission to that husband and a spirit that is in the sight of God of great price, extremely expensive and precious. He knows the price we have to pay to keep our mouths shut and submit. Remember Jesus before His accusers? He spoke not a word and submitted to the cruel injustices and pain that was inflicted upon Him. (1 Peter 2:21-23) He knows! And He honors that behavior as truly as He honors the call of the trumpet; He reaches out of heaven and saves us from our enemy.

In this role of a Helper T with no weapon against the enemy, a wife still has some pretty potent resources in Christ, as powerful as those chemicals that our Helper T-cell sends out to its co-workers. There is a battle plan to be formulated and executed, and she must use the resources given to her if she is to be effective.

Let's look at 2 Peter 1 first. In verse 2 Peter is praying for God's grace and peace to be multiplied to us through the knowledge of God and of Jesus our Lord. We proceed no further without the grace of God - His divine favor and influence working within us and reflecting outwardly in our lives. And that grace and peace only come our way through exact **knowledge** of our God - gained through personal participation in a relationship with Him, which in turn powerfully influences our lives. Then **"according as His divine power"** He gives to us **"all things that pertain unto life and godliness, through the knowledge of Him that hath called us to glory and virtue."** By His power we have been given **all** that we need to live a life that is the whole, true picture of devotion to God, which includes a marriage that honors Him. Peter then speaks of **"the exceeding great and precious promises"**; this power and knowledge enable us to **"be partakers of the divine nature, having escaped the corruption that is in the world through lust."** It is for this reason that he lists the seven things in verses 5-7 that must be added to our faith. Faith in Christ is only the beginning. It has brought you to salvation and keeps you walking daily in trust.

Hopefully, you know how to follow a recipe to make a successful dish. And if you leave an ingredient out, or prepare it poorly, your efforts have been sadly wasted on an inferior dish. (Angel food cake is a good example, really simple, but the recipe must be followed precisely; don't throw those eggs in with the flour to beat them!) So for our spiritual recipe: Add to your **faith**...

virtue, which is moral excellence, excellence in strength and courage, bold in your faith and witness. Remove all immorality from your life, including your thought pattern and any hypocrisy – even vicarious sin of association through books and movies. It taints you and makes you ineffective; you have a bold job to perform. Add to your virtue...

knowledge, different than the previous knowledge in verses 2 and 3. This knowledge is fragmented, only what is known by experience, but those experiences give you clarity of understanding and certainty of each truth and fact that has been revealed. Do you suppose you need some experience with Jesus and His power to accomplish this battle plan? Without it, you will never know what or why you believe. Ignorance is a curse with which many have been self-inflicted. Now that you have faith, virtue, and knowledge mixed well, add...

temperance, self-control, mastering our desires and appetites, keeping in check those so-hard-to-control passions in which we want to indulge. Now how well could that work for you as you enter into a war with the adversary? Next to be added is...

patience, abiding under, the ability to endure, not to surrender to circumstances or succumb under trials and pressures but to press on abiding under until the victory comes. People say they are afraid to pray for patience because

God sends adversity to teach them to endure. Patience, however, is in partnership with hope. It is that quality that allows one to stay under adverse circumstances because there is hope of victory, and that brings joy. This is kind of like beating those egg whites at the right temperature and to the perfect consistency or there is no hope of this cake succeeding. Patience is vital when you can't see the end; you just trust God is bringing it in His timing. Now we are up to...

godliness, devout fulfillment of religious obligation, to worship well, devotion, piety toward God. Piety - now there's an antiquated word modern society never uses. It means faithfulness in showing reverence for God and devotion to worship Him dutifully. Don't we all need to add more reverence in our worship and certainly more faithfulness – gratitude and duty demand it. Worship the Lord in the beauty of holiness, by fulfilling the role to which He has called you. You have a critical job. Do it with all your might in His name. Following this faithful devotion add...

brotherly kindness, the love of a friend for another as a brother through a spiritual bond in Christ. Do you have a spiritual bond of love as well as your physical love for your husband? Christians love Christians differently, bearing one another's weaknesses and foibles, giving blessings, expressing compassion. Add to your philadelphia...

charity, *agape* love, love shown not by doing what the loved person desires, but what the one who loves deems best for the one loved, sacrificially, unselfishly. That is the love God has towards us, giving us what we need for our good not what we want. That is the love a wife must draw upon to serve her husband for his good and the good of their marriage. Love is at the top of the list and surpasses all else, the same love we spent time on in the last letter. This is the most powerful chemical she has. Use it wisely as the scripture instructs. This is the love God expects from believers, reflecting the character of our heavenly Father, His very nature.

Need more resources? Go to Colossians 3:12-15. Remember, God has given you **"all things that pertain to life and godliness."** Here we find listed tender mercies, kindness, humility, meekness, longsuffering (this is patience with people as opposed to patience under circumstances to which Peter was referring), bearing with one another, forgiving as Christ has forgiven us, having love above all else, letting peace rule your heart, and being thankful. These are all "chemicals" that are protecting the rest of your body while you are at war with the enemy in the invaded cells of your marriage. They enable the uninfected areas to resist the adversary by drawing near to God through godly living.

One more set of resources? In Ephesians 6:13-18 we find truth, righteousness, peace, faith, and salvation. Again, the more you read with your Teacher, the more you will find.

Can you see the vital work you must do to organize and direct the battle plan? God has equipped us for battle. We just must approach it according to His directives and plan, step by step, as He has so well demonstrated for us through our immune system. This educated commander role on which we have just elaborated is what activates the rest of our defenses, making them more efficient, causing them to multiply and rise to the occasion, even protecting other vulnerable areas in our marriage.

I have been awfully long-winded again, or since I am writing, I guess you would say I have been very wordy. I shall have to save the next comparison for another letter. Before I go, look at Psalm 44:4-8 with me again. This is a prayer to our King for deliverance from distress, knowing when God commands, it happens. This a prayer of faith, believing that we already have our victory, having pushed down our enemies and crushed them under our feet by His name, not trusting in our own resources but knowing God has saved us, set us free from our enemies, and humiliated them with the shame of an utter defeat. **"In God we boast** (radiate with praise) **all the day long, and praise Thy name forever."** Now is when we do our bragging - in God. Remember you are one flesh with your husband in marriage, and in praying for him, you are praying for yourself and your own life in the battle that takes place against your mutual enemy. Defend your marriage and walk with God.

I have to tell you, it has done wonders for me to review all these scriptures and remind myself of my job. Those that desire my hurt, and yours, have been after me in ways that I am ashamed to admit that I failed to recognize. I let down my guard and defenses and can see the sad results. I have done some serious repenting as I write and am settling back into my meek and quiet mode of submission to my husband. Pray for me as I pray for you. It is obvious I have not conquered this submission thing yet, and you have only just begun. I am hoping you will seriously make an effort, not because your husband is always right, but because it is God's plan. The enemy is watching every move and looking for an opportune time to attack. Be ready. Sound the alarm. Plan the attack. And pray earnestly Psalm 70:1-2. **"O God, deliver me; make haste to *help* me, O LORD. Let them be ashamed and confounded that seek after my soul: let them be turned backward, and put to confusion, that desire my hurt."**

Sounding the alarm with great love,
Momma 2 CK

LETTER 13

Forward into Battle

*M*y Darling Soldier,

It took too long getting that last letter out. Having just reviewed my notes from the "Adam's Prime Rib" Bible study, I realize how much more there is yet to say. The days are fleeting and my life is so full of duties that take precedence over my time with you here, critical time. My own marriage was under assault as I wrote to you. Satan does not like for us to discuss his tactics or proclaim God's truth. I knew it would come, as it always does when we enter his domain on the offensive. He prefers our ignorance or apathy. There are attacks building against you and your precious family. We must press on to the battle, aware of the enemy.

Okay, you need to review the lists you made about the enemies *without* – the "protozoa", "bacteria", and "viruses" - and enemies *within* – the old nature, neglect, pride, and rebellion. Have you added to your lists yet? New circumstances present new areas to defend … a job change, moving to a new hone, sickness… Fatherhood. So does Motherhood! You will add some real challenges to the sanity of your marriage with a developing she-bear attitude towards anyone who dares think your little darling needs a swat across the hind side for the betterment of humanity. When daddy loses his cool with the constant crying of infancy, or the incessant whys of the terrible twos, or the defiant, independent spirit of the fours, well, hang on to your spirituality when the confusing, rebellious 13th year arrives! You will look back on the lists that you compiled in the early years and laugh at the simplicity of what you thought were "problems." But for today and in all of its seriousness (for our enemy is serious at every stage), get your inventory in front of you and evaluate the health of your marriage. If your role as phagocyte can simply do some house-cleaning, go for it. If your macrophage mode needs to be called in, don't hesitate. And if as a macrophage you detect an antigen, by all means, move to your Helper T character and begin your plan of counterattack for whatever the enemy has devised against your marriage to foil the plan of God for your good and His glory. What are you dealing with at the moment?

To get you thinking, let's pull an example out from the "within" list and see what we do naturally and how the devil gets involved. If it's pride that is riding a man, his wife automatically thinks humiliating him (especially in public) will knock that pride right out of the saddle. Wrong. She has just passed off a full load of ammunition to the forces of the enemy. Remember, our ways are not His ways. Your Teacher must have the freedom to train you in His ways. It is most unfortunate how pride burrows its way into a man's life. He is forced to look for things in which to boast (which Satan delightedly provides) because his precious wife has neglected her role as his biggest fan, bragging on his every accomplishment. God is the One who made us with an ego – that thinking, feeling, and willing part of us that distinguishes each one from others. When Satan feeds that ego, pride is the result, producing an egotist consumed with arrogance, conceit, and self-reliance. But when a wife feeds her man's ego, not only does she build his confidence in his work, he is humbled at her praise and reflects it back to her. There is a beautiful adoration of one another that takes place, building up the other's character and confidence, and, at the same time, becoming more dependent upon one another. Unity! It is more wonderful and fantastic than words can convey. It is conforming to the script the Author has laid out. Believe me, that ego will be fed, either by you or

Satan and the world. And the submission principle of Ephesians 5:22-23 is one of the best tools God has given woman to build up her husband's confidence in his manhood. Choose to be used by your Creator to fulfill all of your husband's needs. When you praise your husband you are praising the LORD. The same principle applies in so many areas of our marriages. Our lives are choices and consequences. What choice is the enemy presently posing to you?

The Author of Life has given us a wonderful, yet terrifying, gift in allowing his characters a say in what they will do. If we know the storyline we will make wise decisions. If we are ignorant of His intended outcome or curiously doubtful, then foolishness and disaster prevail. Still, He gives us the right to make choices.

Do they still make the children's books that let the reader choose what the character does next? After reading a couple of pages, you were faced with two or three options. Choose A. and go to page __ to see the result and more choices that led to more results and so on. Or choose B. and turn to page __ for the differing circumstances now giving new choices leading to yet other pages and other choices creating many endings to the same story. The books were amusing for none of the results were real and, of course, you could always go back to the first choice and change it for a better outcome. It was a good way to make a child realize choices had consequences. Unfortunately, our real-life choices cannot be undone any more than you can undo the loss of feathers when Grandma's feather pillow is torn open and shaken in the Oklahoma winds. Life is choices and consequences. Choose wisely!!!

Back on track... Let's take an up-close and personal look at the Killer T cells of our immune system. They, too, have graduated from their "Thymic" training. I can almost see their big "TU" insignia patch on the backs of their camouflaged uniforms. Each one is now specialized, assigned to kill one specific, designated antigen. With their "goggles" in place for accurate identification of the enemy, they target cells that have been infected. They even recognize the mutiny that's occurred when a cell turns cancerous and loses its self-marker. When the alarm is sounded by the Helper T, these soldiers respond straightway. (Don't you like that word, straightway. Mark used it some 40 times in his account of the Gospel – a word that stands out in Mark's telling of the life and working of our Lord, a word of immediacy, a word of prompt action, describing well God's obedient servant!) These Killer Ts are our combat professionals, armed and ready to fight. These cells are filled with potent, lethal chemicals that puncture bacteria cell membranes or destroy our own infected cells before viruses inside can multiply. They take aim with their weapon and deliver bursts of toxin to the enemy. (They are the ones responsible for the body's rejection of tissue grafts and organ transplants.) They are all over anything that is not self, killing on contact with no questions asked or prisoners taken. They stand by their name, Killer.

Now how in the world do you relate to that? Well, let's look at your weapon. An M-16 or bazooka or AK-47 or any other such gun would fit the description of "delivering bursts of toxin" that puncture the enemy. But do you remember I said I preferred to think of their weapon as a sword? That's because our weapon is the same one Jesus used when Satan tempted Him – Scripture, the Word of God, the Sword of the Spirit (Ephesians 6:17). The wife's major force against the enemy, foreign or self, must be one that is directed toward that specific enemy, to puncture and destroy it with the Sword of the Spirit. That was the only weapon Jesus used when the adversary assaulted Him in the wilderness. Jesus knew how to handle the Word of God. It works against the forces of evil, temptations, false doctrines, self-inflicted torments, and even cancers of the soul. It is tried and proven effective every time.

2 Timothy 2:15 is a verse every Sunday School child is taught to memorize:

"**Study** (to use speed, to make an effort, be prompt or earnest, diligent)
to show thyself (to stand beside yourself, to exhibit, substantiate yourself)
approved (acceptable, proved as though tried by fire or adversity
and purified)
unto God, (our Creator and Judge, the One to whom we must give an account)
a workman (one who performs labor resulting in attainment or realization)
that needeth not to be ashamed (not able to be found with fault)
rightly dividing (to make a straight cut, to dissect correctly)
the Word (the orderly linking and knitting together in connected
arrangement as the expression of the inward thoughts and feelings of the
intelligent mind – logos from the verb lego [the toy maker knew Greek!])
of truth (unveiled reality, actual state of a matter transcending
perceived experience)."

Now, as a grownup woman, you must put into practice that verse. A wife must know the Word of God so well that she will not be found with fault. She must speedily make a diligent, earnest effort to be approved for the assignment she has been given as her husband's help. Be assured the devil is quick to attack at first opportunity. She must be just as prompt to keep her marriage healthy. And she must know the Word so well that her cuts will be straight when she thrusts at her target, trained by her Teacher to know the specific enemy well, puncturing it with doctrines of truth that are lethal to Satan's vexations.

"The Word of God is quick, and powerful, and sharper than any two-edged sword, piercing even to the dividing asunder of soul and spirit, and of the joints and marrow, and is a discerner of the thoughts and intents of the heart." (Hebrews 4:12) The Word is living (**quick**) and active (**powerful**), also bringing life through death. Just as the piercing of infected cells, and their subsequent destruction, brings health and life to the body attacked by disease, so the Word of God brings healing and life to the marriage. This Sword is living, energetic power, awakening the conscience and producing fear of the coming judgment. It is the Word of God that separates this mortal body from the spiritual soul, literally inflicting a deadly wound that slays the sinner with the first edge and resurrects him to eternal life with the second edge, all in one swift cut. This Sword cuts both ways, entering where no other weapon can, making the most critical analysis between the natural man that has been caught in the entanglements of this world and the spiritual man that longs to be set free from sin. It cuts off the defiling root of bitterness. It slices away ignorance from our understanding, pride from the humble spirit, rebellion from the heart that desires to be obedient ... It goes deep into the most secret parts to remove the lust of the flesh and a carnal mind. It is used to remove anything from the heart that would oppose the will of the Father. It cuts through even self-deception and hypocrisy to lay bare the intent of the heart.

That word, **sharper**, means cutting with a single blow as opposed to chopping or hacking on something. That puts me in thought again on 1 Peter 3. If a husband does not obey the Word, the wife can win him by her manner of life lived before him, chaste, in submission to him and in the fear of God, not by hacking away at him through repeated naggings. Those only drive him further away to get away from the pain of the constant chopping at his manhood. No, the Word of God slices clean and is effective, exposing friend and foe.

The Sword divides the **joints** and **marrow**. Let's look at definitions and make some analogies. The joints are part of our skeletal makeup that allows us to move and function; the marrow is the soft tissue in the inmost cavity of the bone that gives us blood, strength, vitality, and our immune system. The Word of God is the means that separates the defining characteristics of man and woman and then distributes to them their individual roles so they might come together to be one united body – the man as the framework of the marriage enabling it to stand, protecting all the vital organs with the skin and skeleton, the *joints* in particular enabling the body to labor and function in service to the Creator as God intended (Genesis 2:15) – the woman as the secret vitality of marriage born in the bone *marrow*, sustaining the continuation of purposeful existence, enabling the body to feed and defend itself through the life giving blood (Leviticus 17:11). Mankind has the roles of man and woman so perverted and confused that it takes a mighty swath of the Sword to correct the chaos. Plus we have to be willing to ask for surgery with the Sword of the Lord so it can cut through to the joint and marrow allowing the Author's characters to develop as He intended in the Script.

When the Word of truth is **rightly divided**, this Sword lays open, as if on a table exposed for inspection, the very thoughts and understandings (or lack thereof). When the Scripture says the Word is a **discerner**, it means this Sword literally has "the power to end all controversy." Amen and amen! It clarifies all doubt as to what sin is, what truth is, what our motives are, what our understanding has missed. I need that clarification! Don't you? The Word pours truth into a life like sunshine into a cave. I'm remembering back when our log house had high ceilings with exposed beams through the central section – living room, dining room, and kitchen - all with matching ceiling fans (with those little lights on the bottom) about 10 feet above the floor. That was not good light for a kitchen, just pretty. For two or three years I operated my kitchen under those high lights. Then a loft was added over the kitchen, which lowered the ceiling to about seven feet. Of course, I now needed a light fixture. Never let it be said that my husband short changes or goes halfway on any project. He put up five fluorescent fixtures around my new ceiling with two four-foot bulbs in each! What did I get? LIGHT! Light that exposed dirt and crud I could not see before; light that made me uncomfortably embarrassed at the effects of the feeble cleaning that had accompanied those former weak lights. The bright light exposed me and I began to clean and polish what I saw. That is just what the light from the Word of truth does to a repentant heart wanting to serve God. The Scriptures will make us wise unto salvation, instructing us, convicting us, making right what was wrong, and training our character to be clean before God, in an appropriate attitude of conforming to His authority and all that He commands or appoints (2 Timothy 3:13-17). It puts an end to all controversy in your mind and heart.

So if the Word of God is your weapon of success, does this mean you preach the Word to your husband when you find an attack taking place? Heaven forbid! That's the preacher's job, or anyone else God so chooses. He can use a donkey if necessary to speak to a stubborn man. If asked for your advice, then certainly share that which God has given you. However, your most powerful area to use the Sword is within your spirit, without speaking a word out loud. You can't thump your husband over the head with your Bible. For goodness sake, forever settle that he is not the enemy! Use the Sword as a weapon on the adversary. The Word is a tool of cleansing and perfecting for our own lives; it is not a weapon to be used against your husband, but against the adversary opposing the will of God in your lives.

Our weapon is not of this natural world, **"but mighty through God to the pulling down of strongholds; casting down imaginations, and every high**

thing that exalts itself against the knowledge of God, and bringing into captivity every thought to the obedience of Christ" (2 Corinthians 10:3-5). This weapon will batter down that fortress Satan has built against us. It will put an end to the calculated plans and purpose of the foe. It will take captive every perception, opinion and purpose and put them into compliance and submission to our Lord and Savior. The promises are fantastic! Psalm 107 is one of my favorites and right in the middle of this song of the redeemed we find **"He sent His word, and healed them, and delivered them from their destructions."** He is so good and He so freely gives us His Word.

But if a wife does not know the Word of God, which reveals the nature of God and the plan of God, better than did Eve, she will be deceived and ineffective in living by His principles. There is only one way to happy, victorious living and it is revealed in His Word. O, to be so diligent as are our T-cells that have matured to recognize the tens of millions of different antigens that they might effectively defend our bodies! Wives must be diligent in this spiritual training and development so we can quickly recognize Satan's diverse attacks on our marriages and rally all of our rich resources in Christ to defend what God has joined together. It is our calling – why we were fashioned in the first place as our husband's help, aid, encircling for protection. Arm yourself, Sis. The battle is hot!

One more word of caution here before we move on. I don't know how familiar you are with Scripture at this point in your life, but I'm going to pull a reference out of the Old Testament that is rich in application for a soldier in a war. Moses led the people of God out of Egyptian slavery to take them to the Promised Land, the inheritance promised to the descendents of Abraham. Joshua led them into the Land, conquering the enemies of God and His people. There were lots of battles – won when walking with God by faith – lost when there was sin or compromise in their lives. But they possessed the Land flowing with milk and honey that had freely been given to them by God, living in houses they didn't have to build and eating fruit from vines and trees they didn't have to plant. That is the Christian life, freely given to us by God (we don't earn it), filled with fruit we didn't grow (love, joy, peace, patience ...), living in victory as we walk with God in faith!

But there were giants and walled cities and wicked lifestyles to battle in the Promised Land. The Christian life also has giants, fortified strongholds, and wickedness that we must conquer. God fought for and with the Israelites, and He will do the same for us; but He expects us to follow His battle plan and fight for our inheritance. Joshua took them into the Land, but the people failed to possess it as their own, allowing their enemies to dwell among them. Wickedness in the Land and their lack of faith lured them into forsaking the LORD! Oh, what a downward spiral the nation took! How could they come so far and quit fighting for what was theirs? They failed to walk in God's Word. Jesus has given us the Promised Life. Don't let there be a "but we failed to possess it." We can't fight a battle and then give up the war because "it's easier to live with the problems than eliminate them." It is not!!! God's way works and He proves Himself faithful to give victory when we conquer our enemy in His name and power! More on that in letters to come...

I am excited about the next soldiers we are going to examine but before we do, spend some quality time with the Author of our story and let Him encourage you in the midst of it all. He has won the battle. Trust Him to provide the victory in your present skirmish.

Swinging the Sword with you in love,
Momma 2 C K

The Power of the Victory

ear Fellow Warrior,

I fear I have burdened you with more than you wish to know, but I must continue with another analogy to explore. I pray you are not too weary yet for there is much still to understand and put into practice. The war is raging. Our battles are sometimes just skirmishes; sometimes they are hot and heavy to bear. But the victory is ours; the Author has recorded it as such for those who live by faith!

There are times, as I pray for my own husband, that all I can ask of the great Conqueror is, "Lord, I believe; help my unbelief." The struggle in this invisible combat with an invisible enemy is often overwhelming. Sometimes I wish I could physically kick something tangible and see the effect of my kick – see the enemy cry out in the same pain inflicted on me – see the results of a blow to the nose of my foe. (And, unfortunately, sometimes I do lash out – at my husband, my kids, a friend, a clerk just doing her job – none of which is the cause for my agitation.) But this is a war for our faith. If only we could hold faith in our arms securely or hide it in a safe. But faith is totally intangible, just like our enemy. We must trust that the blows of the Word of God are really effective on this foe and our hearts. We must believe every Word of God and feed on it as our bread of life. I try to hold myself to a higher standard so you will be encouraged to follow me, yet still I stumble as the vigilant wife. The trials come for we must grow in our faith and confidence and sometimes the only way to do that is to fail as Peter did when he denied the Lord (fear and confusion at the trial), as Israel did in the battle of Ai (overconfident and sin in the camp). What victories followed confession! Keep your eyes fixed firmly on Jesus. He is our ideal, the model of perfection in winning the war. And you will find Him waiting for you in the Word.

Now, back to our immune system... As your Helper T-cells send out these chemical messages to alert the rest of your defenses, they have also instructed them to multiply. So the process begins, your temperature rises, and your white blood count climbs in massive numbers. More phagocytes are called in to clean up the debris of the battle. Killer Ts are reproducing themselves and joining the fight. And now we are introduced to the B-cells...

Not all immune cells are sent to the thymus "West Point" for processing. Our B-cells are processed in the bone marrow and then sent directly to front-line defense bases - the lymph nodes and the spleen. The encyclopedia called these lymph nodes and spleen "kind of immunological conference centers." As the blood passes through these bases, our magnificent macrophages bring antigens to be identified. The immune cells gather and confront the enemy in these centers. The B-cells staff these bases, milling around the lymph nodes just waiting for a macrophage to deliver an antigen or for the call of a Helper T through a lymphokine called B-Cell Growth Factor (BCGF), which triggers the B cells to begin multiplying. Now they are making clones of themselves called daughter cells. I think there is an analogy in there somewhere but we'll save that for another day. Maybe you can share it with me one day.

These B-cells cannot kill the invading organism, as can the Killer Ts. But without their addition to the defense team, the body could not overcome the assault, much less defeat the enemy once and for all. Each B-cell has antigen-specific receptors, and when one matches up with the enemy's antigen, remarkable things begin to happen. The Helper T is now sending another chemical message, B-Cell Differentiation Factor (BCDF), which instructs some of the Bs to quit multiplying and start dividing. This division draws out plasma, which produces weapons called antibodies, as well as memory cells, which we will get to later. It's the production of these antibodies that concerns us now.

The B-cells are now churning out weapons that will interact with this one particular invader. Antibodies are made of heavy and light amino acids (which we shall not go into because that was way beyond my comprehension). These antibodies have a strong chemical attraction to one specific type of foreign matter – the one that is besieging the body at the moment. They are shaped like Ys. The V top is called the variable region because it varies greatly from one antibody to another. This region has unique contours that match up with a specific antigen - the lock and key effect again. The bottom of the Y is the same in all antibodies because it links it to the immune system. At the peak of operation, each B-cell can produce 2000 antibodies per second! That's over 7 million per hour, all targeted at one specific enemy! Multiply that times thousands of B-cells at the control panel and you have billions of antibodies springing into action. Our little B factories are super efficient at what they do! But then they must be since just one bacterium can generate a million offspring in just eight hours.

These unique protein gems – antibodies – that have just been created are then sent out to circulate in the bloodstream, scouting in search of antigens to match their lock. They neutralize the enemy by binding directly to their surfaces - locking onto their key, not only preventing them from attacking other cells but also making them more ingestible for our phagocytes (who are enjoying a feast during this battle). The antibodies signal Killer Ts and macrophages to destroy and consume their captives, and they also mark the invaders for destruction by complement, which is a serum of proteins in the bloodstream made up of 30 different components. I don't have the education to understand all there is to those components, so I am just taking by faith what scientists have learned as they study man's blood. When gathered in just the right sequence, this complement creates holes in the enemy which allows salt from our own body to enter, causing swelling and presto – it detonates like a bomb; death to the invader. Gosh, it exhausts me just thinking about all the activity going on inside. Have you ever wondered why you are so tired when you have a cold? There is a whole lot of work going on inside, behind the scenes and under the skin. What a wonder God created when He made the human body! Remember Psalm 139:14? **"I will praise Thee; for I am fearfully and wonderfully made: marvelous are Thy works; and that my soul knoweth right well."**

Okay, enough science; let's move back into the spiritual realm and do some comparing. Keep in mind that a wife has that power to either be a crown for her husband or rottenness in his bones (Proverbs 12:4). This powerful influence can only be used for good when it is united with the plan and purpose of the Author. We discover each new page of the script for our lives as we spend quiet time before our Maker. This quiet time (QT) is like the organs of our spleen and lymph nodes – a "kind of immunological conference center" for our spirits. Can a person live without a spleen? Yes, but one lives in greater risk of infection. What area does Satan most want removed from a believer's life? - the quiet time before the Lord. And where is it, that when cancer is detected, it is almost a certain death sentence? - the lymph nodes, that complex network connecting the flow of lymph fluid throughout our bodies. These wonderful nodes filter out bacteria, viruses, cancer and other unwelcome things from our bodies - until they are put out of commission by some cancer. And what area of our life is so vital that should one of those spiritual cancers of stress, depression, guilt, or bitterness take up residence it would take over and spread throughout one's spirit and marriage? - that quiet time before the Lord, the time alone with the Word of Almighty God filtering out the spiritual bacteria and deceptive viruses and all other sin and yucky stuff that hinders a walk with the Lord. I am not talking about a five or ten-minute slot set aside to read a devotional book, though I love to read devotions and testimonies of others. Nor am I talking about a dutiful sit-down reading of the scheduled scripture for the day or a quick grab at spirituality as one falls asleep at night. This quiet time is a frontline base where we can confront the enemy with our "immune system" resources.

In her macrophage mode, a good wife detects an enemy within the ranks of her marriage, displays the enemy's marker, and permeates the body with the potent and compelling agape love. As the Helper T, she identifies the particular enemy, sounds the alarm to her defense mechanism, and sends out the urgent messages that will not only increase the use of the Sword of the Spirit in the ensuing battle but will call out even more love to overcome and consume. Now as we move into our B-cell role we will see that nothing could better staff our spiritual conference center than that of a praying wife through her time alone with God. Prayer must be in a constant state of "milling around" in all areas of her influence in this marriage. And when an alarm is activated, those quiet times, a storehouse of potential power, must multiply her prayers tremendously and rapidly for prayer is where God filters our will and makes it His.

At the end of our list of armor in Ephesians 6, verse 18 tells us to pray always. This is the follow-up resource to the Sword and completes the armor that God has given us to defeat the enemy. 1 Thessalonians 5:17 tells us to pray without ceasing. Prayer must be ongoing and persistent (Luke 11:5-13 & 18:1-8), believing and anticipating God's answers (Mark 11:24). We have already talked about the aspect of prayer as part of our macrophage character, receiving and engaging in communication with the brain (Jesus, the head of the Body). The Lord's admonition to pray persistently and expectantly with those two parables of the neighbor and the judge back in Luke 11 and 18 seems to have fallen on deaf ears. And we aren't hearing any better today. Paul reminded the Philippians to lay aside those anxious worries and take everything to the Lord in prayer, thanking Him for His answers in the midst of our prayer (4:6). It takes faith to say thank you before the answer is received.

You've heard the old adage "There's nothing left to do now but pray." Mercy! That should be the first thing we do about everything that passes through our lives, good, bad, huge or trivial. God is interested in hearing from us about it all. He is our best friend and not only has a great listening ear but perfect advice about every situation. He wants us to talk to Him and then listen for His answers. Prayer changes things; prayer unites people; prayer relieves pressure; prayer casts out demons! (...although in the case of demons Jesus did say we needed to include fasting, Matthew 17:21. We will have to pick up on that fasting principle later.) Nehemiah is my prayer champion. When you read the book of Nehemiah, you find him praying at every point – agonizing in burdened prayer for Jerusalem, a flare-prayer before answering the king, prayer whether facing the enemies of God or encouraging the Israelites to work. Prayer sustained him and strengthened him to perform the calling of God on his life.

This B-cell phase of our prayer life takes on a fresh dimension with each new call to arms. This kind of prayer multiplies and multiplies, consuming our purpose for being. An alarm has been sounded. A breach has occurred. The enemy is within. This kind of prayer also lays open the very heart of the one praying so she can see herself in a discerning light, for one that is not in one accord with the Lord can never hope to have those prayers answered (John 9:31; James 4:3; Proverbs 28:9; Micah 3:4). For a terrifying scripture that should put some fear of the Lord in us all, read Proverbs 1:27-33. [You are looking this up in your Bible, right? you know – exercise, study …] Wouldn't you want to know that when distress and anguish come upon you, when a whirlwind hits full force, that you can call upon the Lord for deliverance? Salvation only comes to those who fear Him, who love His knowledge and counsel and His rebuke. When we make light the sin in our own lives, seeing the fault in everyone else, especially our mates, failing to ask God to change us and conform us into the image of our dear Savior, refusing to confess our own failures and faults and pointing instead to our husbands', totally oblivious to the fact that God wants to perform miracles in our own hearts, then we can never hope to appeal to the courts of heaven for deliverance from the oppressor. This B-cell kind of prayer separates the plasma out of our daily devotional life, that pouring out of our spirit that transcends the pull of sin's gravity and allows us to soar into the heavenly realm and boldly come before God's throne to commune in effectual fervent prayer to the Father (Hebrews 4:16; James 5:16). It is this kind of prayer that releases the greatest power on earth, our "antibodies." We will come back to the antibodies in just a minute...

Let's look at the encouraging and admonishing words from Jesus that John recorded for us concerning prayer the very night before the cross: **"Whatsoever ye shall ask in My name, that will I do, that the Father may be glorified in the Son. If ye shall ask any thing in My name, I will do it."** (14:13-14); **"If ye abide in Me, and My words abide in you, ye shall ask what ye will, and it shall be done unto you. Herein is My Father glorified, that ye bear much fruit;"** (15:7-8); **"Verily, verily, I say unto you, Whatsoever ye shall ask the Father**

in My name, He will give you. Hitherto have ye asked nothing in My name: ask, and ye shall receive, that your joy may be full." (16:23-24). Do you get the impression that Jesus wants us to ask for help? But we must ask in His name, abiding in Him and His words abiding in us. He wants to prove Himself strong because it glorifies the Father. He wants to answer our requests that He might fulfill our joy. We can have confidence when we ask according to His will because John assured us (1 John 5:14-16) that He hears us, and if He hears us, whatever we are asking for, He will give us our requests, even when asking Him to forgive a brother's sins (or a husband's). Those are mighty powerful words. Got anything you need to take to the Lord of Glory, the Great I Am? Make sure you are faithfully remaining in Jesus – and that His Word is living in you.

Can we ask for selfish desires or frivolous whims "in the name of Jesus"? That phrase is more than an appropriate ending to our prayer. It is a reminder that we are standing before our Father in heaven requesting Him to move into action whatever He deems necessary to grant that request – standing as it were in the name, the character of Jesus, as His representative, as though Jesus Himself were making this request of His Father by our mouths. That is a sobering thought! What would Jesus pray? Am I abiding in Him so as to fully know what He would ask the Father to do in a particular situation? Though precious and necessary, we aren't talking about casual conversations with God while strolling down the avenue of life, enjoying the scenery and the Company. We are talking about a war zone with wounded and fatalities lying all around us. Bombs are dropping and devastating lives. There is no greater terrorist than Satan. The need is urgent and God's will stands opposed. How, when, and what do we pray?

James has some pretty important things in his letter about how to pray. Beginning in chapter 1 verse 6 he warns us to ask in faith – there is no room for doubt. This asking business must be serious. Don't ask if you don't sincerely, deeply desire that for which you are asking. Can you believe God is going to do for you that for which you have prayed? We just read some potent verses in the Gospel of John and 1 John. Either you believe them or you don't. James says if you doubt you are like a wave of the sea being tossed about. You are unstable. Don't expect anything from the Lord. James then ends his book in chapter 5 still emphasizing how to pray, fervently – actively and energetically. You can have the same power with God as did the prophet Elijah! Prayer! How priceless! How vital to living this starring role to which He has called you!

Because I don't know your relationship with your own father, good, bad, indifferent, I am using what I wrote to Susie at this point... "Can you imagine coming to your daddy when you were a little girl with a real heart's desire, laying your request out to him, hoping with all your heart for a yes answer, and then saying to him, 'As much as I want this, you probably won't give it because you don't really think I am important enough to listen to or you probably can't afford it right now or you don't think I've been good enough or...' Get the picture? All it took was for you to admire that Apple Annie porcelain doll in a magazine when you were just eleven. Dad delivered it to you for Christmas in spite of its ridiculous price and eight other children and several grandchildren to buy for on an extremely limited budget. He delighted in giving you something that pleased you. Can't you think of some pretty serious times that dear ol' Dad came through for you? Do we think so little of God that He would not meet our every need, especially in the midst of a battle for our home and marriage?" Susie's daddy never let her down, unless he had to say no to her request for her own good or during discipline, as I imagine was true in your life, too. But more often than not, she had what she asked for. And he's just a human daddy. What do you have to ask of the omnipotent Heavenly Father today?

When do we pray? Look back to Psalm 107 again. Yes, read it again, please... In the innocence of our childhood we wander and get wearily lost, yet when **"they cried unto the LORD in their trouble, He delivered them out of their distresses. And He led them forth by the right way..."** (v.6, 7) In our stage of rebellious youth we get bound up in sin and are chastised severely by the Father but: **"Then they cried unto the LORD in their trouble, and He saved them out of their distresses. He brought them out of darkness and the shadow of death, and brake their bands in sunder."** (v.13, 14) In our prideful, grownup state of adulthood we indulge in behavior that sickens our souls to the point of death yet: **"Then they cry unto the LORD in their trouble, and He saved them out of their distresses. He sent His word, and healed them, and delivered them from their destructions."** (v.19, 20) Even in our mature years, just doing the business of living and enjoying the wonders of God, He sends the stormy wind and waves that swallow up all our wisdom, so: **"Then they cry unto the LORD in their trouble, and He brings them out of their distresses. He makes the storm a calm, so that the waves thereof are still. Then are they glad because they be quiet; so he brings them unto their desired haven."** (v.28-30) We simply must cry out to the Lord. Four times the Psalmist repeats **"Oh that men would praise the LORD for His goodness, and His wonderful works to the children of men! For He satisfies the longing soul, and fills the hungry soul with goodness."** Unfortunately, those praises don't come when things are good and healthy; they come after the times of crisis when our souls are crying out in need and in pain. We are driven to Him when we are empty and in despair. No prayer touches the heart of God like the one that comes from the depth of the soul through trial and trouble. That is the kind of prayer that allows God to show Himself strong. That is when God is the closest and we experience the greatest joy.

So, be it our innocence and ignorance that make us lose our way; or our stubbornness that puts us in bondage; or pride that sickens our marriage relationship; or just being caught up in living a beautiful life and thinking we have finally figured it all out; we will need deliverance and the Lord is always there waiting for our cry. Praise His Holy Name! When do we pray? Always, in every stage of life, when the storms rage, we cry out to our Deliverer. And the prayer of praise must adorn our lips anticipating His answer.

These prayers are not a weapon but the means of releasing the mighty hand of God through the power of the Holy Spirit, the Comforter, the Helper, the greatest power on earth or heaven. It was in the midst of those scriptures in John as Jesus made His promises concerning prayer that He also promised He would send the Spirit. It was through intense prayer in the name of Jesus during the critical birthing of the Church that the promise of the Spirit was first released on the day of Pentecost in Acts 2. Did God demonstrate His power that day, or what?! Peter was transformed from a man whose big mouth led him into pride in his relationship with Jesus (which Satan quickly attacked, causing him to bear the shame of denying the Lord), into a man whose mouth was used by the Spirit to proclaim the glorious gospel of forgiveness and salvation to thousands who were delivered from Satan's grip.

So just what are we to pray for in the midst of battle? - Power from on high, not a weapon but a Discerner, a Director, a Neutralizer. We, too, must delve into the realm of those intense prayers of the saints of old, prayers of total need and dependence upon our God. Unfortunately, credit cards have made the concept of dependence upon God a foreign thought today. Yet, there's no other way to have the hand of God upon us if our marriages are to be the union He purposed in His heart. It is those prayers of total dependence that will release the power of the

Spirit of God, our spiritual Antibody for anything and everything that can ever come against us! This is unimaginable, unsearchable power that has been granted to us that, sadly, few believers ever experience. It is the Spirit that will neutralize the enemy, preventing attack in other areas of our walk with Him and the marriage that we have vowed to keep true. He makes us safe from further attack by defusing the adversary. He also directs the wife to slip into her phagocyte mode and enables her to consume the effects of the attack by her own self-sacrificing love. By the way, a Spirit-led wife in the heat of battle will consider it a feast to sacrifice her own will and desires for the sake of her marriage, because she knows she is doing God's will – and doing God's will is always as satisfying as a good meal (John 4:32-34). Wow, the Lord is talking to me again...

I sure needed this little talk we're having. One can never be reminded enough Who is the One with the power in this battle. The Spirit is our life giver. It is the Spirit that revives each sinner from dead works into a living relationship with God Almighty. Nothing we can do adds to the work of God. **"Not by might, nor by power, but by My Spirit, saith the LORD of hosts."** (Zechariah 4:6) I think we touched on this way back there at the beginning of these letters. Wives cannot change their husbands for the better. Only the Spirit of God can do that. The more we try, the more obstinate men become and a better foothold we give to the adversary. We need to learn to do what we have been told to do and let God do what only God can do.

The first time that really sank into my heart was when I was reading the account in John 11 of Lazarus being raised from the dead. I ask questions when I am reading. I've found God usually answers them for me. So I asked why Jesus told the people to roll the stone away. Wouldn't that have been an imposing act - to have the tomb open up at His bidding? After all, the storm obeyed His voice.

Why did He tell them to remove the grave clothes from Lazarus when He loved touching people and expressing His love to them? The Lord gave me something that went deep into my soul that day. It's this: God will not do for us what we are capable of doing ourselves; God does what only God can do. Anyone could put some muscle behind that stone and move it – they had put it there in the first place. Anyone could remove those grave clothes; only Jesus could raise the dead! The sooner we learn that, the busier we can be in doing what is expected of us – those things we can do. We are then able to rest in faith and expectation that God will do what only He can do. Only God can defeat our foes, whether it be Satan and his demons or our own selfish, prideful hearts.

Before we leave the book of John look at chapter 16 again, verses 7-11. The Spirit is here to bring conviction of sin. That is not the wife's job! The Spirit is here to convict of righteousness. That neither is the responsibility of the wife. The Spirit is present in this world today to admonish that there is punishment of sin and of the coming judgment. Nowhere in a wife's job description does the role of passing judgment fit in. Yet women spend most of their marriages trying to expose their husbands' sin, be their consciences, reprimand every deed, and then execute what they deem appropriate judgment. I'm not saying we can't give advice or encouragement in a godly direction, but we both know that is not what women usually do. We need to get out of His way so the Spirit can do what only the Spirit can do. He has given us plenty to busy ourselves without taking on His job.

I'm not sure how that fit into our subject at hand, but it didn't cost anything so take it. I think maybe the Lord is reminding me of a lesson He has already taught me that needed to be reviewed. Just keep in mind, it is in that quiet time we spend before the Lord that the Spirit can be released most effectively to do His job – in our hearts and in our marriages. So to receive this decisive power

(Acts 1:8a), we shut the world out and continue with one purpose in prayer and supplication (Acts 1:14a). If you want to read a powerful verse, read Romans 8:11. If the Spirit of Him who raised Jesus from the dead lives in me, and He does, this same Spirit gives life to my mortal body, and I take that to mean here and now as well as for eternity. Satan wants to make us physically ill as well as spiritually – any means will do to weaken our relationship with God and one another. The Spirit (the Breath of God) is here to give us life through the words of our Savior (John 6:63).

Look at 1 Corinthians 2:9-16. Mankind's natural nature – thinking and attitudes from the fallen, unregenerate mind – cannot comprehend or accept the things of God. We, on the other hand, as children of light, have received the spiritual teachings of the Holy Spirit and are enabled to know the mind of the Lord. Wow! Are you taking advantage of what the Spirit is offering here? Look at it this way: Does anyone know you better than you? Of course not. That's why Jesus warned us about judging one another. One of my biggest peeves is when I am told why I did something when that reasoning hadn't even crossed my mind. No one knows my logic or motives for saying or doing except me. And no one knows the mind of God except God. But He has miraculously and graciously given to us part of Himself in the person of the Holy Spirit so we may know His plans and His purpose for saying and doing what He does – and that we might know the deep things of God and what He has prepared for those who love Him. We need to spend time with this precious Gift, giving Him the liberty to instruct us and guide us in the right course of action, or we are going to disastrously distort God's perfect script. With the power of the Spirit released in a wife's life, direction will be given to both the "Killer T" and "Macrophage" modes of her ministry; she will be able to discern when and where to use the Sword of the Word so she isn't slicing when she should be consuming in love.

I am pretty sure there is something really deep about those heavy and light amino acids that make up our antibodies that could be compared to the Holy Spirit, but what I haven't studied out and understood leaves me without an analogy. Maybe later... For now, it is enough to know these antibodies have been made available to keep my body free from disease – well and functioning to the best of my physical ability. So, too, has the Holy Spirit been made available to me to keep me free from sin, holy and functioning in the grace He has given for my spiritual life. We do not control His working; He controls us. Without Him, we can do nothing, but by His power extraordinary results take place in our lives. We can never run ahead of Him or act independently without grieving Him and reaping heartache. That's why we have been told repeatedly to walk in the Spirit, be led of the Spirit, be strengthened by the Spirit, be filled with the Spirit... (Romans 8:1-14; Galatians 5:16-18; Ephesians 3:16; 5:18b; Colossians 1:10-12) Thank You, Father, for sending Your Spirit to dwell within me! I now pray my precious daughter will understand how to walk in Your Spirit, to be led and strengthened and filled, grieving not the Holy Spirit of promise. Forgive us for our past neglects and anoint us anew.

There is more to be said - one more crucial job these antibodies perform at this point in the battle, one more vital role the Spirit performs to free us completely and eternally. But I must let you ponder on this one a bit. Write down your thoughts and questions. Take them to the Lord, then jump right into letters 15 & 16... absolutely, fantastically exquisite if I can get it from my heart and head and out my fingertips into printed words.

Yours in love and intercession,
CK Momma 2

Learning the Secrets of God / Finding the Second Twist

*M*y dear Adventurer,

I am so greatly encouraged that you have stayed with me this far! We must take time for an interlude at this point. Our immune system is so awesomely wonderful and does such a superb job of keeping us healthy – more so than we will ever understand! But lest we think too highly of ourselves (since we are comparing our wifely character to this virtuous host of protection), I want to prepare you for another twist in our plot. This is a beautiful but humbling turn in God's masterpiece that He has written. You must look for the hidden clues to His mystery – His most precious secrets. Satan is nearer than you would like to believe, and he would delight in making you think you are the all power-ful force in your marriage. Keep alert. We are going to take a side road in our study; don't fall off my wagon...

This letter writing has been a hard journey for me. The devil doesn't like it when we probe into his realm so he begins his series of attacks hoping to dis-tract us, weaken us, and trip us up so as to discredit our testimony. I know I've said that before, but it's worth repeating! Putting this Bible study into letter form has brought new trials into my own marriage, pressurizing it in ways I never could have imagined. I knew to expect troubles because of what I am attempting to write. Satan has tempted, trying to discredit and discourage me / God has tested to prove me. Somehow I just didn't expect the tests to be so terribly tough this time or the lessons so difficult to learn. However, I personally know the Author of my life and I know where He is taking me, even though I can't see it. Each chapter is for my good, changing me from this vile creature that I am (Philippians 3:21; Romans 7:24), conforming me into the image of His Son (Romans 8:28, 29). I praise Him for the growth. I do so want to mature while still here on earth so I might be all God has created me to be in that heavenly city. Reminds me of a song: "One day Jesus will call my name; as the days go by, hope I don't stay the same. I want to get so close to Him that it's no big change, on that day that Jesus calls my name!"

It is a pleasurable thing to watch a young girl grow over the years, developing into a gracious woman. Are you still blossoming, already in full bloom, or is your flower beginning to fade somewhat? There's a unique joy in watching a mother with her own child, taking pleasure in every stage of development - from discovering toes and tongue, to crawling, to running, now confident, yet so full of questions. Time brings such changes in one's growth, quickly in infancy, much slower the older we become, but always changing, always growing – physically, mentally, emotionally, socially, spiritually.

Life begins at conception, not the day we enter the world. That's what makes abortion so wrong. I hope you already knew that. The baby in the womb is not just a mass of tissue. How precious to feel life within oneself – that tiny baby kicking, rolling over, hiccupping, growing and stretching while all his cells are developing to equip him for life in a world of light beyond that darkness.

Our time on earth parallels greatly to a mother's womb, a place of incubation to grow and develop so we, too, can function well in the world to come. What Christians call the second birth, the day one places faith in Jesus as the source of salvation, is really more like the conception of a new life. You then begin to develop into the beautiful creature you will be when Jesus is revealed, either at His second coming or when He calls you home (1 John 3:2). We looked at 2 Peter 1:2-11 back in *Let's Meet the Staff*. That puts it pretty plain about our need to mature after we have expressed our faith in Jesus. Faith is just the point of beginning. Faith has made you a partaker of the divine nature. There are areas in the spiritual life that must be developed, just as surely as the physical body must develop. It progresses from faith in Christ to loving as God loves – maturity, perfection in God's eyes. It would do well to reread these verses and refresh.

In the light of the next four verses (12-15) of this same chapter in Peter - "**I will not be negligent to put you always in remembrance of these things, though ye know, and be established in the present truth. Yea, I think it meet, as long as I am in this tabernacle** (body of flesh), **to stir you up by putting you in remembrance; knowing that shortly I must put off my tabernacle...I will endeavor that you may be able after my decease to have these things always in remembrance.**", I too have a mandate to share all I can with you, to stir you up. There are just some things we must share with the next generation. My time is getting shorter every day...

I am praying earnestly that these letters will be as beneficial to your spiritual nourishment as the food you received through an umbilical cord so long ago. In spite of sickness those first few months (and carelessness in the diet later), your mother's body still gave you what you needed from resources that were stored up within her so you could develop completely before entering your new world outside the womb. Draw on the good things that God has graciously reserved in my life (as a spiritual mom [Titus 2:3-5]) and other godly teachers to help nourish your development in this present world that you may become all God has purposed for you. There is so much growing to be done in such a short time before we enter our new, eternal world. Each stage of development should bring joy and excitement in the prospect of what we will one day be.

This letter is a preface on the subject of our next letter in hopes of giving you a glimpse of the glory of the intimacy with which we have been privileged to share with our God. Jesus said that He came to give us eternal life, **"and this is life eternal, that they might know You the only true God, and Jesus Christ, Whom You have sent."** (John 17:3). Eternity does not begin for the believer when we get to heaven; it commences the moment we give our life to the eternal God and begin a relationship with Him. I wish someone had taught me that much earlier in life. In that relationship we find our joy, our strength, and our victory over sin and Satan. That is our Promised Land right here on earth; we don't have to wait for Heaven to enjoy peace and eternity.

Find a good, quiet spot to read this. Keep your Bible close at hand – and a pen. It's all right to mark up the pages of your Bible. It will jog your memory in future days of the good things you learn and bring gratitude to your heart that the King of glory still speaks out of heaven to each one who diligently searches for Him. Hebrews 11:6 reminds us, **"He is a rewarder** (one who repays or compensates benefits for efforts) **of them that diligently seek** (search out, investigate, crave) **Him."** If we put out the effort to search out all that we can know of God and the Pearl of great price, He graciously rewards our every endeavor.

I want you to do some digging for buried treasure with me. We are going to revisit a verse I touched on way back there, Proverbs 25:2. Don't you find it curious that it says, **"It is the glory of God to conceal a thing: but the honor** [same word as glory] **of kings to search out a matter** [same word as thing].**"** Now the Hebrew word translated into English as **glory** and **honor** is an interesting word. It means weight – in the sense of importance and influence – and comes from a root word that means to be heavy, weighty, renowned, esteemed, to show oneself great and mighty. The main idea behind this word is to be wealthy - heavy with goods, property, money, importance and influence. Strong's Concordance gave the definition of **glory** as weight or copiousness. That word took me back to the dictionary; it means having an inexhaustible and lavish abundance of wealth, fullness, thoughts, and words. That does describe our God, doesn't it? But why does it say it is His glory to conceal a matter? Why would God hide things from us and how does that reveal His inexhaustible and lavish abundance? The Scripture then tells us this glory, inexhaustible and lavish abundance of wealth, fullness, and influence belongs to kings who will search out what God has hidden. I might just throw in here that Revelation 1:6 calls believers kings and priests unto God. The next key word that is translated as **search out** gives us a clue as to why it would be weighty for us. That word means to examine intimately; to penetrate; to understand the meaning or truth of a matter by going through something, perhaps after some difficult or slow process. God wants us to want Him enough to search out His truth until we understand it, even if it is a slow, difficult process.

Now in today's "instant everything" society, that verse in Proverbs doesn't have a remote chance of being understood by most people. Few want to wait or put out effort for anything. Pop frozen food in the microwave, order supper via the "drive-thru", liposuction rather than diet, no waiting on mail or film development with instant pictures on cell phones, instagrams, emails, skype, face-time or Face Book, and on and on and on...! And how many times have you heard or said, "This computer is so-o-o-o slow!" But, it is guaranteed that there were a lot of someones who took the time to search and examine a subject, going through a slow process of discovery and learning, to create all of these modern conveniences that have made the rest of us lazy, undisciplined, spoiled, and ignorant. In our quick lifestyles we need to remember there is glory for those who will take the time to search out, examine intimately, and be willing to go through a difficult and slow process to understand the meaning and truth of what God has for us. I hope and pray you are willing.

Have you ever wondered why Jesus taught in parables? There were truths about God and heaven and eternity that needed to be learned. The long await- ed Messiah was proclaiming those truths, but He veiled them, concealed them, covered them in stories that left His listeners scratching their heads and won- dering what He was saying. Why? That's the same question the disciples asked. The Pharisees, too, said, "If you are the Christ, tell us plainly." (John 10:24) They were tired of the sheep analogies, the door illustration, the parables of lost coins and seeds sown, the charge to "eat my body and drink my blood"... What in the world was Jesus saying? Well, it is the glory of God to conceal a matter and the glory of kings to search out a matter. God only reveals Himself in all of His glory and majesty to those who are willing to diligently seek Him at all costs. In some matters it may be an instant revealing, but it is usually the slow and difficult process that brings the greatest glory into our lives, giving us an inexhaustible and lavish wealth and fullness of the riches of God. Read Ephesians, at least chapter one (preferably the whole letter), and write a note by some of the riches Paul reminds us are ours: we are chosen, adopted, ac- cepted, redeemed, forgiven, made to know the mystery of His will, given an inheritance, sealed with His Spirit, made alive, loved, delivered, given a seat in the company of Jesus Christ as His bride! (Are you in that quiet spot with a pen?) Reading that powerful letter to the Ephesians will pull anyone out of de- spair, making the problems of this world pale in the light of the riches of glory purchased for us by the blood of the Lamb. God is so good!

Jesus told us more parables of the kingdom of heaven in Matthew 13:44-46, describing it as a treasure hid in a field and as one pearl of great price. The seeker was willing to give all he had to make that treasure his. Proverbs gives us more insight on something hidden to be sought out: "**If thou seek her** [wisdom] **as silver, and search for her as hidden treasures; then shalt thou understand the fear of the Lord, and find the knowledge of God.**" (2:4-5). If it is hidden, you can be sure it is precious and held in reserve for only those who seek God, His wisdom, and His kingdom. Hold on to that phrase "understand the fear of the Lord"...

Have you ever heard the quip, "This'll bless your socks off?" I don't know if that's a reference to Moses standing on holy ground in the presence of God at the burning bush or just a cute saying. But I can tell you it will put one on holy ground, blessed beyond measure when Psalm 25:14 is understood: "**The secret of the Lord is with them that fear Him; and He will show them His covenant.**" Are you ready for this? That **secret of the Lord** means: a session with the Lord, being in the company of the Lord as though on a cushion or couch, implying an intimacy with the Covenant Maker as a friend in close conversation or serious consultation, sharing things that are hidden from others. Wow!!! Read that again! Doesn't that put you in mind of Jesus' invitation in Revelation 3:20? "**I will come in and sup with him and he with Me.**" Do you remember how they ate their meals? On low couches or cushions on the floor, and not just to fill their bellies with food but to engage in conversation and fellowship to fill their souls. They discovered the thoughts and hearts of their fellow diners!

And who has this privilege of intimate companionship with God? Those who have learned from wisdom to "fear" nothing but God Almighty, giving Him the reverence, honor, and worship due to such an awesome, powerful God. In that closeness of intimate conversation and serious consultation with the Lord, He makes known His promises and purposes, His plans and pleasures, His priorities for - and expectations of - our lives, and especially His precious covenant that sealed our salvation through the blood of our Savior. That covenant was made secure by the blood of Jesus poured out from His broken body on the altar of the cross, redeeming us from our lost estate, releasing us from our guilt and despair, and making us at peace with our God. (Colossians 1:20, Romans 5:1) Bask in the glory of that truth for a little while.

Now if this covenant assures us that God has saved us by the blood of the Lamb, set us free from the bondage of Satan, and propelled us on our way to the Promised Land, then why all of these troubles, and trials, and battles? Can we know what God is doing? Of course! He has told us in His Word. Exodus 14 holds some keys to our questions...

The plagues are over. Pharaoh's own son is dead and he releases the Hebrews to go serve their God. They have been set free and have begun their great exodus to the Promised Land. And they lived happily ever after. Not so.

For some strange reason God instructs Moses to have the children of Israel turn back and camp at a hard name to pronounce (that means mouth of the gorges), between the Egyptian city Migdol and the sea. Why would God do that? Well, I'm glad you asked. Though it looked like the enemy had been defeated, the battle wasn't over. God was going to harden Pharaoh's heart one last time for a very specific purpose. The enemy was going to come at God's people with all of the fury and hatred they could muster, and God declared He was going to gain honor over Pharaoh and all his army that they might know first hand, experientially with all their senses, that God is Jehovah, the covenant

Maker and Keeper. (By the way, that word translated "army" here is the same Hebrew word describing that wife in Proverbs 12:4 and 31:11! Didn't I say you were an army for your husband?)

The people did as Moses said, still quite bold with their new found freedom and excitement of the journey to the Promised Land. Yet when Pharaoh's army drew near they were very afraid. Do you remember ever being very afraid? Dear Moses had the advantage because he had heard from God and knew the plan. He encouraged them: be not afraid – stand still, and see the salvation of the Lord... the Egyptians you see today you shall see no more forever. The Lord will fight for you, and you shall hold your peace. Read on... The Lord overthrew the Egyptians in the midst of the sea. Not so much as one remained. Thus the Lord saved Israel that day and they saw their enemy dead, destroyed!   The reason God parked them by the Red Sea was to put them in a position of vulnerability, of impossibility, their back against a sea and nowhere to run. They panicked and railed against Moses for bringing them out of Egypt, out of their slavery! But, remember, they were sore afraid. We don't think well when we are afraid. God must teach them to trust Him if they are to grow up strong. As a child, fear drives one into Daddy's arms; but fear makes the confident youth question the father, angry over exposure of personal fears. Growing up is a fearful experience! Satan has his demons pursuing youth aggressively. Embarrassing and vulnerable situations usually result as parents implement a plan of rescue, bringing back dependence and trust, giving freedom from the grip of the enemy. It's easy to look back and see that God knew well what He was doing with the Israelites, but it was tough in the midst of it all. It still is today ...

The point of this excursion we have taken to Exodus is this: The Hebrews did all God told them to do in Egypt, from despoiling the Egyptians to applying the blood of the Passover Lamb to the door of each home. They headed for the Promised Land the minute Pharaoh turned them loose. They followed Moses wherever he led them, even in turning back and camping at the mouth of gorges before the Red Sea. Now they could do no more. Only God could take it from here. Only God could completely destroy their enemy. Of course, He could have sent fire and brimstone to destroy Pharaoh and his army back in Egypt and make them as Sodom and Gomorrah. But He chose to bring them out to the Red Sea and let Israel see Pharaoh's destruction with their own eyes. They could not have done what God did even if every man and woman had taken up arms. They did what God told them to do and God did what only God could do. Isn't that fantastic! They saw their oppressor destroyed – completely!

That's what God wants to do for us today!- what I, as a parent, desired to do but just couldn't ('cuz I'm only human). God destroys completely the enemy that comes to overtake us. He will gain the honor over the adversary. We must do our part and then hold our peace – be still and see the salvation of the Lord. Yes, it is scary. Our foe is a formidable one. But let your fear drive you into the arms of your Father Who knows all and wants your deliverance to be secured. He will fight for you in ways you are incapable of even understanding. Just trust Him.

What are you fighting today, my Sister/Daughter? What is in hot pursuit of your marriage? Have you experienced a "cut" in your relationship that has allowed one of those bacterium of temptation to explode when things don't go as you planned? Or maybe the temptation has prevailed to let feelings dominate your thinking and actions. Plus, if you are parents, the temptation to bicker over discipline has great potential to drive you apart. Beware! Maybe there is a virus hot on your trail, one of Satan's lies that sounds good and smoothes the way for his slithering entrance into your marriage. Has he hissed to you lately that you and your husband are total opposites and will never come to agreement on anything? Remember, Satan will include truth but always twists it into perversion. Of course, you are opposites. How could you complete one another otherwise? Has he whispered to your husband that there is an escape clause for any marriage? After all, God wants us to be happy and live in peace. Or maybe he has attacked the heart of your marriage by feeding you the lie of "he's not my boss and I'll do what I like!" My submission to my husband is watched by others; seldom does anyone understand – "Stand up for yourself; don't let him walk all over you!" I don't always understand myself. But I know God's Word has instructed me, and if I don't do my part, God can't do His. Take time right now to read Matthew 13:58!!! It's not a matter of understanding; it's a matter of faith – believing God – for without faith it is impossible to please Him. I choose to please Him. I pray you will, too. Be on the watch for any cancerous stress or jealousy or bitterness. What are you fighting today? Don't ever let it be your husband, my Dear. You are a team as one body. Work together and watch God fight for you!

Yes, even when you obey Him, God will allow you to be backed up against a sea with nowhere to go – but to Him. That's the only way He can prove to us He is our victory; He is the power that overcomes. Yes, you may be very afraid. But you have the same privilege Moses had of receiving a word from God and knowing the battle plan. Instead of cowering in fear you can sing praises to God as did the singers marching before good King Jehoshaphat's army. They watched God fight for them, too. He is always ready to defend those who obey His strange commands: camp in the gorges before the sea, put singers before the troops when marching into war, march around the walls and shout to defeat a city, submit to a husband to strengthen a marriage...

So what is the new twist in our story? Learning the secrets of God? Well, that's the beginning of understanding this turn of thought. The twist is the opposite of the first one when we learned that woman is man's protection! We have pursued that thought throughout these letters. But lest we become puffed up, God has put a check on the limit of our help. Keep in mind the glorious position God gave to Lucifer as one of His chosen angels and the pride that welled up within him that cost him his place in heaven. We must remember Who is in control. Yes, God desires and expects us to do the job He created us to fulfill. But He has reserved the privilege of deliverance for Himself – and that is the topic of our next letter.

Are you willing today to begin a deeper search? Will you open your heart and gird up your mind as we travel through this living parable – that of our immune system? Are you willing to proceed through a possibly slow and probably difficult process to understand the hidden glories of God that will provide an inexhaustible resource in your life that will overcome the foe? You may have to spend some time rereading and praying over some of the scriptures to get a clearer picture in your mind and heart. God's ways are not our ways. We must spend time with Him to know Him and His ways. And be ever mindful that Satan will use anything to distract you or lead you down the wrong way, including your own heart and self-will. Beware of what the world is telling you to do; it will most likely be in direct opposition to His will. We can know His will. He desires that more than anything. The Lord Jesus wants you more than anything and is waiting for you to meet with Him. He already has your cushion fluffed and waiting.

Diligently seeking Him with you in love,
CK Momma 2

The Secret Weapon for Ultimate Victory

*P*recious Daughter,

How are you progressing, my Dear? Have you found some time to sit at the feet of Jesus? Did you take a good look into Exodus 14? I just wanted you to get a glimpse of some important facts: sometimes God leads us into some precarious situations that make us wonder what's going on; God knows exactly what is going on. He wants to show Himself powerful; He wants to deliver completely by destroying the enemy. That is just what He did for the Hebrews backed up against the Red Sea. Birthing a child, losing a job, dealing with in-laws, selling a home, moving into a new home is much like being backed up to the Red Sea and watching Pharaoh's army come at you, isn't it? But then to come down with the flu in the midst of final paintings and packing and moving...how much is one woman expected to take? Some things just must be struggled through – you know, character building! God certainly gives us plenty of opportunities to identify some enemies, doesn't He? How are you doing?

Your body does a superb job of giving you a good parable every time an attack takes place by a mean germ. When were you last sick with a cold or the flu? You can feel pretty pathetic and three days later actually look and feel quite chipper. Your body counterattacked. Your Helper T-cells recognized the antigens displayed by your macrophages and sounded the call to arms as good commanding officers. Your Killer Ts multiplied and entered the battle in full force. Your temperature rose as the activity increased with additional macrophages entering the battle and those B-cells multiplying. The Bs churned out your own antigen-specific antibodies that targeted that specific invading enemy (unlike the antibiotics physicians prescribe that destroy even the beneficial bacteria in our bodies). There was a spectacular defense going on within your body! Don't you wish you could have seen it? The power of the antibodies, combined with the skilled Killer T-cells and these marvelous macrophages have the germs well under control.

But under control is not good enough. You don't want to continue battling this germ for the rest of your life. If you are already battle weary from this ongoing fight, what happens when another germ jumps you – and then another, and another? No, there must be absolute victory declared over this foe. You must be free of it and there is only one source for that freedom.

We left off in *The Power of the Victory* with our B-cells producing potent antibodies. These antibodies latch onto the germ to disable it from attacking additional cells, neutralizing the enemy; marking the enemy for destruction by the Killer Ts; and making the foe a tastier treat for the macrophage. Remember, these antibodies have no curative power. They can't fix what has gone wrong or undo the consequences of disease. They are preventive agents, protecting against additional damage while signaling Killer T-cells to eradicate the antigens they have tagged for destruction. Antibodies also contain a substance that enhances phagocytosis (the consuming of antigens by phagocytes) – it just makes them taste better and easier to ingest. Phagocytes enjoy consuming their captives after they have been duly marked and marinated by the antibodies. But this marking of the invaders isn't only for the Killer Ts to identify them. It also emphasizes the crucial job of the antibodies as they call out of the bloodstream the most powerful and effective resource our body has, the complement.

This complement is a serum of proteins made up of 30 different components within our blood which, when gathered in just the right sequence, is the secret weapon that overcomes the foe completely. When complement enters this battle it creates holes in the enemy, which allows salt from our body to enter. The salt causes swelling and the enemy detonates like a bomb. The result is death to the invader; victory to the body! The battle is ended; the germ has been conquered.

As complex and efficient as our immune system is in its creation, it cannot totally eradicate the enemy without this complement. And as powerful and effective as this complement is, it cannot exercise its absolute authority until the antibodies call for it! The antibodies must first be generated by the division of B-cells before they can exercise their power to summon the complement. The B-cells must receive the message from the Helper T-cells to reproduce and then divide or the antibodies are never created. If the Helper Ts never receive the message of an invasion, the immune system is never activated. It must begin at the beginning with the consuming macrophage. God has given us a marvelous body that displays His order in creation. Let's learn from it, and the earlier, the better.

Okay, we have already compared the work of the antibodies to the work of the Holy Spirit, doing a job that no other part of our immune system can do, a power released when called upon by fervent prayer as a woman's heart cries out to God. But remember the Spirit is neither a weapon nor a cure-all. His purpose is not to fix what has gone wrong nor erase the consequences of sin or the temptations of the enemy. He is the agent of prevention, protecting our hearts, minds, and spirits from further damage. Once the onslaught of the enemy has been neutralized, the Spirit clearly tags the enemy for both destruction and removal. He directs us to use our Sword appropriately to defeat each temptation and evil influence. His entrance into this battle also enhances the wife's ability (in her macrophage role) to shed the love of God liberally throughout her marriage. It is His sweet touch applied to this bitter enemy that allows us to swallow the otherwise bitter cup that this war brings. Knowing His hand is controlling actually makes the battle cleanup enjoyable and pleasant to consume. (I know that's impossible to believe now, but being controlled by the Spirit enables the impossible to become sweet reality.)

This involvement of the Holy Spirit in our conflict now brings into action His highest assignment: collecting from the all-powerful blood of our Lord Jesus the necessary components - our spiritual Complement - to bring a final end to this adversary. This Complement is the second twist in our story, the turning point upon which victory hinges. Even with all of the mighty resources with which God has empowered the woman to keep her marriage healthy, the war could not be won without this final step. Remember, God has reserved the glory of victory for the name of our precious Savior.

Jesus indeed used the Word of God to defeat Satan's temptations. We follow His example in using our Sword. It brings us victories in the heat of battle, but it does not end the war. Satan did not disappear from the ministry of Christ after those three temptations in the wilderness. Luke 4:13 says the devil departed from Him **"for a season"** – until another occasion. As we read the Gospels, we can see the constant harassment of the devil throughout the Lord's ministry, using religious leaders, foes, and even friends to entice our Lord to say or do something contrary to the purpose of God. Even in the garden before His arrest, we see the struggle Jesus had against the cross He was called to bear. Jesus won each skirmish, but Satan was not conquered until the sacrifice was made, shedding the blood of the Savior – that unique, precious blood perfectly brought together in exact proportions of divinity and humanity, coupled with authority and meekness, empowered by complete submission and conformity to the will of the Father in obedience and suffering – all gathered in just the right sequence. It was that priceless blood that brought complete victory over Satan and all the forces of evil. Jesus has earned the right and has the authority to bring that victory to us in each battle we face. As we faithfully walk in His will, doing what He has called us to do, praying in the power of the Spirit, Jesus is faithful to administer His overcoming blood to conquer once and for all the evil that has come against you and your marriage.

I wish I had the time and knowledge to dig out what the implications are in the analogy of the complement that is drawn out of our physical bloodstream by antibodies and compare it to the atoning blood of Jesus that the Holy Spirit draws into action to destroy our enemies. The word that scientists came up with for this special serum of proteins – *complement* – must also have been divinely inspired, as was the *Helper* T. What better word could describe what the blood of Jesus does; it is the element that completes our salvation – **"It is finished."** The last word Jesus uttered on the cross means completed, accomplished from the initiation to the end in perfection! What God had planned and set into motion from the foundation of the world (Revelation 13:8, Matthew 25:34), was now fulfilled to perfection as the blood of Jesus was called out to complete our salvation.

That number 30 must surely have significance as well, but I am in about the second grade in my study of numbers in the Bible. I know the number 3 means Divine perfection and completeness: Father, Son, and Spirit is the complete Godhead; body, soul, and spirit is the complete man; it takes three lines to complete a plane figure; there are three dimensions of space - height, depth, and width; time consists of past, present, and future; ...and the number 3 includes resurrection: on the third day of creation the dry land rose from the deep and the fruit rose up from the earth, Noah's three sons raised up the population of the earth, and, of course, the Lord rose up from the grave on the third day. I also know the number 10 is ordinal perfection: ten generations from Creation to the Flood; the Ten Commandments; the ten plagues on Egypt; ten fingers and toes; the mathematical base of ten digits... Three and ten are both perfect and complete numbers. And 10 x 3 (30) is ordinal perfection intensified three times by Divine perfection: Joseph was 30 years old when he rose to power in Egypt; a priest could not serve in the ministry of the Lord until he was 30; David was 30 when he became King; Jesus entered His ministry at the age of 30 and was betrayed for 30 pieces of silver. I bet some smart person could sit down and come up with 30 things about the blood of Jesus that would correspond with the 30 components that make up the complement in our immune system that would really wow us, but I'm not that person. So onward we go. (Meanwhile, be alert to numbers in the Scriptures; they are clues to the secret things we spoke of in our last letter. The Father is really big on math!)

We have talked much about our fearsome foe already. But in light of the devastation he determines against us and the frightening skill and subtlety with which he does his dirty work, it bears reviewing. Remember what the word Satan means – an adversary, an enemy who fights determinedly, continuously, and relentlessly, opposing God's plan. In the shedding of His precious blood, Jesus offered us absolute freedom from the bondage Satan brings to enslave us. It's an old song but full of absolute truth – *There Is Power in the Blood*, by Lewis Jones: "Would you be free from the burden of sin? There's power in the blood, power in the blood. Would you o'er evil a victory win? There's wonderful power in the blood. Would you be free from your passion and pride? Come for a cleansing to Calvary's tide..." The blood washes us white as snow, removes the crimson stain, pays the price of God's judgment against sin, and guarantees victory over evil. But why blood? Isn't blood gruesome and morbid?

Follow with me a trail of death and life and deliverance through blood: Hebrews 2:14-15 **"...through death He might destroy him that had the power of death, that is, the devil; and deliver them who through fear of death were all their lifetime subject to bondage"**; 9:11-14 **"But Christ ...by His own blood entered in once into the holy place, having obtained eternal redemption for us. For if the blood of bulls and of goats ...sanctified to the purifying of the flesh: how much more shall the blood of Christ, who through the eternal Spirit offered Himself without spot to God, purge your conscience from dead works to serve the living God"**; 9:22 **"...without the shedding of blood is no remission** (forgiveness)**"**; 1 Peter 1:18-19 **"Forasmuch as ye know that ye were not redeemed with corruptible things, as silver and gold, from your vain conversation** (useless behavior, conduct without profit) **... but with the precious blood of Christ, as of a lamb without blemish and without spot"**; 1 John 1:7 **"...and the blood of Jesus Christ His Son cleanses us from all sin."** We have been **"bought with a price"** (1 Corinthians 6:20; 7:23), the precious blood of Jesus, and we need to understand the impact that blood has in our lives – the absolute, utmost, unlimited liberty that has been purchased for us.

Satan had no idea what power he was unleashing when he stirred the Jews to crucify Jesus. **"We speak the wisdom of God in a mystery... which none of the princes of this world knew: for had they known, they would not have crucified the Lord of glory."** (1 Corinthians 2:7-8) **"Having spoiled** (stripped of everything) **principalities and powers, He** (Jesus) **made a show** (exhibition) **of them openly, triumphing over** (conquering) **them in it."** (Colossians 2:15).

Are we victors, or what?! Satan has been stripped of his power; the blood of our Savior has conquered him!

Jesus said, **"...In the world ye shall have tribulation, but be of good cheer** (take courage); **I have overcome the world."** (John 16:33) Before we add more verses to that one, let me define some synonyms that have just enough difference in their meaning to get excited about. We have talked about defeating our enemies, triumphing over them, and overcoming. *Defeat* is what we must do on a daily basis and suggests beating or frustrating temporarily, which Jesus did during His temptation after His baptism. Triumphing over means to *conquer,* which implies finally gaining control over something, usually after a series of efforts against a systematic resistance. But the Greek word translated **overcome** in John 16 means *subdue,* which means to conquer so completely that the spirit of resistance is broken! Jesus has overcome, subdued the forces of evil completely, as the complement we so desperately need. **"The Lamb shall overcome them: for He is the Lord of lords, and King of kings and they that are with Him are called and chosen and faithful."** (Revelation 17:14) And 1 John 2:13-14 lets us know that we, too, have overcome: **"...the Word of God abideth in you, and ye have overcome the wicked one."** And chapter 4, verse 4: **"Ye are of God, little children** (darlings, Christian converts)**, and have overcome them: because greater is He that is in you, than he that is in the world."** Now look at chapter 5, verse 4: **"For whatsoever** (any, every, all) **born** (conceived, birthed, given life) **of God overcometh the world** (subdues, conquers so completely that the spirit of resistance is broken)**: and this is the victory** (the conquest, the victor taking control and putting the conquered in obedience, the decisive superiority in any battle or contest) **that overcomes** (subdues) **the world, our faith** (conviction of reliance upon Christ for salvation).**"** Try rewriting that in your own words and make it your personal promise of victory in your notebook of "lists"/ prayer requests.

With the Word abiding in us as children of God, that spirit of resistance really can be subdued completely. In fact, the seven churches in Revelation 2 and 3 are admonished seven times to overcome if they are: to eat the tree of life; be free of the second death; eat of the hidden manna and receive a new name; have power over the nations; be clothed in white raiment having Jesus confess them before the Father; be made a pillar in the temple of God with Jesus sharing His new name; and sit with Christ in His throne. Revelation 12:11 says, **"And they overcame him by the blood of the Lamb..."**

But again, why blood? Did you know there are actually denominations that have removed the concept of blood from all their hymns and teachings? It is offensive – barbaric they say. They focus on the "love of God" instead. But the love of God and the blood of the Lamb are synonymous. God Himself shed the first blood on earth when He clothed Adam and Eve with the skin of an animal, not only to cover their nakedness but their sin. Abel's offering of the slain lamb was accepted while Cain's offering of the fruit of the ground, the work of his hands, was rejected. God wanted mankind to understand well the cost of sin and the concept of death because of that sin. There is, however, another side of blood - not one of death but life.

Hang in here with me, Darling, as we take another trail through a few scriptures to see what God thinks of blood. **"The life of the flesh is in the blood"** (Genesis 4:10; 9:4; Leviticus 7:26-27; 17:10-14; Deuteronomy 12:23-28). **"...the voice of thy brother's blood crieth unto Me from the ground."** (Genesis 4:10) Even in the New Testament (Acts 15) when there is a question about Gentiles keeping the Law, circumcision, and all the other things that even the Jews could not keep, the only restrictions the apostles placed on these new converts were: stay away from those things polluted by idol worship, stay sexually pure, and don't eat meat that was strangled because it would still carry the blood. Why do savage warriors drink the blood of an animal before they fight? They believe the blood of that animal feeds their own bodies with the power and strength of the creature. In their own perverted way, those heathen are more in tune with the view God has of blood than most Christians. The blood signifies life, vitality, strength. It is the blood that carries life-giving oxygen and nutrients to every cell in our body. When the blood quits circulating through our body, we die. The heart is a vital organ because it pumps the blood. It is not in the stopping of the heart that brings death; it is the stopping of the blood. If the blood does not carry oxygen to the brain, the brain dies. If circulation is shut off from a foot, that foot dies... You get the idea. The life of the flesh is in the blood. How could doctors so foolishly once believe in bleeding a patient? Isn't that what cost George Washington his life?

Not only does blood carry life to each cell, it carries away the waste created as the cells use oxygen. It is constantly cleansing the body of toxins formed during the living process – carbon dioxide, urea, uric acid and such. If you were to try to use muscles that had been deprived of the cleansing action of the blood, you would find not only lack of strength but extreme pain because of the retained toxins accumulated in those muscles. As a little girl I remember hanging my arm over the back of my chair at school until it went "dead". When I tried to use it - what pain! There must have been something wrong with my brain. I suppose all kids have wound a string or rubber band around their finger at some point, just to watch their finger turn blue. But isn't that what we do as Christians when we allow something to hamper the flow of the power of Christ in our lives – we don't receive the life-giving "oxygen and nutrients" that our spirits require and we are deprived of the cleansing that removes "waste and toxins" from our walk with Him. I have seen some blue Christians, haven't you? In fact, I have been there myself, empty and dry but still trying to perform my spiritual tasks. There was no strength. There was great pain. We can only continue in that state a short while before permanent damage is done. We must let the blood of Christ do within us what our own blood does for our bodies, consistently, relentlessly, day by day, moment by moment. That was the analogy He was giving on that last night when He said we can do nothing apart from Him, no more than the branch can produce grapes if it does not have the sap of the vine flowing through it. The life is in the blood.

We are saved by His death, yes - reconciled to God, but we live by His life! The life of His blood has been given to us. I don't think I can even begin to give you a glimpse into the mystery of what I just said. I am just beginning to realize it for myself after all these years. Turn to Romans 5:8-11 and let it speak to you. Mark in your Bible somewhere some definitions to be remembered: (v.9) *justified* – recognized by God as righteous; *saved* – delivered, protected; (v.10) *reconciled* – to cause hostility to cease, to harmonize or settle a quarrel, to restore to the original! God Himself established peace with man, which hitherto had been prevented by the demands of His justice as Holy God. He took upon Himself our sins and became the atonement. We are now at one with Him, restored to the original state of fellowship. If we were reconciled to God by the death of His Son, much more shall we be saved by His life! What joy!!! If only the Church could get the full grasp of what Jesus wants to do through her as His body on earth, with His life-blood flowing to each member, vitalizing and energizing us to do His will!

Isn't it just like God to choose something so contrary to our thinking as blood to be the very thing that washes us white as snow? Women learn early that blood stains. If you don't treat a bloodstain with cold water quickly, you will have a permanent black stain. Yet God says the only way to remove the sin that has stained our lives is to be washed "**in His own blood**" (Revelation 1:5). And how powerful Hebrews 9:14 speaks to us with **"how much more shall the blood of Christ ... purge** (cleanse) **your conscience from dead works to serve the living God."** That's worth just sitting around and thinking about for a while – meditating – chewing on again and again and again, until the full, wonderful truth sinks deep into one's heart and soul.

If we as women are going to serve God in the capacity in which He has called us as wives, we must be purged in our heart of hearts from dead works. The works that are dead are those things not touched by His will and purpose. Can you name some deeds you have attempted that just fell flat because God was not consulted? Jesus said if you just give a cup of water "in His name" you will receive a prophet's reward. Again, He has given women an extra insight into His ways by our monthly cycle. If an egg is not fertilized, no life is conceived; it passes from the body fruitless - dead. That is exactly what Isaiah meant when he said in 64:6 that **all our righteousnesses are as filthy rags** – those filthy rags were the foul-smelling menstrual cloths that women were relegated to wear when a child was not conceived. Any righteous deeds we attempt apart from Him are just like that unfertilized egg, no matter how "good" they appear to be to the world. (Matthew 7:22-23) We need to enter into an intimacy with Him that brings abiding fruit for His kingdom; we need to be cleansed from unfruitfulness. Seek Him and the power of His cleansing blood. How I love William Cowper's beautiful song: "There is a fountain filled with blood, drawn from Emmanuel's veins; and sinners, plunged beneath that flood, lose all their guilty stains..." Every verse is beautiful – grateful for the cleansing power of the blood of our Savior. Songs seem to keep popping up in this letter. Is this a reminder of Psalm 61:8? Are you singing? Remember the battle of Jehoshaphat! (2 Chronicles 20)

Let's go back to our spiritual immune system for marriages... In the midst of whatever conflict you happen to be fighting, when battling a force that is contrary to God's perfect plan, you can count on it multiplying quickly and viciously. We must do all we have been given to do and then call on the Holy Spirit to do what only He can do. It is then, from this precious, perfect blood of the Savior, that the Spirit calls for the "complement" to come to the rescue. You now have that final overcoming force that ends the war against that particular foe that has come against you. His blood is all powerful. He won this battle before you were ever attacked! But it is only by the blood being applied that we gain total victory. If we are sick and weak and besieged by the enemy, it is because we have neglected so great a salvation. We have come short of His rest (putting to rest, calming of the winds, repose), Hebrews 4:1-11. We have failed to believe there is rest and freedom from the dominion of the winds of sin, Satan, the flesh, and even the yoke of religion and all its toilsome ceremonies and servitude.

Let's finalize the job of the complement: When complement comes together from the blood of our Savior and enters this battle, it creates holes in the enemy, which allows entrance for salt from our own marriage. The salt causes swelling and the enemy soon detonates like a bomb. The result is death to the invader; complete victory to the body! The battle is ended; the evil, the temptation, the false doctrine, the cancer - whatever has been your tormentor - has been conquered. So what is the salt? This was some fun research... I learned a lot in looking for this.

I bet you didn't know salt was required in the sacrifices of the Israelites; I read right over it for years. In fact, in Leviticus 2:13 it says the salt was not to be lacking from their offering; **"with all thine offerings thou shalt offer salt."** Numbers 18:19 speaks of a **"covenant of salt"** for ever before the Lord.

2 Chronicles 13:5 tells us God made His promise to give the kingdom of Israel to David for ever by a **"covenant of salt."** Then Jesus tells us in Mark 9 that **"every sacrifice shall be salted with salt. Salt is good: but if the salt has lost his saltness, wherewith will ye season it? Have salt in yourselves and have peace one with another."** Add Matthew 5 to that, **"Ye are the salt of the earth..."** And Colossians 4:6, **"Let your speech be always with grace, seasoned with salt, that ye may know how ye ought to answer every man."** Okay, what is it with salt? Let's see what salt does.

Do you remember any of your chemistry? Let me refresh your memory. Salt is the compound sodium chloride. It is essential for life and health for man and animals. Every cell of your body contains salt; it keeps our bodies functioning properly. It maintains the fluid in blood cells, and helps transmit electrical impulses between your brain, nerves and muscles. It helps the digestive process, preserves the acid-base balance in the body and helps the blood carry carbon dioxide from the tissues to the lungs. Without enough salt, our bodies cannot perform its vital functions. Without it we die. And our bodies cannot produce the salt we need; we must rely on it being furnished from an outside source! Of course, salt makes food taste good, enhancing the flavor of whatever you eat. No other seasoning can satisfactorily take the place of salt in bringing out the distinct taste of varying foods. Salt keeps flesh (meat) from putrefaction (preserving it from rotting). Its preservation power has made it invaluable throughout history, keeping foods such as meat, fish, and dairy products safe to eat. Because of that ability to preserve, salt was the emblem of incorruptibility and permanence. Hence, a covenant of salt signified an everlasting covenant, permanent, perpetual and inviolable, not to be profaned or treated with irreverence. Salt's power to strengthen food and purify it signified that the sacrifice being made was offered in might and purity.

Now here are some more interesting uses for salt: Salt melts ice, keeping our way safe. Salt softens hard water to make it useful for cooking and cleaning. Salt is an excellent cleaning agent, by itself or in combination with other substances such as vinegar, alcohol, lemon juice, or baking soda. Salt removes tea and coffee stains from cups. Salt smothers a grease fire. Salt relieves the pain of a bee sting, sore throats, and toothaches. Salt rubbed on your windows keeps the glass frost free. Salt rubbed on your griddle keeps your pancakes from sticking. Just a pinch of salt in egg whites makes them beat up fluffier. Salt kills weeds in your lawn, grass in your sidewalk, and poison ivy anywhere. Salt removes odors from sink drainpipes. Salt controls fermentation in baked goods by retarding the growth of bacteria, yeast and molds. Soaking stained hankies in salt water before washing restores their color. Salt is an abrasive and also burns like fire on an open wound.

And that's just a few common uses for sodium chloride! We could learn a lot from our great-grandmas if they were still around (and if we would take the time to listen to them). Furthermore, we didn't even touch on salt baths, or hot salt domes and salt ponds used to create energy, or salt brines used as antifreeze, or salt being used in high powered lasers! What a day in which we live! Moving right along, let's do some comparing...

As Christians, we all have been given salt to circulate through our lives. I didn't give much of a definition of sodium chloride, just its usefulness. But we need to look well into what this spiritual salt is. Salt is the grace of God, but what are the elements that make up the grace of God? Grace is defined as "free, unmerited loving-kindness and favor expressed by Divine influence upon our hearts and its reflection in our lives, affecting our sinfulness and bringing joy to replace guilt." I've touched on the definition of grace in earlier letters, but have you ever really thought about that definition? Check out Ephesians 2:4-9. #1 – it's free; we can't earn God's grace. #2 – it's unmerited; we don't deserve His love and favor. #3 – it is God's influence working in our hearts for our good. #4 – if grace is truly grace, its effect in our lives creates such gratitude of the heart that it will reflect the image of God's character for all to see. Reread that definition. Think about that word influence. Webster says influence literally means a flowing in, into, or on, referring to something spiritual or too subtle to be visible – like inspiration. It is the operation of an invisible power known only by its effects, like gravity on a dropped object or the moon on the tides – or God in a heart. God's invisible influence moving on a heart causes a change that is reflected in that life: a renewed heart restrained from sin and a virtuous disposition. The affect of grace in a marriage is as evident to all as surely as the tides of the ocean reflect the power of the moon.

What exactly are those effects of grace? The grace of God is essential for life and health for all of God's children. It keeps us functioning properly. It maintains the operation of the Spirit in our lives, transmitting the impulses between our Lord and our feelings and actions. The grace of God helps us digest His Word, balances our physical-spiritual makeup, and carries away trash from our daily living. The grace of God seasons our hearts and makes our speech and actions savory. The grace of God preserves us from the corruption of sin that would putrefy our lives, our testimony, and our service to Him. Since the nature of man is corrupt (and called flesh) it must be salted with grace for it to be sacrificed to God, preserving it by removing evil. Now, to be a living sacrifice to God (Romans 12:1), our corrupt affections must be mortified (Romans 8:13) and we must have in our souls the savor of grace, the only quality which renders us valuable and agreeable to the taste. Grace works out all corrupt, stinky dispositions and any and every thing in the soul that would try to reduce us back

The Mystery of Marriage through Adam's Prime Rib

to our pathetic, sinful state of separation from God. Without grace, our lives would be as offensive to Him as tainted meat with the stench of rottenness. It is in that grace that we can offer ourselves as that living sacrifice, offered in strength and purity. He has given grace to every cell in His Body - the Church - that we might function as He intended. Without grace, we would be dead. And this next sentence is the one I find most amazing of this whole analogy of salt and grace. Grace is something we *cannot* produce ourselves; we must rely on it being furnished from a source *outside of ourselves* - from our God and Savior. **"Therefore being justified by faith, we have peace with God through our Lord Jesus Christ: By whom also we have access by faith into this grace wherein we stand and rejoice in hope of the glory of God."** (Romans 5:1-2) No one can earn grace; no one deserves grace. God just gives it freely as a gift to all who trust Him, because that's Who God is. Therefore, as a gift from God, it is permanent, everlasting, perpetual, not be profaned or treated with irreverence (Hebrews 10:29).

Now here are some more interesting things grace does for us: Grace melts an icy heart, making the walk with Jesus secure. Grace softens a calloused spirit to make it useful for service to its Creator. Grace is an excellent cleaning agent, by itself or in combination with many other means such as trials, adversities, persecution, or humiliation. Grace removes the stains of sin from vessels of service. Grace smothers the fires of anger, bitterness, revenge, and a gossiping tongue. Grace relieves the pain of sorrows, the hurtfulness of ugly words and misunderstandings. Grace applied on the windows of your heart keeps your view of the world frost free. Grace applied to your tools of service keeps your fruit from sticking. Just a pinch of grace in those little goodies of life makes them fluff up fuller and go further. Grace kills weeds of condemnation and poisonous lies, removes offensive odors, and controls the growth of temptations and evil. Soaking stained experiences in grace restores their original beauty. And, yes, at times grace will burn like fire as it sometimes must act as the corrosive element that removes proud flesh. The grace of God makes us good and useful to others as the salt of the earth. Now go back through these last two paragraphs and substitute "grace" with "Divine influence." It works!

God has given His grace to your marriage as well as to each individual - you two have become one new body. Of all things, He desires the Christian marriage to "work" because it reflects His relationship with us, as Christ with His Church. Anything less than a man and wife living in harmony gives the adversary opportunity to blaspheme God's Word and His wondrous plan for us. Our Complement comes into this battle with power from on high to blast holes in our foe with a vengeance that belongs to an offended God. Those holes allow the grace of God which is abiding in our lives to enter into that enemy. And to be totally frank, grace (God's divine influence) within the enemy just isn't healthy for said enemy. That adversary will swell up and blow up in unrecognizable pieces that are quickly gobbled up by the macrophage. It is possible to be rid of that enemy forever with a properly functioning immune system. Remember we overcome by the blood of the Lamb. A major problem in overcoming, however, is the fact that the enemy comes in so many different forms and is mutating just enough each time in hopes of catching us off guard and getting the upper hand.

One quick example from my own marriage: I have a good looking husband! He has always had trouble with females being drawn to him, as a little boy, a teenager, and in his manhood. We had our share of trouble over that before we were married. I thought it was behind us when we said "I do"; but with my insecurities and his good looks and outgoing personality, Satan knew exactly where to attack our marriage. We survived the attack and came out on the other side fairly unscarred and more confident. However, the enemy would mutate just enough that there would be another successful attack – nothing too severe but still making our marriage nauseated. Again we found victory. When Wayne was called into the ministry Satan changed his tactics and tried again. God warned him through a dream of a trap awaiting him and he was able to escape it with no effect from the enemy, only a wholesome awe and fear of the Lord. Years later, one final attempt came from the adversary that had mutated so much neither of us recognized it until it had its tentacles almost embedded in our marriage. (Watch out for that 13th year of marriage, Sis – it's a year of confusion!) God graciously showed me what was happening, and the battle was on. Yes, the victory was sweet, but oh, the battle was hard, the body was sick and miserable. Yet this time, by the power of the blood, we became overcomers! We had defeated the foe at each point of attack, frustrating his efforts temporarily; but we needed to conquer him. Jesus has the power to do that for us, to subdue the enemy so completely that the spirit of opposition to God's will is broken. We are victorious in an area of our lives that has been attack free ever since. Praise the Lord!

I reiterate from the last letter: as complex as this role of a wife is and as efficient as our Creator desires a woman's mission to be in protecting her marriage, she cannot totally eradicate the enemy without this complement from the Lord's own blood. Moreover, as powerful and effective as this spiritual complement is, it cannot exercise its absolute authority until the Holy Spirit has first been given liberty to function by the fervent prayer of the wife. In order to pray rightly, this virtuous wife must be in abiding fellowship with her Lord to discern the urgent needs of her marriage. If there is no discernment, there is no call to arms, no fervent prayer, no power of the Spirit released, no blood of the Lamb applied. If the woman never recognizes the enemy and understands there has been an invasion, the spiritual immune system is never activated. It must begin at the beginning with the consuming macrophage of love. What a marvelous body God has bestowed upon us to display His order - yes, it works even in marriage. Are we learning anything yet? Get your immune system in order! The blood is sufficient for every battle. What a job we have!

Now the ultimate question: If Satan was subdued by the blood at the cross, why do I constantly need to be delivered again and again? Wouldn't it be wonderful if the world could be eradicated of all the protozoa, bacteria, and viruses that stalk us? It will be one day, just as surely as Satan's devices will be stopped totally one day. But for now God has enabled our bodies to overcome one ailment after another, one victory at a time. I reminded my Susie more than once that those chicken pox scars on her body were a reminder that she was an overcomer. The cold you had last year will never affect you again because you overcame it. One germ at a time, your body responds with a healthy immune system to annihilate another foe. So it is with Satan's attacks, one victory after another. With our spiritual immune system functioning, each step leads us to our secret weapon that utterly destroys that foe. We get to "see" it dead on the shore of the Red Sea of His blood. Hallelujah!

We are so blessed to live in this modern age of science. The more they learn of the earth and the universe, the more proof is given to the accuracy of the Bible. The more they learn about the human body, the deeper and more exact are the truths of the analogies revealed to us. Why, just the uncovering of the DNA of cells has opened doors of unbelievable and far-reaching magnitude in unlocking mysteries that were before unsolvable. How can this master code engrained within each living cell not have a Code Maker? The analogies implied enable us to understand God and ourselves and His Church. Be overwhelmed by His love and goodness, grateful to live in this day of scientific knowledge!

Again, reread and let the goodness of these verses sink deep into your heart and spirit. Whatever comes against us, we have the victory! We have the secret weapon to end all weapons!!! Personally, I find great relief in knowing it doesn't all rest on me: the Spirit of the living God and Jesus Christ Himself are at my beck and call! WOW!!!

I am excited about the next letter and the promises that come with it. But I must first close this one, right? Until next time...

Eternally victorious in Him,
CK (2nd momma, grand momma)

P. S. There are over 130 verses dealing with grace in just the New Testament. So many scriptures - time won't allow me the privilege to deal with them. Humor me and look up just these few to think about and chew on for a while.

- *Luke 2:40*
- *John 1:14, 16*
- *Acts 4:33*
- *Acts 15:11   Acts 20:32*
- *Romans 3:24*
- *Romans 5:2, 20-21 (Romans is so good! But isn't it all?)*
- *1 Corinthians 15:10*
- *2 Corinthians 6:1*
- *2 Corinthians 9:8 ! 2 Corinthians 12:9 !!*
- *Galatians 2:21*
- *Ephesians 2:7-8   Ephesians 4:7, 29*
- *Colossians 4:6*

- *2 Thessalonians 2:16*
- *2 Timothy 1:9; 2:1*
- *Hebrews 4:16*
- *Hebrews 10:29*
- *Hebrews 12:28*
- *James 4:6*
- *1 Peter 5:5 2 Peter 3:18*

dot, dot, dot again...

The Mystery of Marriage through Adam's Prime Rib

Assurance from our Commander

*J*ust a note, my Dear,

The following is a chapter from the Psalms that has spurred me on and given me great confidence. I have mentioned it in past letters but I want to reemphasize it right now – for reference when you are in the heat of battle. For sake of space I only printed those verses that apply in such a wonderful way to the spiritual battle in which we are engaged. Read the whole chapter, recounting the many ways and times the Lord delivered man.

Psalm 18 - To the chief Musician, A Psalm of David, the servant of the LORD, who spoke unto the LORD the words of this song in the day the LORD delivered him from the hand of all his enemies, and from the hand of Saul:

1 And he said, I will love thee, O LORD, my strength.
2 The LORD is my rock, and my fortress, and my deliverer; my God, my strength, in whom I will trust; my buckler, and the horn of my salvation, and my high tower.
3 I will call upon the LORD, who is worthy to be praised: so shall I be saved from mine enemies.
6 In my distress I called upon the LORD, and cried unto my God: He heard my voice out of His temple, and my cry came before Him, even into His ears.
7 Then the earth shook and trembled; the foundations also of the hills moved and were shaken, because He was wroth.

17 He delivered me from my strong enemy, and from them which hated
    me: for they were too strong for me.

18 They prevented me in the day of my calamity: but the LORD
    was my stay.

19 He brought me forth also into a large place; He delivered me,
    because He delighted in me.

28 For Thou wilt light my candle: the LORD my God will enlighten
    my darkness.

29 For by Thee I have run through a troop; and by my God have I leaped
    over a wall.

30 As for God, His way is perfect: the word of the LORD is tried:
    He is a buckler to all those that trust in Him.

31 For who is God save the LORD? or who is a rock save our God?

32 It is God that girds me with strength, and makes my way perfect.

33 He makes my feet like hinds' feet, and sets me upon my high places.

34 He teaches my hands to war, so that a bow of steel is broken
    by mine arms.

35 Thou hast also given me the shield of Thy salvation: and Thy right
    hand hath holden me up, and Thy gentleness hath made me great.

36 Thou hast enlarged my steps under me, that my feet did not slip.

37 I have pursued mine enemies, and overtaken them: neither did I turn
    again till they were consumed.

38 I have wounded them that they were not able to rise: they are fallen
    under my feet.

39 For Thou hast girded me with strength unto the battle: Thou hast
    subdued under me those that rose up against me.

40 Thou hast also given me the necks of mine enemies; that I might
    destroy them that hate me.

The Mystery of Marriage through Adam's Prime Rib

42 Then did I beat them small as the dust before the wind: I did cast them out as the dirt in the streets.

46 The LORD liveth; and blessed be my Rock; and let the God of my salvation be exalted.

47 It is God that avenges me, and subdues the people under me.

48 He delivers me from mine enemies: yea, Thou lift me up above those that rise up against me: Thou hast delivered me from the violent man.

49 Therefore will I give thanks unto thee, O LORD, among the heathen, and sing praises unto Thy name.

The battle is challenging, sometimes to the point of despair. But, as we have seen, the victory is ours with God in command. When He is bringing you through a testing time, don't be discouraged. You cannot fathom what is in God's mind for your future or what He is creating from the materials of your life. Oh, the storyline He has carefully plotted out for you and your precious family! Don't bring disaster by attempting to take the pen out of His hand to rewrite your character. That would be like your little child, who so wants to help Momma paint her beautiful watercolors (and by the way, is confident he could do every bit as well), taking the brush with his small, untrained hands and ruining a masterpiece – not on purpose, but in ignorance, impatience, and inability. It would be ruined none the less. Not only does he lack the skill, he doesn't have the capacity to see what is in your mind's eye, nor the insight or foresight required to create what only you can create. {My own Susie is an exceptional artist, whose firstborn was in the "terrible twos" as I wrote this letter to her} Don't be an impudent child and bring ruin to your life!

No, trust Him. He is the Master Writer, Artist, Sculptor, and Judge. Never doubt that He wants the best for you! God doesn't doodle; every stroke of His pen has purpose to mature you into the Bride that will be fit for His Son as His wife and Queen.

Such joy there was in His heart when you were birthed into the Kingdom! I have had physical birthing joy over nine babies, though painful, each one euphorically joyous! But now, as a mother of grown children, I can understand: there is an even deeper rejoicing in God's heart over the maturity of His children. Trust Him. Feed on His Word and grow up in His grace. Give Him a free hand with your script and follow it through the conflict into the climax and on to the end. The resolution of it all will be glorious indeed. He will bless you and reward you and reveal to you the greatness of His salvation. You can't even imagine the epilogue He has written just for you when all is said and done! (I have been privileged to see a glimpse of the rough draft of my own!) Physical enemies are nothing compared to our spiritual adversary, but both the physical and spiritual sufferings we endure in this life are not even deserving to be compared to the glory that will be revealed (Romans 8:18).

Gird up your battle gear and encounter first hand what glorious rejoicing engulfs us when we experience each victory over yet another invisible, despicable foe. Hang in there, Baby...

Trusting our Commander,
C K

Sweet Peace and Rest

Peace and Rest Precious Warrior,

I guess I've laid some pretty heavy stuff on you in these letters. Just remember "heavy" means glory and honor when you are speaking about spiritual matters. Have I overloaded your circuits with too much information? At least you don't have to take it in all at once; just refer back to your letters and the Scriptures often. God knows where you are and will speak to you at your point of need.

What did you think marriage would be when your sweetheart gave you that ring? With starry eyes and a heart full of hopes and dreams, no one ever thinks about entering a war zone when you take your marriage vows. Yet almost every marriage spends its existence in war, most unfortunately, with spouse against spouse. Wives nag their husbands and tear them down while husbands grow calloused and treat their wives as something to be tolerated. Both wonder what they ever saw in the other.

We are in a war for sure, but it was never meant to be declared against one another. The real enemy is in the shadows, gleefully laughing at the mutiny for which he is responsible. He has scattered the protozoa of evil across the earth; he has infiltrated every marriage with fast multiplying, enticing bacteria of temptations; he has breathed his vicious viruses of deception into every aspect of those lofty hopes and dreams. We must identify the real enemy at war with God and all who belong to Him. We must fight against him with all of our being. When we faithfully do so, Jesus then steps in and completes the battle for us. What a wonder!

Stepping back into our immune analogy, this letter will bring us into the realm of another T-cell that we met briefly in "Let's Meet the Staff." This soldier is called the Suppressor T because it does just that, suppresses the forces of your defense system that have been in a frenzy of activity. As the infection is contained and then overcome, the Suppressor Ts bring a halt to the immune responses. Of course, with the battle already won there are no weapons involved in the Suppressors' ministry to our body, yet the role of these cells is just as vital in our immune system as any other. As surely as the call to arms was sounded by our Helper Ts, there must be a call to cease-fire and desist all activity in our counter-attack. If not put in check, the immune response will spiral out of control, creating further damage to its own body. These Suppressor Ts send out chemical messages that silence the red alert sent from Helper Ts; call off the attack from Killer Ts; and stop the replication and division of B-cells, halting the production of antibodies. The temperature returns to normal. The debris from the aftermath of the battle is cleaned up. The Suppressor Ts have proclaimed a solid victory against this particular foe. They carry the sweet aroma of peace and rest from the conflict. The body has won this round and begins to slow down and glory in the success.

It would be disastrous for our body to continue in this full battle mode of warfare for very long. You know well how tired the body gets when sick. All of your energy is exerted within the body – you have little ability to pursue even the daily duties on the outside. Your focus is all turned inward until the battle is resolved. Plus, all these chemicals are being released into your body, building up your troop force and preparing reserves to come in as replacements. There is stress put on all your organs and systems. At some point, victory must either be declared or surrendered. And, of course, we naturally cast our vote for complete victory. When it is evident the antagonist has been overcome, then the Suppressor T steps up to front and center with its melodious sound of peace. The enemy has been subjugated; the treaty has been signed. There is an observable absence of conflict. A time of repose and well-deserved rest is in store. Harmony has been restored to the body. After all this war talk I hope you can enjoy just thinking about this part. As healthy as we have been, it sure seems we have had our share of battle-weary days. If there were no times of rest in between the conflicts... Well, thank God for His faultless plan when He put this body together.

There has been a lot of research in recent years on this Suppressor T-cell. They are now calling it the Regulatory T-cell, but I like the old name, Suppressor, because that is exactly what it does. Scientists have recently created an antibody that inhibits the ability of Suppressor cells to slow down the response of the other cells; it other words, it cancelled suppression. The molecule recognized by this created antibody was glucocorticoid induced tumor necrosis factor receptor (GITR). Suppressor Ts have high levels of GITR. When the antibody binds to that GITR in the T-cell, it prevents the Suppressor T from downgrading the activity of its fellow soldiers - the Helper Ts and Killer Ts and those productive Bs. The poor mice on which they were experimenting developed autoimmune gastritis. Why on earth would scientists want to develop something to prevent the Suppressor from doing its job? Because they are learning that if there is an excess of this type of cell in the body, the immune system is shut down too quickly, or is never allowed to engage in full battle; it can't fight off the germs. The body is also prone to develop malignancies. There is simply too much suppressing of the immune system and cancers can grow out of control. So the big guys in the experiment department are trying to find ways to correct this excessive shut down which plague some people. The body must have a balance in its forces. Every soldier is important in its place and proper balance of each regiment is vital to victory. We can't have the Suppressors acting too quickly before the battle is won, nor too slowly, endangering an overload of the system. When our immune system is cooperating as the proficient army that God ordained it to be, we see the battles won and the glorious tranquility that follows.

Okay, are you ready to apply these soldiers' jobs to your own? What is a wife to do after she has recognized the enemy, sounded the alarm, consumed in love all that is possible, turned to the Word, cried out to the Lord in fervent prayer, seen the effects of the Spirit's touch in the conflict, and then watched as the power of the blood was applied so God's grace could perform miracles? When the responses have been proper and the temptation or deception has been defeated, the wife must be the first to acknowledge that all is well, reassuring her husband of her love and confidence in him. Peacemaking in the home and heart of her husband must always be priority after an assault from Satan or the world or even himself. Just as an immune system spiraling out of control can be disastrous, so also can the ongoing pursuit of something that has already been resolved. Rest and peace must come after the battle. There must be a calmness of the Spirit, a rest in the Lord.

Take a look at Proverbs 14:1. We do one of two things: we either build our house as wise women or we pull it apart and destroy it as a fool. The word house could be a tent, hut, house, mansion, or palace. It is a dwelling place in the widest sense and is used to describe every home, from the spider's house (Job 8:14) to God's house and everything in between. But it isn't just the house – it includes everything inside that makes it a home fit for habitation. It includes the family. We are back to that powerful influence we have as women. We make or break the home! May God give us wisdom (and may we use it)!

Proverbs 17:1 speaks of quietness in the house with only dry bread as being better than feasting where there is strife. Quietness doesn't mean the absence of noise; it is the absence of strife; it is security of defense. That is the peace and rest that comes to settle over the home when the battle has been won and there is surety of safety. Twice in Proverbs 21, verses 9 and 19, we see "It is better to dwell" statements that are not too flattering for women. The first advises one to choose the corner of the housetop (the peak of the roof) than to live inside with a brawling woman. The second bit of advice is to go live in the wilderness rather than with that same brawling woman who has added to her contention anger and fretfulness and spite. Gee whiz, what kind of woman wants to treat her husband like that? One who wants to pick a fight? One who won't let the fight end? One that can't accept that the fight is over? That woman drives her husband out of the house into precarious situations. Satan is taking note. He will take every advantage that he is offered. We must be on guard and, when the battle is over, cover our homes and families with sweet peace. One more verse from Proverbs: chapter 31, verse 12 says, **"She does him good and not evil** (the opposite of good, giving pain or causing unhappiness) **all the days of her life."** That's the virtuous wife whose worth is far above rubies – the wife of great force, the valiant army, the band of soldiers.

Look at these verses in Leviticus 26: 3, 6, and 7. **"If you walk** (figuratively applied to the characteristics of one's lifestyle and continuing relationship with God) **in My statutes** (boundaries, limits, instruction as a rule of action or conduct laid down to be strictly obeyed)**, and keep** (exercising great care over, careful attention paid to obligations) **My commandments** (what is due, terms of a contract, clear-cut directives, condition of God's covenant), **and do** (perform, toil to accomplish) **them;... I will give peace** (health, security, tranquility, a harmonious state of soul and mind, both externally and internally) **in the land, and you shall lie down and none shall make you afraid: and I will rid evil beasts out of the land...And you shall chase your enemies, and they shall fall before you by the sword."** When you have lived in God's boundaries and instructions that He has written into this script just for a wife, and you have taken great care to pay attention to His clear-cut directives addressed to you, and then toiled to accomplish that which He has asked you to perform, then comes the peace, health, security, tranquility. None will make you afraid. You know God is bringing to an end those evil experiences that bring pain and unhappiness. You know you have the ability to chase those enemies from your marriage by the power of the sword God has given you.

When it is evident the antagonist has been overcome, then a wife must don her Suppressor T-role and step up front and center with a melodious sound of peace. The trial has been overcome, the temptation defeated; deliverance has come. There must now be an observable absence of conflict. A time of repose and well-deserved rest is in store. Harmony has been restored to the body of this marriage. This is when you can kick your feet up and enjoy some well-deserved rest! After suffering from battle fatigue it is sweet to enjoy some peace.

Proverbs 13:12 can help us understand what is happening in the heart of marriages. **"Hope deferred maketh the heart sick, but when the desire cometh, it is a tree of life."** We all have great hopes when we get married. That's why we marry. But when our dreams of happily ever after are delayed in coming, if they aren't enjoyed as soon as expected, or if they too soon depart, the mind becomes uneasy, the heart sinks, and we are ready to give up all hope of enjoying the desired bliss of marital union. That's where most of our marriages are today, either at the brink of divorce or already plunged into that sewer. Hearts are sick. But when that which has been longed for comes, it gives an inexpressible satisfaction and delight. It is as the tree of life in the Garden of Eden, strengthening and energizing the marriage for the duration of life. The marriage is healthy regardless of the outward circumstances; trials that come only make one stronger. **"The desire accomplished is sweet to the soul"** says verse 19. And your desire for a peaceful, idyllic marriage is well to being accomplished when you are doing what God created you to do – when you have been that mighty host and won a victory!

Jesus promised us peace in Him in John 14:27 and 16:33. The peace He is talking about is the absence or the end of strife; a state of untroubled, undisturbed well-being; deliverance and freedom from all the distresses that are experienced as a result of sin. Again He reminds us that He has overcome the world. No doubts need to ever mar your peace. Rest in the knowledge that God's grace is all-sufficient and this skirmish is won. Bask in the peace won for the present and take advantage of the reprieve to ready yourself for the next attack from another demon on assignment.

You have to love Matthew 11:28-30, **"Come unto me, all *ye* that labor and are heavy laden, and I will give you rest. Take my yoke upon you, and learn of me; for I am meek and lowly in heart: and ye shall find rest unto your souls. For my yoke *is* easy, and my burden is light."** The rest Jesus gives us is a ceasing from labor, a time of refreshment and relief, time to rest up from our toil – or in this case, our battle. When we yoke up with Jesus, our burden becomes light. We take on His character of meekness and lowliness in heart. Remember that other verse that we dealt with on meekness in 1 Peter

3:4? Here is where that quiet spirit comes in – keeping one's seat, undisturbed and undisturbing. That is the personality of the Suppressor T; there's no reason to be disturbed or to disturb the body. Everything is under control. Take a seat and rest up. Learn from Isaiah's words from the Lord in chapter 30 verse 15: **"In returning and rest shall ye be saved; in quietness and in confidence shall be your strength: and ye would not."** For goodness sake, don't be like Israel; they would not return and rest in their God. Quietness and confidence is strength because it testifies to our faith and trust. The Father really appreciates trust from His children. He especially likes the world to see that trust.

Can you see the relevance of that tidbit I threw in there earlier about scientists trying to control our Suppressor T-cells? When a wife is too quick to shut down the other responses, there isn't time to defeat the enemy. She often fails to evaluate the severity of the attack, thinking this is just a phase or this too will pass. She cancels any thoughts of alarm and no defense is taken. She is never engaged in full battle. I'm afraid that is where most women are, totally unengaged in the spiritual warfare because they suppress any fears or warnings or are just totally ignorant, off in la-la land. The marriage is prone to develop malignancies. Temptations and deceptions are allowed to grow to the detriment of the marriage.

"A prudent wife is from the Lord." (Proverbs 19:14) Have you ever looked up the definition of prudent? I didn't think so. It isn't a word we use much in conversation. It means to have wisdom, skill, or expertise; to have understanding, insight, or intellectual comprehension, cautious of the consequences from deeds done; knowing the reason for something. You have to be skillful and intelligent in your role as a wife. You must understand the reasons behind what you must do. You must be cautious in your words and actions knowing they have consequences that are eternal. Furthermore, in commanding your valiant army you must have balance in your great forces. Every aspect of your soldiering is important in its proper place if there is to be victory. You can't take your rest too quickly before the battle is won, nor be too slow about it. That would put you back there in that category of the brawling and contentious woman in Proverbs 21, never allowing the peace and rest to come, endangering an overload of just how much this marriage can sustain. We just have to be the virtuous, prudent woman that God ordained us to be, a gift to man from the Lord. The battles can be won and a glorious rest awaits each victory.

Back to our immune system: In addition to the joy of being set free from this present skirmish as our Suppressor Ts sound victory, we now experience the blessing of new recruits being added to our defense system. Our final regiment of soldiers to appear on the scene is the battalion of newcomers that were born during this illness. They will remain with us for life. These lifers are called Memory cells, created when the B-cells were churning out those antibodies as the result of the preceding conflict. These Memory cells bring a tremendous, liberating advantage to our body, which is an incredible reward for those who have endured the suffering – they are now "overcomers." God has graced these cells with a permanent memory and their sole job is to search for that one specific antigen that has just been conquered should it ever again seek to do our body harm (which it most probably will). These cells are diligently searching out every nook and cranny of the body. Should that particular disease make an entrance into the body of an overcomer, it is met at the door by these Memory cells that instantly nip it in the bud. When the two cross paths, the resulting conflict is so slight, so quick, and so complete that your body never even knew the bad guy was present! These Memory cells made an instant meal for the phagocytes to enjoy. The germ had no effect on the body. There was no need to sound an alarm again because the battle had already been won. The antibodies created in the original attack are forever present in the bloodstream and do their job quickly and efficiently, as the experts they were designed to be.

In years gone by, people who survived an attack of smallpox or scarlet fever, diphtheria or cholera, whooping cough or the German measles, or any other such dreaded killers, were invaluable assets in caring for those newly infected. These survivors were now immune to the disease and had no fear of contracting it again. Even today a victim of the bite of a poisonous viper or a rabid animal will pay any price to someone who has survived such a bite because the blood of the survivor now carries the antibodies to defeat that deadly toxin. When that overcoming blood is injected into the victim's body, it offers forces to defeat the onslaught that would otherwise kill.

I've mentioned Susie's encounter with chicken pox before, but I bring it up again because she has a physical reminder on her skin that she experienced the dreadful pox as a child. Her mother stupidly dressed her in soft, comfy sweats, thinking I was doing her a favor. What a mess getting those fuzzy things off with itching, oozing, and scabbing sores. I am so sorry! She has some dandy scars from that chapter in her life (but that's because she wouldn't leave those scabs alone). Do you have scars from something your body has defeated? Can you look at your scars and be glad? They are a constant reminder of your fearfully and wonderfully made immune system working for you. God knew the ugly things we would face in life and made provision for our bodies to overcome, all the while growing stronger and healthier through each encounter. I don't think very many people have the proper reverence for this awesome creation that God has fashioned. Never again will Susie break out in those awful sores – nor will you be afflicted with the germ you encountered and beat, nor last year's flu bug, nor on and on and on... You now have a whole regiment of soldiers proudly display-ing their badges of honor for each victory that has been won in your life. You are an Overcomer. And a really neat addendum to this reward is that your babies are born immune to everything you have previously fought. The milk they get from you is a special insurance for them. God has graciously offered them pro-tection from these evils because of your accumulated antibodies until their tiny bodies are able to develop their own immune resources. Isn't God so good!

Okay, ready for our memory cell analogy? Now we get to enjoy the bless-ing of new experiences being added to our defense system. Our final aspect of soldiering appears as lessons learned, born during this assault. These learned lessons will remain with us for life, created as the result of our recent triumph. And, oh, what a tremendous, liberating advantage they bring to us! What an incredible reward for those who have endured the suffering! We become "overcomers." God has graced us with a memory that will long retain what we were taught in this trial as a valuable lesson. Should another attack come from this foe just conquered (which it most probably will), we have the blessing of learned experience on our side. This memory part of our defenses is created as part of the Holy Spirit's involvement in our battle. He is our Teacher, guiding us into all truth, bringing all things into remembrance (John 14:26 & 16:13). Diligently search every nook and cranny of your marriage; the Spirit will help you immediately recognize this defeated antagonist when you see it. It is He that strengthens you: **"That He would grant you, according to the riches of His glory, to be strengthened** (empowered, increased with vigor) **with might** (force, miraculous power) **by His Spirit in the inner man."** Ephesians 3:16. Meet the intruder at the door and instantly nip it in the bud, forcefully and with vigor. You know exactly how now. It has no advantage, no foothold. The resulting conflict is so slight, so quick, and so complete that your marriage will never even know the bad guy was present! You have made an instant meal for your phagocytes to enjoy, and it is sweet to swallow. Through the power of the Spirit you have gone **"from strength to strength"** Psalm 84:7. (Hey, that's the same Hebrew word describing a wife as virtuous in Proverbs 12:4 and 31:10 – a great force, an army, a mighty host, full of virtue, strength!) The temptation or deception will have no effect on your home. There is no need to sound an alarm again because the victory is factual truth. The sweet memory of victory is present and ready to do its job.

Just as surely as your body remembers those past defeated germs, each experience you gain will be a constant reminder of success, stirring up confidence and trust in the Lord and His ability to see you through every temptation and trial. God is faithful and will not let you be tempted above your ability to cope (1 Corinthians 10:13). Some trust in physical help, but we will remember the name of the Lord (Psalm 20:7). Do you have trouble remembering all that the Lord has done for you? Of course, you do. We all do – depositing those memories in the recesses of our minds. Don't let the devil bury them. Go to your river of experience and drink up the refreshing memories that gave your childlike faith strength for salvation. Don't forget what God has done for you! Did you ever do any scrap-booking? My Susie was the great scrap-booker of all time! Wish I had the time and space to tell you of the books she created. If I need a good nostalgic cry I can open one of those scrapbooks and wash my heart with memories of love. Open your book of remembrances and reflect on the obstacles you have cleared and the valleys you have crossed and the mountains you have ventured to climb. You know you didn't do it alone. Who was with you each step of the way? Remember some choice mercies of days gone by. You just might have the greatest darkness you have ever known coming upon you, but those memories will shine through the darkness **"until the day dawn, and the Day Star arises**

in your heart" (2 Peter 1:19). What a privilege to gain those memories of victory! Experience strengthens our faith; faith in our Savior is the victory that overcomes the world! (1 John 5:4-5) Regardless of the attacks of the enemy, **"we are more than conquerors through Him that loved us."** (Romans 8:37). The more we dwell on the victory we have been granted, the more we can join Paul when he said in Philippians 4:13, **"I can do all things through Christ which strengthens me."** Strengthen your marriage with the victories already won.

Today's society has everything backward, including memories. We memorialize all the bad stuff that happens, from "Remember the Alamo" to the Murray Building Bombing to 9-11. Memorials are built for people to go look at and remember the horrors and sorrows that resulted. But God wants us to memorialize the good things. Thanksgiving is about as close as our country has done. But God's people remembered being set free from slavery in Egypt as they celebrated the Passover... crossing over the Jordan on dry ground... God fighting for them at Mizpah, defeating the Philistines... and on and on. They remembered the victories and were strengthened. Israel's failure came when they quit remembering and failed to teach the next generation all that God had done for them. God forbid that we should fail to remember the victories or fail to teach our children until they have their own memories to memorialize.

Because I don't know your past I again must refer to my own children. They were spiritually sheltered from much as children because their parents had gone through some tough battles - just as they were protected from the measles and mumps as babies because I passed on my immunity to them as long as they were getting milk from me. But our accumulated experiences were no help to them as they reached accountability age - they were on their own. They have to create their own immunity to these trials by personal experiences.

The purpose of all the trials and temptations that God allows into our lives is to strengthen us and grow us up that we might live lives of holiness, free from the bondage of sin, in gratitude to Christ and His grace. Oh, the price He paid to give us the abundant life, both on earth and in heaven! Do take just a minute to read Romans 6:14-22. This is one of those scriptures on grace and fruitfulness that I wanted to delve into a couple of letters ago. Just spend a little while thinking on them and let the Spirit lead you in conviction and repentance and gratefulness. We have been set free from sin and now are servants of righteousness. Our fruit is now unto holiness and everlasting life. Paul reminds us in his first letter to Timothy (4:8) that godliness is profitable unto all things, having the promise of life now and life to come. Sure it's hard. Whoever said bearing the cross was going to be easy. But we know God always causes us to triumph in Christ (2 Corinthians 2:14), and when we fail because we are weak, He understands perfectly! He said His **"grace** (Divine influence) **is sufficient for thee, for My strength** (miraculous power, force) **is made perfect** (accomplished, completed) **in weakness** (feebleness, frailty) (2 Corinthians 12:9). We can actually glory in our weakness knowing that the power of Christ is resting upon us. **"Therefore I take pleasure in infirmities** (feebleness, frailty, sickness), **in reproaches** (insults, injury), **in necessities** (compelling forces, distresses, afflictions), **in persecutions** (the affliction of pain or punishment unjustly), **in distresses** (narrowness of room, pressed in from the sides, calamities) **for Christ's sake: for when I am weak** (feeble), **then am I strong** (powerful, capable)." (verse 10) Now that is maturity, Sister! - taking pleasure in the tough times for Christ's sake, that we might show His strength working within us.

Can I add a note of motherly advice here? Just as a victim of a poisonous viper will die without the aid of antibodies found in the overcoming blood of someone who has survived that bite, so, too, one would do well to seek life-saving help from another Christian who has already fought a vicious battle that is sucking you under. In desperate times, God will raise up a brother or sister in Christ (or maybe a mom or dad) who can give you the aid you need to bring you through your trial. They have been there. Don't hesitate to ask when you have no strength within. And remember, the blood of our Savior has overcome every obstacle that could possibly come against you and your marriage. You can call on Jesus anytime; He is ever faithful to answer. JESUS BORE THE DISEASE, PAID THE PRICE, ROSE VICTORIOUS, AND OFFERS US THE POWER OF HIS OVERCOMING BLOOD!

You should have enough to dwell on for a little while with just these last scriptures from Romans and 2 Corinthians. Apply some thought to your role as your family's immune system. This has been a long, heavy haul. I hope you haven't had to push too much of it uphill. Just spend time with Jesus and it will fall into place. We have now concluded each of the soldiers' duties in your battalion. Our next letter will take us on to our third line of defense. Until then...

Basking in the warmth of sweet memories,
CK Momma 2

Ouch, That Hurt!

*H*ello Princess,

Have you time today for a mother's need to hand out advice? The nice part about a letter (or book) is that you can pick it up or lay it down whenever – and then pick it up again. I hope you are not at the point Susie was when I sent her this letter. Her schedule had become so hectic trying to tend to a growing family while holding down a full time job (to which I am totally opposed when one already has the most important job in the world as wife and mother! I warned you of my opinions.) – and trying to squeeze in time for more college classes! She was fortunate to have brothers who are willing to baby sit. Not once while growing up did she ever think those little brothers would be good for anything. They caused some trials and aggravations in years gone by, but looking back at this point in her life, those aggravations were pretty petty. They were really a resource for learning to deal with life. They also made a good example for our next topic to discuss: dealing with small trials early in life enables us to better handle big trouble later in life!

We have covered our first line of defense – our body's part in cleanliness, proper nourishment, adequate exercise, and sufficient rest – all corresponding to the care a husband must bring to the marriage to keep the immune system working properly. Then we laid the responsibility on the woman's shoulders to work behind the scenes to defeat those foes that come against their marriage, loving sacrificially, praying urgently, and trusting implicitly in God's plan and

workings. Now we have come to the third line of defense and this one is super –
but only if we will take advantage of the benefits when they are made available.

How do you feel about shots? You aren't alone. But there have been some
pretty remarkable things accomplished through vaccinations. Don't leave me
before you hear me out, please. There are lots of pros and cons about getting
vaccines. There are vaccines for smallpox, diphtheria, rabies, yellow fever,
whooping cough, tetanus, polio, measles, mumps... you get the idea, with new
ones being fabricated every year. The thought of injecting a virus or bacterium,
even if weakened or dead, into a human body just has a negative connotation
to it. But it has worked.

I agree, there are too many vaccines today with stuff in them that are harmful, even deadly! Yes, there are horror stories that accompany vaccines. You have
to sign papers that state you understand this could mentally incapacitate or even
kill your child. Over 50,000 cases of adverse reactions are reported annually.
Anyone born before 1985 received only 3 vaccines. Today there are 16 with multiple doses of each! By 2010 pre-kindergartens received 156 antigens in their
vaccines. Heaven only knows what the number is up to today! Plus there are 63
chemicals added to those multiple doses. In 1999 the Public Health Service recommended that thimerosal (a preservative containing mercury and a known
neurotoxin) should be removed from vaccines because of the dramatic increase
in autism. Yet in California where vaccines are mandated, autism is skyrocketing
with 97,000 public school students diagnosed as autistic in 2017. And that's not
to mention other effects, such as infertility, organ failure or death. There certainly is a valid concern over vaccines today! You must understand that is only
because the godless, humanistic worldview controlling humanity is governed by
Satan himself who hates mankind and wants to kill, steal and destroy. He coun-

terfeits every good thing God gives us and makes it bad! Too much of our medical world today has succumbed to his lies of "this is for the good of the world". But Satan cannot invalidate what I have to tell you in this letter! Please read on.

Let me take you back to when man discovered vaccines. Here is the scientific definition: a vaccine is a biological preparation that stimulates the body's immune system to recognize, destroy and remember, so that the immune system has a head's up on that particular antigen for future days. (Okay, head's up wasn't in the scientific definition.) We could get real technical here but that isn't my purpose. I want to say just enough about vaccines to make our spiritual comparison. Basically, a vaccine is a weakened or dead virus or bacterium that is injected into the bloodstream that activates the immune system, producing antibodies which easily defeat the weakened enemy. Presto, immunity for life! Actually, the word vaccine comes from the Latin word "vaccinia" which means cowpox. The original fight against the dreaded smallpox was warded off with the less potent pox virus found in cows. Now they call all such precautionary injections vaccinations.

You could do some fascinating reading about smallpox and Edward Jenner's work in developing the vaccine from cowpox. (The internet is full of information.) Smallpox was once one of the worst fears parents had, since mortality among children was the greatest. And, of those who contracted the disease and survived, a third was left blind. George Washington said it was his worst enemy when fighting the British. Both he and Abraham Lincoln were survivors of smallpox. Andrew Jackson and his brother were captured during the Revolutionary War, just children themselves, and contracted the disease in prison. His mother got them released, but his brother died and his mother followed soon afterward, leaving Andrew orphaned at 14. Benjamin Franklin's son also died of smallpox. It affected anyone, from the poorest of the poor to the royalty of Europe with no discrimination. But those who survived were immune. And those who were vaccinated never contracted the disease at all. In fact, smallpox has been eliminated through a concerted effort by the World Health Organization as they sought out people in the darkest, most remote areas of the world to vaccinate. The last case in the U. S. was in 1949 and the last one in the world was 1977. (Unfortunately, America and Russia both have stockpiles of this dreaded germ, I suppose with thoughts of germ warfare!) Through vaccinations, rubella, whooping cough, and diphtheria, which once killed tens of thousands of infants every year, have almost been eradicated. Polio, which crippled and paralyzed thousands every year, was reduced to only 61 cases by 1965, and the last known case of polio in the U. S. was in 1993.

My point is, even when inoculated with an impotent germ, the body still goes into full battle mode - sending out the alert, raising your temperature, producing antibodies – all to fight an ineffectual germ. This is a one-sided skirmish. The germ has no power to reproduce. The impotent enemy was planted into your body for the sole purpose of boosting your inventory of antibodies. And, sure enough, you soon have an accumulation of antibodies and memory cells that are there for life, or at least, many years. The vaccine was not a real threat to your body, just an uncomfortable inconvenience. It was a shortcut to build up your immunity. You did not have to endure the disease!

Fervent prayer accompanied every shot my children received growing up. The twins didn't get their preschool shots for years because of those awful ear infections that kept them sick so much. When they were well I just couldn't bring myself to intentionally make them sick with a vaccination. Personally, because of pressure put on parents to vaccinate on schedule, I think many of those who had severe reactions to good vaccines were probably ill with something already, and their bodies just could not handle the overload. Regardless, the risk is real. During mass inoculations with the smallpox vaccine, the risk was ½ to 2% who actually contracted the disease or died from taking it. But when compared to the 33% mortality rate of those who had smallpox and another 33% left blind, the risk was worth taking.

Hopefully, I have this vaccination stage set, so let's see if I can make my analogy. God deals very graciously with us as children, knowing we are but flesh and that the flesh is weak. We've seen how we can overcome sin in our lives as we engage in battle with the enemy, calling upon the Lord for His resources. That's pretty fantastic. But, you know, we have a really gracious God. He has provided ways in which we can build up our defenses against the devil without going through an all-out assault! When we understand the physical example of vaccines, we have been allowed a glimpse into the realm of a gracious shortcut to a spiritual victory.

God is fitting us for His Kingdom and His methods are varied. He most certainly wants to use His Word, but not many of us listen – like most typical kids. Teachers and parents alike put out a lot of words, but it takes a test to really judge how the growth process is advancing. Of course, God already knows what kind of grade you're making, but He wants us to know as well. So times of testing come to prove us. We call them trials.

Take just a minute to look up Deuteronomy 8. Moses was reviewing the 40 years of wandering in the wilderness of the Hebrew people. These words were an exhortation to the new generation as they were readied to enter the Promised Land. **"...remember all the way which the LORD thy God led thee these** forty years in the wilderness, to humble thee, and to prove (test) thee, to know what was in thine heart, whether you would keep His commandments, or not ... the LORD thy God which brought thee forth out of the land of Egypt, from the house of bondage; Who led thee through that great and terrible wilderness, wherein were fiery serpents, and scorpions, and drought, where there was no water; Who brought thee forth water out of the rock of flint; Who fed thee in the wilderness with manna... that He might humble thee, and that He might prove (test) thee, to do thee good at thy latter end..."

Now, just as surely as a small, weakened dose injected into the bloodstream allows the immune system to quickly overcome that germ so it can never cause disease, so also God injects into our lives trials, testings, distresses, and persecutions, in such a manner that they should provide us with faithfulness, strength, joy, power, boldness, confidence... That particular trial or temptation should never cause sin in our lives, but rather, provide a source of maturity – both in our personal walk with God and in our marriage.

Trials, tests, persecutions? I'm pretty sure you are not liking this part any more than you like the shots! However, Psalm 66:10-12 says **"For Thou, O God, hast proved** (tested, examined) **us: Thou hast tried** (refined, melted, purged) **us, as silver is tried. Thou brought us into the net; Thou laid affliction** (pressure, distress) **upon our loins. Thou hast caused men to ride over our heads; we went through fire and through water: but Thou brought us out into a wealthy place** (satisfaction)." Yes, God does send hard things into our lives to prove us, to refine us, to mature us, because we are precious to Him. His purpose is for nothing but our good, to bring us to a place of satisfaction. Psalm 119 speaks of the goodness of afflictions to teach us God's word and His boundaries for our lives (vs.67 & 71). In Proverbs 1:33 we find sound advice with a promise: **"Whosoever hearkens** (listens intelligently) **unto Me shall dwell** (reside permanently) **safely** (both security and trust) **and shall be quiet** (relaxed in a peaceful state) **from fear of evil** (from dread/terror of wickedness that brings pain, sadness, death)**."** When we listen to God and allow Him to work in our lives as He desires, we can be assured of both security and trust taking up permanent residence in our marriage; there will be no fear of the evil that Satan would like to dump on us. God truly wants a good life for us, especially in marriage. He has a plan to be followed if we will listen to Him with our brains in gear.

What kind of difficulties are you having, my Dear? Do you know how to make the distinction between temptations from the enemy and trials from the Lord? Put them on paper and evaluate them. Which of your trying times are real attacks from the enemy, bringing havoc to your life? Which are inoculations from the Lord, used as agents to increase your faith? Some clues to your answers lie in what brought them about: choices made, words exchanged, walking in faithfulness or rebellion... Have you given the devil opportunity to get his foot in the door? Once he crosses the threshold of your marriage he can sure bring mayhem into your family. And when you sin against a holy God, you bring chastisement. But if you have had no power over what is taking place, if there is nothing you could have done to prevent it, take a deep breath and look upward. Is it the hand of God growing you up, giving you opportunity to develop endurance, making you more like Jesus, bringing glory to His name, providing a testimony for you to share?

[More paragraphs from Susie's letters left intact here because I just don't *know* you yet.] "Use your own short life for some very elementary examples. You understand the results of choices. It is pretty easy to identify wrong choices and the consequences that resulted. Chastisement comes, deservedly so. It always gets ugly when we decide to take control of our own lives, yielding to the temptations of the enemy. Rebellious attitudes and words have sunk you in deep mire more than once. More than once I would like to have had you grown, totally skipping all the growing up process between kindergarten and adulthood. You caused several ouch moments for me as well. [and she hasn't quit yet!] But I wouldn't have missed it for all the gold in the world. Some choices I made I would like to do differently - I'm sure you would, too - but even those times of chastisement grew me right along with you. (Children do that for you. I pity those who have never had the privilege of learning from children. I don't know how God equips them for Heaven...) God is such a good Father and sets the example for us. He chastises His children for their own good to bring them back into right thinking and actions. **"Turn you at My reproof: behold, I will pour out my spirit unto you, I will make known My words unto you."** Proverbs 1:23.

"On the other hand, He also sends trial and persecution into our lives even when we are doing everything right. Why would God lay distresses, afflictions, and persecutions on obedient children? Because those things are short-cuts to maturity! They aren't punishment or discipline for wrong choices. What parent doesn't lay heavier weights and responsibilities on the maturing child? It gives them the opportunity to prove worthy of the parent's trust, to gain confidence in his own capabilities, and to honor his parents. But do children ask for harder jobs around the house or to carry the load for others? No, they are children getting by with as little as possible so they can spend more time in pleasures. Therefore the parent takes control. Would children ask their teacher to give some extra homework so they can learn more about a subject? That example was silly. Do you remember the year we did the unit study where all of you had the same lessons? You were in the 7th grade, Daniel in the 5th, Joey in the 3rd, and

Benj was in kindergarten. As we studied the universe you were given assignments that I would never have put on the younger boys. To have required from you no more than I required from Benjamin would have been totally unfair to your education. No, the teacher is in control of the assignments that will push the students on to maturity in their education. The teacher knows who is capable of that extra work. Isn't God our Father? Isn't the Holy Spirit our Teacher?

Job's ordeal was not a result of sin; he had no control over his circumstances. His faith was in the crucible being purified. Abraham was not asked to sacrifice his son to pay for some sin. He was proving his faith through this act of obedience, even unto the death of the promise. His faith was so strong that he believed God could raise Isaac from the dead because he knew God's promises couldn't die.

"If you want to see if your present trouble in life is from the Lord, ask who is in control over what is happening. Look at the things in your early life over which you had no control: your physical looks (what you inherited from your parents has been a real burden to you, hasn't it?), your parents, your personality, home-schooling, birthed into a large family... those older sisters and brother that spoiled you rotten your first two years, then five little brothers that you learned to use to your best advantage. Be honest. Hasn't God given you an upper hand in dealing with life through some "trials" in your early years? Weren't you distressed about such strict parents? Haven't you felt persecuted by your brothers or sisters? Wasn't home-schooling an affliction in your life? These things were a source of irritation, aggravation, and sometimes a real pain, but never life threatening – well, maybe leaving your friends when we moved out of state was fearsome. That was a real "Ouch, that hurt" trial. [make your own list please, dear Reader] Doesn't our Creator have the right to choose the best method to bring us to maturity? Is He not conforming us into the image of Christ

(Romans 8:29)? Is the Spirit not giving us the freedom to behold the glory of the Lord that we might be changed into the same image from glory to glory (2 Corinthians 3:18)? Is He not changing this body of humiliation to be fashioned like Christ's glorious body (Philippians 3:21)? Are we not to know Him and the power of His resurrection and participate in His sufferings, conforming even unto death (Philippians 3:10)? God has taken on quite a challenge to bring us back from sin and death; to once again conform us into His image. Wouldn't it be wise to let Him be the Potter and allow Him the right to do with our lump of clay whatever a Sovereign God knows to do?"

Let's leave youthful examples behind and move on to some examples from John's gospel. The first is one of sinful consequences: the woman of Samaria that met Jesus at the well in chapter 4. Her life was in shambles, a victim of bad choices, most likely wrong words and attitudes that led to wrong actions, and now she was living with a tainted reputation that separated her from her peers. After five marriages she didn't even bother making vows with this last man. When she meets Jesus, we see some of that arrogant attitude with cutting words and a debating spirit. She was responsible for the suffering in her life brought on by her own choices to sin. This woman was sick unto death and needed the Great Physician to heal her. Through that Divine encounter with Jesus and His perfectly directed words, she found life and forgiveness, and it set off a reaction within her spirit that forever stopped the lies with which Satan had tortured her. She had the full-blown disease of sin and death; but Jesus intervened, and she survived. She became an over-comer. She had a testimony to share, and glory was brought to God through her encounter.

But sometimes God has a purpose to glorify Himself through adversity and it is no one's fault. Take for example the blind man in John chapter 9: He was living in separation and blindness through no fault of his own, struggling to survive on the alms of compassion from passersby. When the disciples questioned Jesus as to the "why" of his condition, the response was neither of the options offered, "but that the works of God should be made manifest in him." This man wasn't blind because of sin; he had no control over his affliction. He was born never to see the beauty of colors in the sunset or flowers in bloom, never to see the stars at night, the parents who gave him life and love, not even able to see himself – a life spent in total darkness. Do you suppose he wondered why, questioned God, or despised his life? How old do you suppose he was? His whole life had been spent in dependency upon others, begging for a living. Ouch, now that hurts! Yet after his encounter with Jesus, I have an idea that he counted his years of frustration and despair as a light thing to bear in order to be a vessel in which God could show His power through the touch of the Master. God had ordained this trial in his life that He might do a work in this man's life, grow him to a mature faith, give him a good testimony, and bring glory to God. This dramatic trial in his life did exactly what God had planned. The attacks of the Pharisees had no effect on him except to strengthen his faith and cause him to worship Jesus. We find him boldly rebuking the same Pharisees that Jesus Himself had rebuked. He is ready to endure the persecution that they exert when they put him out of the Temple. What? You think blindness was a little harsh? This man now has all of eternity to see with perfect eyesight! What is this small span of time we have on earth compared to an eternity in heaven with our Redeemer and God!

But if being born blind was harsh, read on to chapter 11. Lazarus dies! This friend of Jesus has become ill. His sisters send for Jesus; they know Jesus can fix things. They are His followers, believers, His friends. They need Him to come now. But Jesus doesn't come. There was a better plan - one that would dissolve their fear of sickness and death forever. The two sisters had a painful inoculation and suffered grievously as they mourned the death of their beloved brother. It was an agonizing injection as they dealt with doubt and disappointment in the actions of the Lord. Lazarus had his own painful shot as he endured this sickness and walked through the dark valley of death. But all of the vaccinations worked! The Lord knew there was never any real threat of separation through death in this family. Do you think there was ever any more fear of death, or any doubt in the wisdom of their loving heavenly Father? Mary even accepted the coming death of Jesus and anointed Him for His burial before He was ever arrested. The fear of death would never more hold that family in bondage. They were set free, never to be enslaved again. That's what a spiritual inoculation does for you!

I have one more example for you and this one is found in Matthew, Mark, and Luke. This is one of the unfortunate souls that couldn't handle the test Jesus presented to him. He was looking for that short-cut to holiness and heaven. So Jesus gave him the shot – Go sell what you have and give it to the poor. This rich man went away sorrowful, grieved because his many possessions were dearer to him than knowing God. This vaccine should have delivered him from the bondage of the world's wealth. It should have forever instilled a love for the poor and less fortunate. It should have opened his eyes to the wealth of heaven's riches and eternity with God. Instead, he walked away from Jesus sorrowful and lost.

Can you be grateful for those trials that God sends your way? You know He would never tempt you (James 1:13); He doesn't want to see you fall or fail. Jeremiah 29:10 – 13, "**Thus saith the LORD, ... I will visit you, and perform my good word toward you... For I know the thoughts that I think toward you, saith the LORD, thoughts of peace, and not of evil, to give you an expected end. Then shall ye call upon me, and ye shall go and pray unto me,** and I will hearken unto you. And ye shall seek me, and find me, when ye shall search for me with all your heart." Your Father only wants the best for you, to grow up strong and virtuous.

Peter has so much to say about sufferings. **"Wherein ye greatly rejoice, though now for a season, if need be** (it is necessary), **ye are in heaviness** (distressed, opposite of rejoice, inward grief) **through manifold temptations** (various trials)**: That the trial** (means of proving) **of your faith, being much more precious than of gold that perishes, though it be tried** (tested, approved) **with fire, might be found unto praise and honor and glory at the appearing of Jesus Christ: Whom having not seen, ye love; in Whom, though now ye see Him not, yet believing, ye rejoice with joy unspeakable and full of glory: Receiving the end** (conclusion, result, purpose) **of your faith, even the salvation** (rescue, safety) **of your souls."** I Peter 1:6-9. There is a purpose in all of this – your own safety and deliverance from Satan's efforts. In chapter 4 verses 12-14, Peter encourages us by reminding us these fiery trials that come to try us should not be thought strange to us. They should bring rejoicing that we might be privileged to suffer with Christ. We are blessed and He is glorified. James has his own advice in 1:3, 4 - **"Knowing that the trying** (testing, proving) **of your faith** (conviction, reliance upon Christ) **worketh** (accomplishes) **patience** (endurance). **But let patience have her perfect work, that ye may be perfect** (complete) **and entire** (perfectly sound in body), **wanting nothing."** And verse 12 - **"Blessed is the man that endures** (undergoes, perseveres) **temptation** (being put to proof)**: for when he is tried** (approved), **he shall receive the crown of life, which the Lord hath promised to them that love him."**

God develops us in so many ways – exhorting, encouraging, but especially through painful trials. Our faith is put to the test because it is more precious than gold. Our love and faith and patience and endurance and trust in Him are thoroughly examined and given the opportunity to grow in grace and be set free from all the liabilities imposed by our sin nature. Some vaccinations the Lord gives us are mild. Others are more intense and put us to bed, but He knows what we can endure (I Corinthians 10:13). Always remember, He's working in us for our good. As this ordained trial triggers our Helper Ts to call out the Killer Ts and Bs that produce the needed antibodies, so quickly does the battle take place under a divinely controlled injection with a weakened agent, that the entire incident is only a passing fatigue in our eternal journey. It was a small price to pay for the strength and power gained, with resources stored up in our memory cells that dehorn any future attack. We are so strengthened in the inner man (woman/marriage) that regardless of the attack from Satan, we remain faithful to our God and Savior. Even death itself can do no harm because our spirit lives on.

I just have to bring up a passing thought as I mention death. Have you ever thought on Stephen's faithfulness unto death? Think back to the ultimate attack at the beginning of the Church in the book of Acts: Stephen, the first martyr for Christ, was full of faith and the Spirit, already tried and proven. He was the victim of the most vicious attack Satan could muster. Did he succumb? Did he waver? No! He died! you say? No, as a matter of fact, Stephen didn't die that day at the hands of his accusers. He died when he said yes to Christ and received salvation. He died each day to the flesh because he had risen to walk a new life in Christ. Remember the words of Christ in His last prayer for His disciples and for all who would believe their words? John 17:3 **"And this is life eternal, that they might know Thee the only true God, and Jesus Christ Whom Thou hast sent."** I know I am repeating myself, but some things are worth repeating a thousand times over. When you meet the Lord as your Savior and gain entrance into fellowship and knowledge of the Father, your eternal life has begun. Yes, it's all uphill from there, but what a glorious adventure – learning more of Him, enjoying the privilege of sweet communion 24/7 with the God of Creation. No, Stephen didn't lose the battle that day. That ultimate conflict was won and ushered him into the presence of the Lord of glory in total victory! The body was badly abused and quit functioning – but he traded that feeble, mortal body for the heavenly presence of Christ and will receive a new indestructible, eternal body. Stephen's spiritual immune system had worked perfectly. Every trial had strengthened him; every past temptation, evil workings, vile deceptions, even self-destructive cancers had all been conquered by the applied blood of Jesus. He was a medical marvel, spiritually speaking, totally immune to this final battle. Stephen won gloriously as he bowed his knee asking forgiveness for these murderous Jews used by the enemy. How like Christ was this man Stephen! – fit for Heaven and his eternal reward!!!

Am I asking you to accept death today as did Stephen? Of course not! I just want you to see the power released to be like Jesus when you walk in the Spirit. The unpleasant things God allows into your life should strengthen you for victory over those ugly things the enemy sends your way. Cowpox, an unpleasant illness, was nothing compared to smallpox, an ugly killer. But a vaccine of cowpox created immunity to the deadly smallpox. Yes, sometimes there are adverse reactions when trials come. Instead of becoming immune, some are retarded in their spiritual development and never reach maturity. Some feel betrayed by God and even die when trials come – not physically but spiritually – forsaking the Gospel and refusing the benefits God intended for them. "... **let us run with patience** (abiding under circumstances with endurance and hope, not surrendering to circumstances or succumbing under trial) **the race that is set before us, looking unto Jesus the author** (originator)

and finisher (a completer, perfecter, one who brings something through to the goal so as to win and receive the prize) **of faith; who for the joy that was set before Him endured** (remained under to sustain a load of miseries, adversities, persecutions or provocations in faith and patience) **the cross, despising** (thinking lightly of) **the shame, and is set down at the right hand of the throne of God. For consider Him that endured** (remained under to sustain a load of miseries...) **much contradiction of sinners against Himself, lest ye be wearied and faint in your minds."** Hebrews 12:3. To the healthy, faithful Christian, each inoculation the Father presents is a marvelous way of growing a more faithful and spiritual immunity to the deadly attacks that lay before us on our upward journey. It's easier than fighting the enemy in all of his strength.

This world's nasty spiritual germs are so like smallpox. But look what diligent vaccinations have done to eradicate the power of this infectious, deadly virus. The world has seen what can happen when everyone has been inoculated. Wouldn't it be marvelous if we could be spiritually inoculated to Satan's infectious, deadly lying doctrines! Unfortunately, Christians aren't quite as diligent as the World Health Organization. We aren't seeking out those that are vulnerable to the Deception. Even if we could reach everyone on earth, their free will is an obstacle to accepting God's deliverance. And yet, when Christ comes again and sets up His Kingdom, ruling and reigning in perfection with Satan bound in the bottomless pit, there will be a world without deception, just as we have a world without smallpox – for now. However, after a thousand years of peace, Satan will be allowed to spread his evil deceptions hoping to infect as many as he can, as surely as smallpox has been stockpiled for future warfare. But we know the final Victor. Meanwhile, we have some good analogies from which to learn.

Take your shots with gratitude and joy, even when they hurt. You're permitted to say "Ouch! that hurt!" You can be confident there is nothing toxic or sinister in them! The Spirit will rub a cotton ball over it and comfort your boo-boo with a princess band-aid. And don't forget to thank Him, Sweetie.

Inoculated in love,
CK Momma 2

P.S. By the way, neither am I excluding the possibility of dying for Christ, my Darling. With the attacks on real Christianity in these last days, we may well be at physical risk. We live in one of the few countries left where Christians are not being murdered for believing. We are really privileged to live in these end times and possibly be part of the rapture of the church. But privilege demands responsibility and maturity, or it produces a spoiled brat. Grow up, my Dear. "I have no greater joy than to hear that my children walk in truth." 3 John 4.

Whoa! What's This???

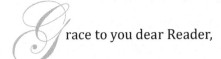race to you dear Reader,

I know – you're thinking "Is there no end? Where is the conclusion!?!" We have covered the workings of the immune system - now what? Well, this letter brings some not so good news, Sweetie. I hope you've done enough planning and preparation, whether for a wedding or a performance, a presentation or a vacation, or just a big party, to understand what we are about to embark upon next. Sometimes your plan works perfectly and comes off in splendor; sometimes something goes awry and there is nothing to do but cry.

What we have done thus far in our study of the immune system is to look at the ideal. However, in spite of the beauty of God's plan for the body to ward off attacks of the enemy and to develop a mature immunity against future attacks, there are complications that arise that even modern medicine can't explain. Webster's Dictionary defines complication this way: "a situation complicating the main thread of a plot; a difficult factor appearing unexpectedly and changing existing plans, methods, or attitudes." This letter begins a look at some of these difficult factors that complicate God's existing plans and change the methods in which the plot must work.

The first hitch in this perfect world of immunity is called allergies, an abnormally high sensitivity of the immune system. All too often our T-cells make an error in recognition, battling against imaginary enemies - substances dubbed allergens - harmless things such as pollen, dust, animal dander, or even food. The allergen itself poses no threat but is reacted to by antibodies that mistakenly identify it as an enemy. The immune system is oversensitive, releasing potent chemicals (such as histamine) to fight off the allergen, with T-cells ordering B-cells to produce more antibodies...thus the runny nose and sneezing with hay fever or the rash and itch with poison ivy. Most allergies are just aggravations; others, like the allergic reaction to insect venom or peanuts, can be deadly.

Allergies result when the enemy is not identified properly, phagocytes have not sufficiently consumed debris, and Suppressor Ts have not halted immune response because there has been no victory. The immune system is disorganized creating confusion! Susie saw it in her own husband's response to red dye in foods; hives covered his body. My husband suffered most of his life because of his allergies to dust and cats. It was just a few years ago that he was introduced to Ester C and MSM that has almost completely cured him. I don't know what that combination did to his immune system but it revolutionized his life! No more handkerchiefs while he's preaching! We don't question why; we just rejoice and thank God for the relief.

Most allergies can be treated with medicines, creams, or shots. However, the best recommendation from professionals is to avoid what causes the adverse reaction – don't eat peanuts, stay away from poison ivy, get rid of your cat, stay indoors, don't smell the flowers... Sometimes treatment to desensitize the immune system will work by getting regular injections of the allergen, each dose slightly larger than the last until a maximum dose is reached and the body no longer reacts adversely. But these shots don't work for everybody. This overactive, confused immune system makes life unnecessarily miserable and sometimes dangerous.

This brings us to another analogy. Allergies are typical of complications that are manifested in the marital relationship. In spite of the beauty of God's script for woman to be man's help, there are complications - difficult factors that change God's perfect plan for the health of this marriage and His method of working in man's life, certainly complicating the main thread of His "plot". He desires to use the love relationship and "oneness" of man and woman in their marriage to mirror to the world the intimacy and unity between Christ and His Church (Ephesians 5:22-33). But Satan creates a nasty situation by throwing in these constant, aggravating irritations in a marriage. His methods to thwart God's ideal plan have proven to be very effective in wearing away the testimony of peace and cooperation as husband and wife live in frustrations day in and day out.

All too often a wife makes an error in recognition and begins to battle an imaginary enemy. That area of her ministry corresponding to the phagocytes has failed to engulf and consume the effects of relatively harmless habits (picking toenails, absent-mindedness ...) or personality traits (extrovert, introvert, detail man ...) or indulgences (guy time, golf, fishing...) that pose no real threat to his spiritual health. She then reacts as though those were an enemy. In her oversensitive state, she releases potent "chemicals" (anger, jealousy, judgment, nagging, bitterness) into his life creating negative reactions equivalent to congested sinuses, sneezing, itchy eyes or a rash... He is irritated; he feels stifled; he can't breathe; she drives him crazy and away from her! Most of these erroneous attacks are just aggravations from a contentious wife; others, like the reaction to jealousy or condemnation, can be deadly to a marriage.

Do you remember those verses from a couple of letters ago in Proverbs about better is a dry morsel with quietness than a house full of feasting with strife, better to live in a corner of a housetop than a house shared with a contentious woman, and better to live in the wilderness than with a contentious and angry woman??? (Proverbs 17:1; 21:9, 19) Sounds like Solomon had "allergy" problems!

These attacks on a husband come when the "intrusion" is not properly identified, the wife's phagocyte mode has not sufficiently consumed in love, and her Suppressor T ministry has not called for peace because there has been no victory. This wife's aid and protection ministry is disorganized to say the least, creating confusion!

Most "allergies" in a marriage can be treated. The husband can rub some cream of consolation on himself through friends in the same predicament; he can pray for his wife and check out his own spiritual nutrition that might be weakening her; or he can seek counsel. However, the best recommendation from professionals is to avoid what causes the adverse reaction – don't pick your toenails, write yourself notes, don't be so forward, don't be so shy, loosen up on the details, give up your guy time, don't smell the flowers... Surely there is a better way! Perhaps this over-reactive woman could be desensitized with some good shots of study in the Word, learning to love her husband as admonished in Titus 2:4 and relying on the Spirit of God to unite them in unity, peace, in honor preferring one another. It very well could take many treatments of a progressively increased infusion of the Word over a long period of time before she becomes desensitized. Personally, I have learned to benefit from my husband's outgoing personality to be included in situations in which I am too shy to interact. When the obvious outcome of picking at a toenail results in pain or blood, I can turn on my compassion and be appreciated. When my husband wants some guy time, I take advantage to catch up on things I can't do when he's home (or I see to it that time with me is more attractive than time with the guys!) You get the drift. Keep in mind the two becoming one, with all their differences, strengths and weaknesses, to make one whole. Find out what the real enemy is and get into that battle. There are plenty of them if you've a mind to fight. This overactive, confused immune system makes a marriage unnecessarily and senselessly miserable and sometimes threatens its survival.

You've seen a husband subjected to some irrational anger and nagging, and his response is typical of every man. How about yours? If you will be honest, you have also seen how a correction in your own attitude can change the entire atmosphere of the home. More diligence and regularity in your Q.T. and your Teacher will inspire you so you can learn to control your mouth – **"In the multitude of words there wanteth not sin** (sin is not lacking): **but he that refrains his lips** (keep your mouth shut!) **is wise."** Going back to the basics of that ardent, fervent love will revolutionize his life! Don't question how this works or why; just rejoice and thank God for the relief.

This is a good place to insert 1 Peter 3:1-4 again. Are those verses becoming familiar yet? I know I have used them repeatedly but we have come to a time that I cannot put off the need to dig a little deeper. This time let's take it apart with definitions. "**Likewise, ye wives, be in subjection** (be subordinate, obedient) **to your own** (the one belonging to you – nobody else's) **husbands; that, if any obey not** (disobey through unbelief) **the word, they also may without the word be won** (gained) **by the conversation** (behavior) **of the wives; while they behold** (inspect, watch) **your chaste** (pure, free from defilements or impurities) **conversation** (behavior) **coupled with** (resting, remaining, within the definite limits of) **fear** (reverence). **Whose adorning** (sum total of one's person and beauty) **let it not be that outward** (external) **adorning of plaiting** (elaborate braiding) **the hair, and of wearing** (decorating oneself) **of**

gold, or of putting on of apparel; But let it be the hidden man (private, concealed person) **of the heart** (the thoughts and reasonings, the understanding and judgments, the affections and designs, the will expressed in things loved and hated, in what brings joy and sorrow), **in that which is not corruptible** (not subject to the same kind of deterioration as the body), **even the ornament of a meek** (the attitude of spirit in acceptance of God's dealings with us as good and not to be disputed or resisted; a condition of mind and heart which demonstrates gentleness - not in weakness but power under control; a virtue born in strength of character) **and quiet** (keeping one's seat; still, undisturbed and undisturbing) **spirit** (the element which enables one to think of God, perceive, reflect, feel, desire), **which is in the sight of God of great price** (extremely expensive)." Says a lot more than one would think, doesn't it!

We are admonished to not use a word to gain victory with our husbands, but rather to be submissive, meek and quiet (a pretty good description of a properly working immune system as opposed to this particular "complication" we are considering). Let me paraphrase those verses above in light of the preceding definitions. A wife's conduct, when obedient to her husband, free from the pollutants of this world, and resting within definite limits of reverence to her Lord, can win a disbelieving husband as he watches and inspects her behavior. Her beauty should not rely on the external things, such as hairdos, jewelry, or clothing, to express who she is, but on the internal character of how she thinks, her understanding of people and how she judges them, where her affections and intentions lie, what brings her joy and sorrow, what she loves and what she hates. This beautiful heart will exude an attitude of acceptance that God's way and will is best, thus creating a gentle spirit enabling her to control the power she possesses, never disturbed (able to remain seated) and never disturbing her husband. This quality of beauty in the Father's eyes will not be corrupted by age or circumstance. She will carry it right into heaven with her. This is what is precious, extremely expensive, in God's eyes; He knows what it is costing you to follow His script. Honey, with this kind of behavior, you are going to make your husband inspect with curiosity, wonder, and desire to know just what is going on in your private life.

Before we leave these verses I want to share what the Greek word picture is of the English rendering we call "meek." There is no timidity or weakness involved in this word. To the culture of that first century in which Peter, Paul, and Matthew used that word in their writings, there was a very definite understanding. It pictures all of the power of a wild horse captured by someone who could tame it to be easily managed in order to harness its power for good and toward man's purpose, willingly submitting to the rider, led and controlled by a small bit in the mouth. The horse retained all of its magnificent power, but that power was now channeled for a purpose. Peter was showing us that the unrestrained and unbeneficial influence that woman has over a man's life can be brought under control by the Spirit, made gentle, and easily managed in order to harness that power for the good work of God's purpose, willingly submitting to the reigns of the Holy Spirit, led and controlled by a small tug on the heart. The wife retains all of her magnificent influence, but that power is now channeled for man's good. God has a really great work to be done and wants to use your natural abilities, harnessed by His love and grace, to make all of your power count for all of eternity. Allow the Spirit to tame you and hold your reigns for His purpose.

That's what a man needs, but all too often he gets that contentious, out of control woman that makes him want to have a running fit. Look at I Corinthians 14:33 – "**For God is not the author of confusion** (disorder, instability),

but of peace (quietness, rest, set at one again) **...**" Let God set you and your husband at one. Know the enemy, do your job efficiently, seek peace, and get your act together. Disorganization causes confusion! Don't be oversensitive to harmless outside forces. Marriage needs stability and order.

But as aggravating as allergies are, there are greater complications that throw a devastating kink into this marvelous design of our protective army: autoimmune disorders. The mission of our white blood cells is to protect the body from harmful antigens. However, in an autoimmune disorder, the immune system fails to recognize certain cells as "self" and begins to attack the very body it was designed to protect. The result is an immune response that destroys normal body tissue.

There are more than 80 diagnosed immune disorders but we are only going to touch on three. (I'm sure there is an analogy to be applied for all of them, but these will suffice for our purpose here. Give me just a minute to give a brief medical description of each of these three and then we will proceed to apply the analogies.) These autoimmune disorders present a real challenge to the medical profession and are pretty much a puzzle to the scientists who study them. There is little to help them understand why the body turns on itself other than slight changes in certain proteins in body tissues. There has been research that confirms that genetic predisposition is a contributing factor.

Multiple Sclerosis is caused by the body's own immune cells mounting an attack against the fatty substance that surrounds the nerve cells, causing nerve signals to slow or stop. What do our nerves do for us? Have you ever jerked your hand from a hot stove? Your nerves saved you from a severe burn. Nerves form a network of pathways for passing information through the body. They coordinate all movements, thoughts and sensations of your body. They sense your external and internal surroundings and communicate information between your brain, spinal cord, and other tissues. All of your involuntary functions (breathing, heart beating, blood pressure), as well as your voluntary movements (scratching your head, swatting a fly, running), are coordinated by your nervous system. [Running really takes a lot of messaging back and forth between the brain and nerves because the coordination demands such rhythm, another reason I am not a runner.] Nerves connect your senses (eyes, ear, nose, mouth, skin) to your brain, the spinal cord to your limbs and organs, and even regulate your thought processes. Because MS can damage nerves in any part of the brain or spinal cord, symptoms can occur in many parts of the body – *numbness, muscle spasms, coordination problems, tremors, vision problems, memory loss, poor judgment, difficulty reasoning, depression, slurred speech, trouble chewing or swallowing.* As of this writing, there is no known cure, but therapies help slow the disease.

Rheumatic Fever is caused by an unusual body response following strep throat or scarlet fever. It is an inflammation of the heart muscle, which can cause congestive heart failure, as well as other complications. And how important is this muscle that we call the heart? This pump sends life-giving blood throughout our body. We've already covered the importance of the blood. It carries oxygen and nutrients to all of our cells and carries away the waste. If the blood doesn't circulate as it should, you die. Yes, an attack on the heart is a mighty big deal. The streptococcus bacterium's cell wall sometimes contains M protein, which is highly resistant to our phagocytes, making it particularly aggressive, breaking down our protective mechanisms. As the strep makes its way through the bloodstream, B-cells manning the lymph glands lock onto them and present the bacteria's antigen to T-cells, which in turn activate Bs to become plasma cells, stirring up the production of antibodies to target the cell wall of the streptococcus. These antibodies lock onto their prey, not only preventing them from attacking other cells but also making them more ingestible for our phagocytes. However, these antibodies which have been generated against the M protein may cross-react with their own body's connective tissue and motor proteins that help in muscle contraction. This reaction is responsible for many damaged heart valves. These antibodies actually attack the body's own heart muscles, as well as other tissues, skin and the brain. Survivors of rheumatic fever often have to take penicillin monthly to prevent another streptococcal infection which could possibly prove fatal.

The third autoimmune disorder I want to touch on is Rheumatoid Arthritis in which an immune response is mounted against the body's own tissues, specifically the synovium - a thin membrane that lines the joints. As a result of the attack, fluid builds up in the joints, causing pain and inflammation. RA may affect many different joints and cause damage to cartilage, tendons and ligaments – it can even wear away the ends of your bones causing joint deformity and disability. Think what our joints do for us. As the skeleton provides scaffolding for our body, maintaining its shape (so we don't look like jellyfish), and protecting our vital organs, the joints between bones make the skeleton flexible. Without them, movement would be impossible; we would be as rigid as a board. Our synovial joints (wrists, ankles, shoulders, hip, elbows) move in many directions giving us great flexibility. These joints are filled with synovial fluid, which acts as a lubricant to help the joints move easily. Cartilage, the rubbery substance in our joints, supports our bones and protects them where they rub against each other. What a fantastic body God has given us! But with Rheumatoid Arthritis comes inflamed joints, causing heat and difficulty in movement. Fibrous tissue develops in the joints, the cartilage is destroyed, and joints become swollen and painful. The tissue begins tethering with loss of movement and erosion of the joint surface, causing deformity and loss of function. This disease involves abnormal B-cell – T-cell interaction. Somewhere in the immune process, there is a production of rheumatoid factor (RF), protein made by your immune system that can attack healthy tissue in your body. Thus, the name Rheumatoid before Arthritis. Healthy people don't make RF. Mechanisms that normally maintain tolerance of "self" are overtaken. Once the abnormal immune response has become established, plasma from B-cells produces rheumatoid factor in large quantities, which activate macrophages, which continue to contribute to inflammation. When the inflammatory reaction is established, the joints thicken and the cartilage and bone begin to disintegrate. If you didn't follow all of that, just know that it was a really simplified interpretation of medical jargon that I had a really hard time following myself; all we really need to know is something went haywire. It is a dreadful attack on the joints, as well as inflammation in the lungs, heart, and eyes. Crippled, twisted hands result from this dreadful condition. People with rheumatoid arthritis are more likely to have a heart attack or stroke as well. There is no "cure" but lots of treatments, including depleting B-cells from the body.

Though genetics plays a big role in falling prey to various autoimmune diseases, the genes do not cause them; they just make you more susceptible to factors that may trigger the disease. Not all people with these genes develop the disorder; and not everyone with the disease has these genes. There is still a great curiosity as to the causes. Environment and cigarettes also appear to have an influence. Autoimmune diseases have become the number one cause of death. Also interesting, the majority of victims are women! Hmmm... The treatment of most autoimmune diseases is typically with immunosuppression – medication which decreases the immune response. However, that leaves one open to attacks from real enemies – protozoa, bacteria, viruses, cancers... It is a dangerous road to travel, all because something went haywire in the immune system.

Now I want to relate all of that to the relationship between the husband and wife and how it affects their marriage. When a woman protects her marriage from harmful substances, such as temptations and false doctrines, as the mighty host she was created to be, her marriage rocks along just as planned. But when she fails to recognize her oneness with her husband and begins to attack him, she is, in effect, attacking herself, as well as the body she was designed to aid/protect (Genesis 2:23-24). She becomes a hypersensitive immune system creating autoimmune disorders that destroy.

We are only going to look at three examples, though there are multitudes. These "disorders" present quite a curiosity in the Christian world and are a puzzle as to why a woman who loves her husband would turn on him. Unfortunately, there is some undeniable evidence that a genetic predisposition is a contributing factor.

Proverbs 14:1 says, **"Every wise woman builds her house: but the foolish plucks it down** (pull down in pieces, destroys) **with her hands** (the open hand, indicating power)."** A woman can do a horrendous amount of damage with her power of influence and authority in the home if she plays the part of a fool, if her power has not been tamed and brought under the control of the Spirit. Wisdom comes from the Father and His Spirit enables us to build up rather than tear down. Speaking of tearing down, look at James 3:5, 6 and see what he says about the tongue. Scary! The tongue is a fire among our members and defiles the whole body. Can you count how many times you have used your tongue to burn someone? How about its use on your husband?

The Mystery of Marriage through Adam's Prime Rib

Getting too personal? Well, let's include me in this personal check-up. Just as autoimmune disorders tend to be genetic so are wives' failures. It usually runs in the family! **"Behold, every one that uses proverbs shall use this proverb against thee, saying, As is the mother, so is her daughter. Thou art thy mother's daughter, that loathes her husband and her children; and thou art the sister of thy sisters, which loathed their husbands and their children..."** (Ezekiel 16:44, 45). A woman must take an honest look at her ancestry, how her mother affected her father's physical, emotional, and spiritual health. We all have propensities to sin that are passed to our children – lying, stealing, failure to obey, rudeness... degrading one's husband, constantly correcting... Have you identified weak areas in your mother's life that hasn't been good for her marriage? Make a point to change them in yours. I saw them in my mother and I've worked very hard to not follow in those same steps. I have certainly seen some sad examples of daughters following in their mothers' footsteps and destroying some good men, as have you if you think about it. Look and learn.

Now for some specifics... Just as Multiple Sclerosis is the result of damage to the nervous system, a woman must take care that she does not damage her husband's spirit – that part of eternity breathed into man, who he is and how he controls and expresses himself, the real him. **"For what man knows the things of a man, save the spirit of man which is in him?"** (1 Corinthians 2:11). The spirit of a man defines his character. God has identified that spirit as **"the candle of the Lord"** enabling man to see into his soul to search out who he is (Proverbs 20:27). Proverbs 16:32 reminds us that a man who has dominion over his spirit is better than one who captures a city, or in today's vernacular, better than one who is famous and successful in heroic deeds (or football!). It is more important that a man rule his spirit well than be successful in the world's eyes. His spirit coordinates all movements, thoughts, and sensations in his life.

It is his spirit that discerns not only his outward actions, which are visible to others, but his most inward thoughts and affections, enabling him to **"stand fast in one spirit with one mind striving together for the faith of the gospel."** (Philippians 1:27). His spirit connects all of his physical, emotional, intellectual, and spiritual senses to his God, that he might regulate his thoughts and transform his lifestyle into that good and acceptable and perfect will of God as the head of his home (Romans 12:1, 2). What happens when those connections are damaged and his responses become slow or even stop? Can his spirit be attacked and not cause severe problems? Psalm 143:3 & 4 are such desperate words of a defeated man: **"For the enemy hath persecuted my soul; he hath smitten my life down to the ground; he hath made me to dwell in darkness, as those that have been long dead. Therefore is my spirit overwhelmed within me; my heart within me is desolate."** God forbid that his wife should be that enemy, and yet many times it is she who attacks him - the very army created to lift him up. Remember the verse we used concerning joy and laughter being good medicine? It was Proverbs 17:22. Look at the second half of that verse. **"A merry heart does good like a medicine: but a broken spirit dries the bones."** When a man's spirit is smitten it causes shame, disappointment and confusion in his vitality of life. Symptoms of an overwhelmed or broken spirit can be manifested in many parts of his life – *numbness* to what once brought him joy and pleasure; *involuntary contractions* of his authority and power; *trouble coordinating* his plans and hopes and duties; *tremors* at the thought of being vulnerable again; *lost vision* of his dreams; *memory loss* of the good times he once had with his wife and his God; *poor judgment* at home and work and relationships; *difficulty reasoning* because of questions left after disappointments; *depression*; *slurred speech* when he tries to speak to the Lord or testify of His goodness; *trouble chewing or swallowing* the truths of God's promises as he doubts his own character and usefulness. **"The spirit of a man**

will sustain his infirmity; but a wounded spirit who can bear?" (Proverbs 18:14). What wife wants to see her husband in that diseased condition of his spirit? What would be the cure? What will be the judgment God meets out to a wife who has turned on her husband's spirit?

Then we have the strength of the heart that comes under attack much like Rheumatic Fever. A nasty temptation has come into his life and his dutiful wife has done her part in helping him overcome. However, in the process of the battle her discernment has aroused suspicions, and the very element that brought victory no longer views something in her husband's heart as a "self" cell of their marriage. What does the heart represent? All of our thoughts and reasonings, understanding and judgments, affections and designs, the will expressed in things loved and hated, what brings joy and sorrow, fear and anger. It is the seat of his treasure (Luke 12:34), the birthplace of faith (Acts 16:37; Romans 10:10; John 3:5-18); the haven of our secrets (1 Corinthians 14:25); our source of meditation on the Lord (Psalm 19:14); the chamber where music abides within man (Ephesians 5:19); the foundation of man's will to do God's will (Ephesians 6:6); that part of man that gives him full assurance of faith (Hebrews 12:22). The heart of faith believes all things (Mark 11:23). A man's heart is his lifeline to his Creator as God speaks to man and man responds to God. 2 Corinthians 4:6 reminds us that **"God, who commanded the light to shine out of darkness, hath shined in our hearts,"** giving us the light of the knowledge of the glory of God in Jesus Christ. He has allowed us to know Him in His glory through Jesus (John 14:9). We are to love Him with all our heart! (Matthew 22:37; ...) We are to love His people (John 13:34-35; 15:12, 17; Galatians 5:13; 1 Peter 1:22...) We are to love His appearing (2 Timothy 4:8). Proverbs 14:30 says **"A sound heart is the life of the flesh."** So what is a man to do when his heart is attacked? His understanding, affections, judgment, and love all become sick. His heart becomes slow (Luke 24:25); hardened (Mark 16:14), waxed gross [thickened and calloused] (Acts 28:27); far from God (Matthew 15:8); deceptive to himself (James 1:6), departing from the Lord (Hebrews 3:12). Proverbs 13:12 reminds us of a very important principle: **"Hope deferred makes the heart sick: but when the desire comes, it is a tree of life."** Hope is a very strong thing. It is the expectation of life, for today and all our tomorrows, the dreams of the heart, the promises to be kept. When they don't come, the heart becomes sick, robbed of strength, worn down, diseased, threatening despair of life itself. The heart "muscle", his will, his intellect, his feelings, can be usurped and attacked by the one who holds its strings! How unthinkable! How absurd! Could a wife be so confused in her job that after warding off an attack against some Satanic temptation and creating the spiritual resources to prevent further attacks, possibly cross-react with her own husband's mechanism that powers his hopes and use those very resources to actually attack his heart? Unfortunately, yes.

Look around you. You see it everywhere! You are friends with women just like that. You have been dangerously close to falling prey to Satan's device yourself. In all of a man's masculinity and macho toughness, there is a heart that bleeds when wounded. The reaction of this dysfunctional mighty host has irresponsibly brought irreparable damage into their marriage. Survivors often have to take "antibodies" from another source on a regular basis to prevent another temptation which could possibly prove fatal to their marriage. This is so contrary to the script that God intended!

On to our third spiritual autoimmune disorder... This one relates to the joints, bones, and cartilage of the marriage. The joints are that part of our skeletal makeup which allows us to move and function. Remember, the man represents the framework of the marriage enabling it to stand, protecting all the vital organs with the skin and skeleton. The joints, in particular, enable the body (both husband and wife) to labor in God assigned activities, those works required and expected of a marriage in service to the Creator. These joints, and the cartilage that connect them to the bones, give him the productivity which every man needs to prove himself. This is what demonstrates his force and power, who he is through his accomplishments, his performance – his works. And what does God's Word say about works? There are, of course, dead works and works of the flesh, but we are talking about the good works that glorify the Father (Matthew 5:16; 1 Peter 2:12), that bring us unto salvation through belief (John 6:29); that fulfill our purpose after salvation (Ephesians 2:10); that make our lives rich in Him (1 Timothy 6:18), that make us a pattern for others (Titus 2:7), that bring us rewards and follow us to heaven (Matthew 16:27; Revelation 14:13). A man must be zealous of good works (Titus 2:14), thoroughly equipped for good works (2 Timothy 3:17), carefully maintain them so he is profitable and not unfruitful (Titus 3:8, 14). And he is to motivate others unto good works (Hebrews 10:24). In refuting the thought that we don't have to "do" anything to please God, James tells us in the second chapter of his letter that works are those things for us to do or attain - what God requires, the proof of genuineness and of faith. **"Who is a wise man and endued with knowledge among you? let him show out of a good conversation** (conduct) **his works with meekness of wisdom."** (James 3:13). No boasting allowed but in meekness - that power under control we have already discussed. Revelation 2:2 through 3:15 reminds us that Jesus knows our works!

A wife becomes one body with her husband when they take their vows. **"And Adam said, This is now bone of my bones, and flesh of my flesh: she shall be called Woman, because she was taken out of Man."** (Genesis 2:23)

If she functions properly according to her design, she is a crown to her man; if she malfunctions in her role, she is bringing ruin to herself as well as her husband. Proverbs again, 12:4 - **"A virtuous woman is a crown to her husband: but she that makes ashamed is as rottenness in his bones."** When she causes confusion in his strength and function as a man, it's as though his bones were progressively decaying, leaving him incapable of performing what God requires of him. Something abnormal takes place in the woman's B-cell mode – her intimate time with the Author of Life – that quiet time of fervent prayer that allows her to discern her will and God's will and unite them as one. In this abnormal functioning of her prayer life, there is a production of some factor that begins working against her own marriage. The prayer and love that normally maintained forbearance for the sake of unity is overtaken by reactions and attitudes that are aberrant. An immune response is mounted against those areas of productive labor in her husband's life, first causing inflammation, a protective reaction from him to the irritation or injury. The result is pain, anger, wounded pride, and loss of function. His strength soon becomes pitted and scarred. A gristly stiffness develops in his ability to perform; what was once firm, flexible, and resilient connections between his works and strength are destroyed. His hampered attempts at proving his genuineness and faith - those zealous deeds required by God as a husband and a Christian - become painful to him, overwhelming, and depriving him of his effectiveness. This condition tethers a man as though he were a chained animal only allowed a short radius in which to move about, binding his freedom. There is a loss of ability to move as the Spirit leads, an erosion of opportunities to do the works of God, a repulsive deformity in his performance and accomplishments - both in the sight of God and of the world watching him. Haven't you seen some husbands whose abilities have been crippled and twisted from what is natural and normal as the head of his home into dependence upon what this demanding, deviant wife

The Mystery of Marriage through Adam's Prime Rib

now dictates? What a dreadful condition for God's highest creation! What cause for humiliation and discouragement. Men in this condition are also more likely to have attacks against their hearts, that lifeline to their Creator which we just covered. There is no cure for this state of abasement in this man's spiritual life, only treatment, which includes reducing the wife's influence in his life.

Are there answers to the whys of these miserable conditions? There are clues. Though Ezekiel 16:44 plays a big role in falling prey to various autoimmune disorders in a marriage, not all women with these propensities to follow in their mothers' destructive ways develop a dysfunction. And not all marriages with a disorder have wives with these obvious inclinations. But it pays to look beyond Mom. Susie never got to know my mother. Mom died too young. Susie is so like her. My mom set her mind on what she wanted and went after it. She was an achiever and a promoter, successful in whatever she set her hand to do. I always wished I were more like her. However, as much as I admired her, I saw destructive actions taking place in her marriage. I also couldn't help but take note of my beloved grandma and saw a pattern of mother and daughter that wasn't pretty. Even though Mom tried to live opposite of all Grandma was and did, when it came to their marriage, they both wanted to dominate their husbands. I determined to make a conscious effort to make serious changes in how I would relate to my husband, and by God's grace, broke the cycle. I know people think I need to exert myself more and that this submission thing is over-rated, but I've seen what domineering women can do. Just be warned, my Dear, if there are latent tendencies toward marital "autoimmune disorders" in your ancestry, beware lest they be repeated. Watch and take heed. What pleasure that would bring the devil to catch you in that trap of wanting to control your husband. That was part of woman's curse back there in Genesis 3:16; woman would desire (reach out to control) her husband, but he would rule her. (That same word is used in the next chapter speaking of sin crouching at Cain's door reaching out to control him!)

Also, there are grave consequences when we submerge ourselves in a detrimental environment and bad habits that choke our ability to breathe in the Breath of Life. Satan's tactics are varied and many and very confusing. Marital autoimmune disorders may very well be the number one cause of the death of a marriage. Also interesting - it is the woman who becomes the ultimate victim, crippling not only her husband and marriage, but destroying her very purpose of creation! How ironic! So what is the treatment? Most marital autoimmune disorders are typically treated with an immunosuppressant – a prescription which decreases the influence of the wife in his life. Wow! That's drastic. How tragic! That leaves one open to attacks from real enemies – evil, temptations, deceptions, stress, bitterness, pride... It is a dangerous road when something goes haywire in this mighty host, this virtuous, valiant force intended to be man's crown encircling him for protection.

But, as I have said before, I now repeat. We expect better things of you and your beloved. Just consider this as part of your education and an extreme warning. Your marriage just can't afford for you to be part of the problem; the devil is hurling plenty at you every day. If you can't see or feel his attacks, maybe you need to be more diligent while on guard duty. It's easy to fall asleep on the job. If he should get his hands on you... well, remember Eve. Be mindful of the fact, you are not alone in this labor of love. Jesus has not left us as orphans. You have been given the Spirit of God Himself to guide you each step of the way. Take advantage of that Gift. **"Ye are of God, little children** (darlings), **and have overcome them** (confidence of final victory): **because greater is He that is in you, than he that is in the world."** He will enable you to be that crown you were fashioned to be! Let Him harness your powerful influence in this marriage and use it to your good and His glory.

Bridled and Harnessed,
C K

P.S. The letters you hold were written to offer some training, warnings, and encouragement, but you also need to be in a spiritual family (local Church) to help you hold fast, without wavering, to God's faithfulness in what He has promised. Assemble with believers that will watch over you, fanning the coals of love so you may do the good works that God has set before you. (Hebrews 10:23-25) They will admonish and encourage you and help bear your burdens. Partner with like-minded women in fellowship and prayer. Time is short! The Day of the Lord is drawing closer.

Our lives are not our own. We will give an account to Him for how it was spent. Destroy imaginations (fears, criticism, distrust, compulsiveness) and every thing that rises up against the knowledge of God. Bring every thought captive to obey Christ! (2 Corinthians 10:5) Make every word and act intentional for God's glory and honor.

Praying for you,
2ⁿᵈ momma

Mutiny on the Bounty

ear Darling Daughter,

We're closing in on the last of the "bad news" letters. I don't like this negativity. I much preferred the process of winning battles against the enemy – being victorious even though each skirmish is fatiguing. There is always such joy when the conquest has brought victory and peace within the body. It feels so good to be healthy! However, I must press on through the ugly reality of the body gone awry, and you must stick with me to grasp the warnings God has afforded us that we might see how to remain healthy – in body, mind, and spirit (1 Thessalonians 5:23; 3 John 2). My mandate to warn you of the enemy's descent upon you and his varied tactics comes from Ezekiel 33:1-6 – especially verse 6: **"But if the watchman see the sword come, and blow not the trumpet, and the people be not warned... his blood will I require at the watchman's hand."**

The seriousness of our topic today sends terror to families when they just hear the word "cancer". Cancer comes not from a virus, or bacterium, or even protozoa, but from within the body itself, in spite of an efficient, diligent immune system. The distinctive trait of cancer, which is manifested in more than 100 separate diseases, is malignant tumors composed of abnormal cells that proliferate rapidly and invade surrounding tissue. Without quick recognition and elimination of these cancer cells, they can spread to other body sites, causing organ failure and death. These cells are from our own body, once loyal, now turned traitorous, and rampantly growing out of control, taking over territory that does not belong to them, destroying good, healthy cells around them. There is a war going on with "self" attacking "self."

Thus, the subject of this letter: mutiny on the bounty. The definition of bounty is: generosity evidenced by a willingness to give freely. I think that is a pretty good description of our body and its functions, freely giving to all parts whenever and whatever is needed. Your heart tirelessly pumps your blood, which indiscriminately distributes to each of your cells the oxygen that your lungs faithfully inhale... and on and on, all giving generously. The definition of mutiny: open rebellion against constituted authority, organized opposition to authority, a conflict in which one faction tries to wrest control from another, insurrection, uprising, revolt, rebellion. When every part of the body is in sub-mission to every other part, there is harmony, peace, success, unified growth. But when one part rebels and infects others, pulling them into the revolt, the result is an attempted "take over", sometimes repressed but sometimes, unfor-tunately, successful.

What happened? Why the insurrection? There is a genetic change in the cell itself. Something happens to cause this cell to change from self to opponent. Again, heredity plays a role in this alteration. If family members have cancer, be on alert! I know a lady whose mother and aunts had all suffered breast can-cer. She too fell victim, but was a survivor. Her daughter had a lump come up on her breast and the fear that struck this girl's heart was certainly understand-able, having lived through the horror of watching her mom lose her hair and suffer the distress of treatments. Beware and take care of your immune sys-tem! Contributing to the growth of these mutinous cells is the neglect of one's health (weakening the immune system) and lifestyle habits (smoking, worry, tanning, not using the body as God intended...), as well as exposure to toxic

The Mystery of Marriage through Adam's Prime Rib

chemicals and excessive radiation. These all can trigger genetic changes that affect cell growth. Altered genes then direct cells to multiply abnormally, taking on the aggressive and destructive characteristics of cancer. Small pockets of these silent cancer cells are constantly arising within us, but as they turn cancerous, the antigens on their surface change just enough to alert vigilant phagocytes and T-cells, which ceaselessly seek out and destroy these mutinous cells, just as it does bacteria and viruses. Our phenomenal phagocytes gobble up anything that is suspicious, whether in the bloodstream, the tissues, or the lymphatic system - whether it is a living microorganism, some pollutant that enters our body, or even "self" turned traitor. However, as mentioned in one of our earlier letters, too much smoke in the lungs or too many undigestables, like asbestos, and the phagocytes are overwhelmed. They can't keep up with their housecleaning duties, or they are destroyed in the process of trying. Still our tireless, conscientious, defensive army battles on, as long as it is able, as long as it is healthy. However, every surgery the body undergoes puts tremendous strain on the immune system and takes attention away from looking for those traitors. All too often cancer is detected soon after major surgeries.

I touched on my mom in our last letter. Again, she makes a good personal example of what not to do. Mom neglected her health dreadfully, living on coffee and cigarettes and only one meal a day. She took pills to go to sleep at night, pills to stay awake during the day, pills not to have children, and pills to soothe her nerves with the children she did have. She pushed herself to be "successful", living under horrific self-imposed stress, as well as stress in her marriage, making alcohol a natural part of her life. My momma died a horrible death as colon cancer quickly destroyed her from the inside, spreading to vital organs within weeks. It was merciful that she died just three months after her diagnosis. We buried Mom as Susie completed her second month of life. She was the first grandchild to give her pleasure, but it was too late for her to be a grandma. I have taken my health seriously and the health of those I love. Consider yourself warned, my Sweet, and eat right, get your rest, forsake any temptations to cigarettes, alcohol, medications (legal or illegal), as well as stress, bitterness, jealousy... Your immune system can only handle so much and is only as healthy as you keep it. Those seditious cancer cells are there even now. Is your immune system up? If you fail it, it will fail you.

If a mutinous cell mass can grow to the size of a pinhead, then cancer cells establish themselves in the body with their own blood supply and begin reproducing out of control. Cells become a threatening tumor. (They say it takes a minimum of one billion cancer cells for a tumor to be detected by radiology and physical examinations.) If it can get enough blood supply to feed itself, it grows large enough to destroy nearby tissues and organs through invasive growth and then spreads to distant tissues and organs through the bloodstream or lymph system.

Treatments such as surgery, chemotherapy, and radiation are effective with some cancers, but all of those treatments also kill healthy cells and devastate the body's greatest ally, the white blood cells - the immune system! Meanwhile, victims undergoing these treatments have to be constantly under protection from any germ that would normally be fought off with little effort but could now kill them because they have no defense. Researchers are now investigating other treatments, such as gene therapy (attempting to correct the faulty DNA that causes the uncontrolled growth of cancer cells), immunotherapy (the stimulation of the body's natural defenses), vectorization (aiming chemicals specifically at cancer cells), and nanotechnology (targeting cancer cells with minute objects the size of atoms). Maybe it won't be long before they can actually cure this vicious malady. Yes, there are survivors, but cancer is a killer. Even with treatments thought successful, cancer often returns with a vengeance, a successful insurrection against the body in which it once lived in harmony! When these mutineers set out to take over the ship, they are in reality destroying the ship that keeps them afloat. The only purpose is to steal, kill, and destroy.

We turn our attention now to the spiritual realm (yet still very physical) - what Jesus called one flesh. Marriage was created to be very good, a bountiful experience in the union of a man and a woman by God in purpose and will. To have a healthy marriage there must be a spirit of "bounty" - freely giving one to the other: he, sacrificing self, working diligently in pursuing right thoughts and actions, purifying her and keeping her safe, freely giving whenever and whatever is needed; she, giving all of her resources in bringing tender and beautiful elements into the marriage, submitting graciously to his leadership, building him up and keeping him strong. But when there is a mutiny against this body of marriage – a rebellion against spiritual union, wresting for control, taking over territory without due respect, then the marriage becomes sick, weak, destroyed. There is a war, with self attacking self.

What could possibly happen in a marriage that could cause this kind of insurrection? We know that there is a traitorous nature within us until we are set free from this flesh (Romans 7:18-23). Those very things we don't want to do, we do; the things we want to do, we find we can't. There is a war going on within us. That war is transferred into our marriage as well, because we are human and subject to fleshly desires. **"This I say then, Walk in the Spirit, and ye shall not fulfill the lust of the flesh. For the flesh lusts against the Spirit, and the Spirit against the flesh: and these are contrary the one to the**

other: so that ye cannot do the things that ye would." (Galatians 5:16, 17) There will be areas of mutiny arising within marriage which will have to be won by walking in the Spirit or the flesh will consume us. It has to be a common goal of both the man and the woman, the husband as the first defense protecting externally and the wife as the second, doing her job internally. If victory is not won, things of the flesh will rampantly grow out of control, taking over territory in which they have no right to reside, destroying good, healthy relationships around them. When every part of the body is in submission to every other part, there is harmony, peace, success, and unified growth. But when one area rebels and is not dealt with quickly and put in check, it soon infects other attitudes and actions which join in the revolt. The result is an attempted "take over", sometimes repressed and sometimes, unfortunately, successful.

What causes this insurrection? There's an inherent change in one of the basic functional facets of the marriage. Something happens to cause this "cell" to change from self to opponent. Again, I hate to bring this up, but heredity plays an important role in this alteration. If family members have a "cancer" in their marriage, be on alert! The tendencies of these same types of destructive issues entering into your own marriage are high, especially in light of Romans 7 just read. Early detection is imperative and is the best method to stop the advance of this mutiny. **"O wretched man that I am! who shall deliver me from the body of this death? I thank God through Jesus Christ our Lord..."** (vv. 24, 25). He is able to deliver us from all natural tendencies through the indwelling Spirit (chapter 8).

A great influence in the growth of cancer in the marriage is neglect on the husband's part as the first line of defense. If he is not keeping himself clean and pure in heart, unspotted from the world, if he is not feeding on the Word of God and has become lazy in his service to God, if he is not getting the proper rest through a strong faith and confidence in God's plans, then he has left his wife's influence weakened, unable to do her job of recognizing and removing these mutating, self-feeding cells gone renegade in their allegiance to this marriage. Lifestyle habits are another cause of accelerating this mutiny, as well as over-exposure to the wicked elements of this world and the "too much"es discussed way back there in the beginning of these letters. Things he allows to become habitual in his life that fail to honor God will not only distract him from God's purposes, but also frustrate his wife's efforts to keep this marriage healthy. Included in that is indulging in things of this world that would lead to temp-tation - excessive entertainment is a good example. Exposing your marriage to the vile things of this world, no matter the glitter they offer, is flirting with danger. In weakening his wife's ability to fulfill her purpose, he is disobeying the Word and forfeiting the promises of God. The inability to deny the flesh becomes powerful, destroying the testimony and spiritual growth, frustrating the grace of God (Galatians 2:21) and failing His grace - that Divine influence God freely offers (Hebrews 12:15). Things a couple does and places they go (or don't do and don't go) will bear a great weight in their ability to walk to-gether. **"Can two walk together, except they be agreed?"** (Amos 3:3) They can quickly destroy their ability to walk with the Lord and in His Spirit when not in agreement with Him and with one another. Satan delights in breaking agreement between a husband and wife! Foul things endured will change one's makeup and soon take command and enslave. **"Let not sin therefore reign in your mortal body, that ye should obey it in the lusts thereof. Neither yield your members as instruments of unrighteousness unto sin... Know ye not, that to whom ye yield yourselves servants to obey, his servants ye are to whom ye obey; whether of sin unto death, or of obedience unto righteous-ness?... I speak after the manner of men because of the infirmity of your**

flesh: for as ye have yielded your members servants to uncleanness and to iniquity unto iniquity; even so now yield your members servants to righteousness unto holiness." (Romans 6:12, 13, 16, 19) Sin must be recognized, eliminated and replaced with righteousness.

These factors can all trigger innate changes that affect a rebellious growth. Self-fulfillment, selfishness, and lack of unity will rapidly reproduce seeds of discontent, ungratefulness, resentment, and bitterness taking on aggressive and destructive characteristics against this union. Potential self-destructive ways are offered daily to a marriage – stress, condemnation, compromise, lust, strife, turmoil, jealousy, quarrels – but an alert, healthy wife will recognize those cancerous traits and seek out their destruction through the power God has given her as the helper. Philippians 4:6 gives us one of the best remedies for stress and strife and quarrels and such: **"Be careful for nothing** (don't be anxious about anything)**; but in every thing by prayer and supplication with thanksgiving let your requests be made known unto God."** Even when self-condemnation makes an ugly entrance, remember I John 3:20 – **"For if our heart condemn us, God is greater than our heart, and knows all things."**

Small pockets of these silent discontents are constantly arising within us, but as they turn cancerous, the telltale signs on their surface change just enough to alert a vigilant wife, who ceaselessly seeks out and destroys these mutinous attitudes. This tireless, conscientious army of defense will battle on, as long as she is able, as long as she is healthy, because she loves him – is at one with him in this marriage. However, just as with the body's phagocytes, a wife that encounters too much contamination or too many undigestables, like adultery, and the woman is overwhelmed. She can't keep up, or she is destroyed in the process of trying.

I thought about giving you types of cancer and comparing them with things that come up in the marriage, much as I did with the autoimmune disorders. But the wisdom of time nipped that in the bud. I don't have time to do the research and you are tired of reading! I will give you some quick examples to think about and you can make your own comparisons. There are things naturally within us that were placed there by our Creator:

~the man was given the desire to work and provide for his family...but when that desire deviates just a little, it becomes a driving force that can turn him into a workaholic if it isn't recognized, taking over time that belongs to his wife, children, rest, worship... those desires must be put in check quickly or greed and pride set in...

~the woman was given a desire to please her husband with her appearance (a man really likes seeing and smelling the wife of his youth)...but when that desires deviates just a little, it becomes a driving force that has her spending too much on clothes, hair, make-up, obsessed with her appearance, enjoying glances from others than her husband...

~man and woman both have been given their sexuality and desire for intimacy by their Creator who told them to replenish the earth... You fill in the rest for man and for woman when things get off balance....

Understanding the gravity of her job, a wife is watchful, recognizing the self-markers of their union, and quickly identifying an unhealthy variation. She can then catch it early with a great advantage. However, when she cannot recognize the change, be it her failure in her own diligence or his lack of keeping her healthy, a cancer will grow large enough to destroy positive attitudes and actions through invasive growth. It spreads to other areas of the marriage that were not even involved. Should these rebellious thoughts or actions be allowed to grow to any significant size, they will establish themselves in the marriage and begin reproducing out of control. They become a threatening tumor. Unfortunately, sometimes it takes a whole lot of these attitudes for a tumor to be detected by an outsider. That leaves the early damage control of these renegades in the hands of the one closest, the wife. And should this mutinous faction spread to that "lymph" area of the woman's life, it renders her helpless, cutting off her network of prayer, that quiet time with the Lord that filters out the yuck in life, multiplies her prayers, and divides her heart so she can see everything in a discerning light. It prohibits her ability to produce antibodies that stop the progression of the enemy. Satan will lead this marriage into self-destruction that will permeate every part of their lives, virtually killing their effectiveness as a Christian marriage (or his opportunity for salvation). She must recognize the warning signs and do something about them fervently! "**...The effectual fervent prayer of the righteous availeth much.**" (James 5:16).

Yes, there are survivors even when cancerous actions and attitudes are allowed free reign, but there are more fatalities because most marriages don't even know what hit them, much less get help. You can see people all around you suffering, many marriages already dead. What once lived in love and harmony has succumbed to a successful insurrection! There is no such thing as a little cancer - little attitudes that can go unchecked. They grow until they kill. When these mutineers set out to take over the ship, they were, in reality, destroying the ship that kept them afloat. That is Satan's purpose in life – to steal, kill, and destroy (John 10:10). God's script calls for life and that we might have it superabundantly! That calls for cooperation between these two defenses that God has put in place. We must work together for the sake of our marriages.

1 Thessalonians 5:11-13 gives us good counsel that would appropriately apply to a husband and wife living this life of unity - "**Wherefore comfort** (call to one's side to give aid, comfort) **yourselves together, and edify** (build up) **one another... And we beseech you, brethren, to know** (perceive with the senses, understand, esteem) **them which labor** (feel fatigue from working hard) **among you, and are over** (to stand before in rank, preside over) **you in the Lord, and admonish** (put into the mind, instruct, warn) **you; And to esteem** (to think, respect, reckon) **them very highly** (over and beyond abundance) **in love** (benevolent love shown by doing what is needed for the one loved) **for their work's sake** (work, performance, the result of doing and working). **And be at peace** (live in peace) **among yourselves.**" I know those verses are talking about the Church, but that is also the relationship a man and woman should have – aiding and comforting one another, each building up the other, understanding and giving the proper respect as fatigue is felt because of their labor in this marriage, especially knowing the rule of one over the other in the Lord, as warnings and instructions are given. Our high opinion and respect should be overly abundant, showing love by doing what is needed for the one loved because of the work and performance done in their marriage, enabling them to live in peace in their home. Doesn't that sound like a description of the perfect first and second defenses? But that was an admonition to do, not a description of. In real life, the Church is no better off than our marriages. There is no perfect Church; there is no perfect husband, no perfect wife; only the perfect Savior!

I have used the third person throughout this section, mostly because I want it to stay in third person, never affecting you or me. But we know better. It doesn't always happen to the other person. If you are honest, you can go back through what I have just placed on paper and put in names. No one is exempt from these cancerous cells in their marriage. But a good, healthy immune system can keep them in check so your marriage never has any evidence of mutiny. I pray the following verse may become "your verse" someday, when you truly know what you are and understand His grace given to you. **"But by the grace of God I am what I am: and His grace which was bestowed upon me was not in vain; but I labored more abundantly than they all: yet not I, but the grace of God which was with me."** (1 Corinthians 15:10) That is my prayer and my personal goal in life. God forbid that His grace could be given to me in vain. May His Divine influence in my heart and its reflection in my life be obvious to all and the source of all I do. I pray the same for you, my dear daughter.

Pledging allegiance,
Momma 2

The Enemy's Ultimate Tactic

ear Promised Help,

Everything inside of me wants to quit and move on to new letters – the bliss of motherhood and the role you play in your babies' lives that will last through adulthood and eternity. But I must deal with this last point and I hope to be brief. We touched on this a long time ago, but I am compelled to deal with it again after stressing the critical role of the immune system's ministry to our body. I thought it would make more sense at the end. (Does that excite you – the end? Mothers can be so harpy – just going on and on and on about things. You will understand, my love, as you will have things you just must tell your children...)

My last topic is the enemy's ultimate, successfully proven tactic against the body: AIDS, *acquired immune deficiency syndrome,* the infectious disease of the immune system caused by the *human immunodeficiency virus* (HIV), leaving the body susceptible to a variety of potentially fatal infections. The heart is not affected by this virus, nor the lungs or brain or any other vital organ. This is not a skin-eating virus, nor a threat to the bones. The sole prey of the HIV is the immune system. But it doesn't molest the macrophage nor attack our Killer T-cells. There is no assault on our B-cells that make plasma and produce antibodies. No, it is so deadly because it attacks the one lymphocyte most critical to the immune response, the Helper T-cell, our Commander in Chief, that part of our defense system that alerts all other defenders to report for duty.

Bodily fluids carry the virus to a victim through sexual intercourse, exchange of saliva, the use of contaminated hypodermic syringes, or even by placental transfer between mother and baby. And it was introduced to the world through perversion and continues to spread through rampant homosexual behavior. It was first called gay-related immune deficiency and gay cancer in the late 70's. Then hemophiliacs and drug users began to be infected and scientists came up with the acronym AIDS to identify the disease in 1982. Since then the world has lost over 100 million people to AIDS and millions are living with it right now with little hope of survival.

The following is the battle tactic that the HIV uses so successfully. Please pay close attention as this has more to do with you that you could possibly believe. The HIV enters the body from an infected host through blood, semen, saliva, or even breast milk, and then slips into the Helper T. Remember; a virus is the simplest and most devious of germs. Although it contains instructions for making identical copies of itself, it can not reproduce. In order for a virus to reproduce, it must infect a living cell. Viruses are not technically alive; if you will, think of them as sort of a brain with no body. In order to replicate itself, the virus must hi-jack a cell, and use its reproductive tools to make new viruses.

I'm trying to not be too technical but bear with me as we do a quick refreshing of your biology. Refer back to these definitions if need be as we progress...

~DNA is the blueprint for building new cells, the hereditary material in humans and almost all other organisms. Every cell in your body has the same DNA with information stored as a code consisting of about 3 billion bases. The order of these bases determines the information available for building and maintaining an individual, much like the way letters of the alphabet appear in

The Mystery of Marriage through Adam's Prime Rib

a certain order to form words and sentences. Nucleotides are arranged in two long strands that form a spiral called a double helix, like a ladder with rungs and vertical sidepieces of the ladder. An important property of DNA is that it can make exact copies of itself, with each strand in the double helix serving as a pattern for duplicating the sequence, a critical point if each new cell is to have an exact copy of the DNA present in the old cell. Your DNA is uniquely yours – no one else on earth has the same DNA as you. And each of your cells knows exactly where it belongs in your unique body with its own instructions to reproduce itself – from skin cells and fingernails to blood and bones – all because of DNA. You are a whole new you remade every 7 years, always the same DNA!

~Proteins are the building blocks that are used to make living things.

~Enzymes are the workers in cells, mostly proteins that act as catalysts to bring about specific chemical reactions - one enzyme molecule may convert 1000 molecules a minute, and some are known to convert 3 million in a minute. They are highly specific - one enzyme will only carry out one of the many reactions for which enzymes control.

~RNA is like the construction boss, a molecule similar to DNA; however, unlike the double-stranded DNA, RNA is a single strand of nucleotides that tells enzymes how to build a specific part of a cell, playing an important role in combining proteins, transmitting genetic information, and controlling chemical activities in the cell. (It is also the genetic material of many viruses, including HIV.)

~Nucleus is the small package inside the cell where the genetic material is kept.

Now let's proceed...

After entering the body, the HIV seeks out a Helper T-cell, to which it connects, kind of like a spaceship docking with the space station. It has a marker on it that matches up with the T-cell's outer surface, and begins to transfer its RNA into its unsuspecting host. This virus must successfully take over control of the T-cell's machinery before it can produce new clones of itself. It does so with some very manipulative, deceptive tools – enzymes that know how to steal, kill, and destroy in such a way that the host is totally unaware of its own doom!

The first enzyme does what is called a reverse transcription, taking the virus' RNA and converting it into a counterfeit DNA. After it has disguised its true nature by putting itself into the form that the T-cell understands, then another specific enzyme of this HIV incorporates this false DNA into the Helper T's DNA makeup (kind of like downloading a new program into the computer that overrides the original program). The virus cancels the DNA of its host, issuing its own instructions. This integration has now hijacked the Helper T's ability to reproduce itself. The virus is now in complete control, patiently waiting for another infection to come against the body, activating the T's reproduction process. The virus doesn't destroy the cell until it has done the enemy's bidding; it has, however, stolen its purpose to defend the body. In fact, it needs the cell alive as it robs its nutrients and establishes its own virus factory. When a germ enters the body and the macrophage alerts the Helper Ts, the captured Ts respond right along with the uninfected ones, churning out 1000s of duplicates of the HIV, which in turn seek out more Helper Ts to steal, kill, and destroy.

The deadly genius of the HIV is that it only targets the Helper T. When some germ infiltrates the body, no matter how slight or relatively harmless, the infection triggers the invaded T-cell to multiply. As this cell divides to become two, it really doesn't. The DNA of that cell, which would cause it to reproduce with an identical Helper T-cell, was short-circuited by the virus. Instead, the virus is at the helm issuing its own command and thousands of the HIV are released into the bloodstream. These clones then infect more Helper Ts, repeating the process, until the body loses the very sentinels that would alert all other cells to take their battle stations. Each new bacteria or virus that triggers an immune response gives these viruses, waiting in infected Ts, the opportunity to repli-cate again and again. Each time the defense is getting weaker because these Commanders are not sounding the alarm. The phagocytes and Killer Ts receive no call to arms. The Bs are not being activated so antibodies are not being pro-duced. The enemy runs free. Death is certain. It gives you a whole new appreci-ation for those Helper Ts and that alarm being sounded. What a marvelous body God has given us! What a devious enemy we have that wants to destroy it.

Ready for our last analogy? Oh, you know where we are headed with this, right? One of the primary roles of being a wife is that of the Helper Ts in our marriage. And, yes, Satan wants to slither into our lives to render our entire ministry ineffective. But humor me, please. I would like to complete this anal-ogy venture...

First point – when a man leaves the natural use of the woman, he is an abomination to God. Of course, the Old Testament has its share of warnings about the subject, but Romans 1:18-32 really puts it straight. When mankind has been given all the evidence needed to acknowledge God as his Creator and rejected that proof, refusing to give Him glory, being ungrateful and choosing to worship a lie, why would God not surrender those to the depravity they are seeking, leaving them open to the consequences of their choices? As haters of God they continue to practice unnatural, unholy lifestyles, taking pleasure in others who do the same. What do you call people like that? Reveling in their sin, thumbing their noses in the face of God, they become their own god, remaking themselves as contrary as possible to God's creation. Is there any wonder why AIDS is taking lives? The saddest part is that many innocent people are also dying because of the vile hatred these condemned souls have for God.

In the same manner, men and women today have their roles so perverted and confused that they have become an abomination to their Creator. He has emphatically revealed His plan for man and woman through creation – just by the way they are sexually formed, for goodness sake, not to mention their emotional and psychological make-up. Because of the length of these letters, I will abstain from any more examples, because you can look around and see plenty for yourself. This race has disgraced their Creator!

Men and women both have positions and responsibilities assigned to them as part of God's plan, their own personal DNA to replicate themselves in order to fulfill that plan. You may well be able to come up with better spiritual analogies for the proteins, enzymes, RNA, etc., every bit as good as mine, and I would be delighted to hear your thoughts.

But, if you will, please, for now let's think of the protein building blocks of the DNA for our spiritual body as the Word of God, each verse, chapter, and book building upon another to make us exactly what the Lord intends our particular character to be.

The enzymes, being the workers in our cells, mostly proteins (the Word incorporated into our lives), would be the good works done that act as catalysts to bring about specific spiritual reactions. Each good deed done in faith can change 1000 attitudes, and some have proven to totally revolutionize entire families.

I think I would call the spiritual RNA (the construction boss) our own spirit that directs those good works of when and how to build a specific part of a cell within our ministry. When working in conjunction with God's Spirit, our spirit plays the vital role in combining verses from God's Word, transmitting that information into the new nature, and controlling the resulting activities in each area of growth.

And the nucleus, as the small package inside the cell where the genetic material is kept, would have to be our heart, present in the center of every ministry the Lord has entrusted to us. We just have to remember that our natural genetic tendency is to fall short of the glory of God, to sin. Yet we are set free from that natural "do it my way" nature that we might be nurtured by God's own Spirit to please the Father. Our heart now leads us to "do it His way"! What we do with what God has given us is up to us. When our spirit is revived by the power of God, fueled by the Word of God, and submits to His Spirit to carry out His eternal plan and purpose, things get done! Life and liberty grow, not only in our spirits, but in our physical lives as well. Living becomes the avenue by which we develop into the eternal beings God desires, prepared to dwell with Him forever! (remember the baby in the womb?)

Satan, of course, opposed this plan of God from the beginning. Determined to cancel it, He became the instigator of all that opposes God. He found the way into man's soul, a way to take away his defense. Eve's encounter with the serpent may have been the first time Satan attempted to secure the fall of man, but I seriously doubt it. The devil is not all-knowing, not all-seeing, nor is he present everywhere. But he watched this couple long enough that he saw what Eve was to Adam, the help-meet for him (Genesis 2:18). So he took his deceptive lies to the weaker vessel (1 Peter 3:7) (Genesis 3:1-5). She doubted her Creator and believed the lie (v. 6), losing her ability to be the aid and protection that God created her to be. Her Helper T DNA was hijacked by this viral deception, canceling any hope of replicating her Helper ministry. No threat was recognized, no alarm was sounded, no action was taken to defeat this enemy. Rather, with her own spiritual Helper DNA being deleted and reprogrammed by this lying spirit, she actually served to propagate this false doctrine of liberation to her husband. This fallen angel had to have a host in order to reproduce and he found it in Eve. **"And Adam was not deceived, but the woman being deceived was in the transgression."** (1 Timothy 2:14). The result was devastating! It meant death for them both.

Satan is alive and well today. His tactics have worked well down through the centuries, and his use of them now is intense. His method of reaching the woman and working within her realm of influence is his surest technique. 2 Timothy 3:5-7 plainly reveals woman is the subject preyed upon. **"Having a form of godliness, but denying the power thereof: from such turn away** (avoid). **For of this sort are they which creep** (sneak) **into houses** (homes, families), **and lead captive** (capture) **silly** (foolish) **women laden** (burdened) **with sins, led away** (driven, induced) **with divers lusts** (various kinds of forbidden longings), **ever learning** (always wanting to know more fully), **and never able to come to the knowledge of the truth."** Satan's demons know how to use their master's techniques: **"For such are false apostles, deceitful workers, transforming themselves into the apostles of Christ. And no marvel; for Satan himself is transformed into an angel of light. Therefore it is no great thing if his ministers also be transformed as the ministers of righteousness; whose end shall be according to their works."** Whether they are false preachers, deceitful teachers, or the devil's own demons, their united purpose is to deceive and destroy. There are always weak-minded/hearted people, but especially vulnerable women, on which they can practice their methods, those who are easily flattered and charmed, lending an ear to anything sounding religious, with open hearts to anything that will advance the happiness of the world, all the while burdened with their own sins, under the influence of guilt, yet still being driven by the variegated colors of forbidden desires. They seek to be relieved of their conscience by any means other than confession and repentance. Satan accommodates their desire through his deceptive viruses of freedom, equal rights, pride, humanism, liberalism...

I must add, women are especially susceptible when they are not kept healthy spiritually by their husbands. There are false doctrines being propagated through Christianity for which foolish women are directly responsible because the men in their lives were not healthy, spiritual men nurturing their wives!

Once this deception enters the heart of this Commander-in-Chief of the marriage's immune system, she loses her ability to recognize the enemy. She fails to send an alarm. No Sword of the Word is applied to do battle. No prayer is offered. The Spirit has no liberty to work. Not only has she lost her purpose in Creation as man's help - protecting the health of her husband and marriage - she instead becomes the vessel which propagates the deceptive lies of Satan. She is left powerless to overcome the enemies which have declared war on the purpose and glory of God - to the destruction of herself and all that pertains to her. The enemy runs free! The future holds only a painfully slow, certain death.

What can be said? This last, malicious tactic is not just an over-reactive response to harmless things causing allergies. A man can live with that, as can a marriage. It isn't an auto-immune disease attacking the marriage, crippling the function and beauty of the body. Marriage can also survive that ploy (though survival is not our goal; it's to be an enduring and vigorous success!). Neither is it the failure to recognize mutinous behavior in the body allowing cancers to sicken and shorten life. There is hope, even in cancer, if the immune system is allowed to maintain its health in order to fight. No, this most contemptuous and effective strategy of the enemy leaves no hope, for the Helper or the body. If the immune system is disabled, the marriage, rendered helpless, succumbs to any "disease" that runs unbridled unto death. If Satan can destroy the helper ministry of the woman in the marriage, he devastates both the man and woman, the marriage.

What do we do? Stay alert! Stay with the Script! Know the Author intimately! Stay beside your husband (where was Adam while Eve conversed with the Serpent?)! When you hear a hissing sound, run into the arms of your husband! There is safety when pulled up close to his heart. Get your Teacher Training! Know your assigned roles, the differences between your character and your husband's. Beware of the hiss that would deceive you into believing a perversion of those roles would be better than what your Creator has written for you. Keep your eyes and heart on heavenly rewards and prepare now for the coming wedding feast in Heaven when the Father welcomes you with: "**Well done, good and faithful servant: ... enter into the joy of your Lord.**"

Expecting the Best,
Eternally your 2nd Momma

To Work or Not To Work? Is That the Question?

ear One,

I hope you understand that you are dear to me. Without knowing you, I love you. It's a supernatural love that I can not explain apart from God. And it is in that love that I say (write) things that I believe best for the one loved, although not always received. Okay, this is the tough letter, the ugly one, the controversial one, from the old lady who has her head stuck in outdated yesteryears. But I can not in good conscience send these letters to the publisher without dealing with "the Question." (You are quite welcome to skip this letter since you've already done the hard part of getting this far. This is more friend-to-friend advice for future days...but I hope you come back to it...)

Is there any doubt in your mind that woman has a tremendous job to do? The content of the letters is almost terrifying as we think of the consequences if we fail to do our job. To work or not to work! What is work? According to Webster's, work as a verb is: to fashion or create a useful or desired product by expending labor; to perform or carry through a task requiring sustained effort or continuous repeated operations; to function or operate according to plan/design; to exert oneself physically/mentally, especially in sustained effort, for a purpose or under compulsion of necessity. The real Question is where will you exert yourself and what product will you be creating in your labor? What task or performance is before you that requires your sustained, continuous effort?

Because I don't know you personally, I have to wonder... Do you presently have a place of employment outside your home? Do you "need" to work to pay the bills? Do you prefer to work because you're bored at home, or you need to get out and meet people, or because you just have a lot to offer others? Work = Paycheck, Pleasure, Involvement, Usefulness, Excitement, Adventure, Decision Making, Satisfaction. I am not questioning the right or wrong of where you invest your time and effort. That is between you and your Author. He knows! Work you must because God created you to work. No matter your gifts and talents, or lack thereof, you do have a "job" in God's script. The Question is how and where will you labor? Working in the world, for the most part, provides only temporal needs, the "here and now stuff". Yes, I know there are many who find their work outside the home to be beneficial and making an impact in their world, i.e., nurses, teachers, etc. The mere definition of work declares its noble value wherever it takes place. However, creating a home, making a marriage useful for the glory of God, is a full workload that provides spiritual needs, the "eternal stuff".

Our society is a tough one in which to develop values and morals. We have become a throwaway culture – from paper plates, plastic forks, and Styrofoam cups, to toasters, blenders, phones, TVs, computers, and automobiles. Is it any wonder people have become disposable as well? Where does marriage stand in this throwaway thinking? Sure, throwaway diapers are a great convenience, as are all other disposables to modern folks who don't want to invest the time, money, and elbow grease to keep their things clean, running and stable. Unfortunately, that mindset now includes people, friendships, obligations, and marriage vows. Those things may dissolve over time but not by God's design. When focused on pleasure, ease, and convenience, we lose sight of what is important and eternal.

Commitment to loving others takes time and self-sacrifice. Some wise person once said, "Love is spelled T-I-M-E". That includes friendships, obligations, and marriage vows. Friendships take time; marriage takes more. Self-fulfillment and seeking material fluff and stuff have to die in our minds, hearts, and lives if we are to follow after love, God, and His eternal promises. So where does that leave us with "the Question"?

What sane woman today doesn't go out and get a job? My Susie wanted her own money to spend the way she wanted. She married a man who was taught a wife had to make money to pull her weight in the marriage – contributing her fair share to paying the bills. Yes, a woman is to contribute to her marriage and to society. However, the absolute best contribution that any woman (and only a woman) can make is creating a happy, content home within her house or apartment, building up her husband, and raising the next generation with moral values, a work ethic, virtues and confidence they can't find in daycare or schools. That, my Dear, takes a lot of work and if you have chosen the matrimony route, nothing else must take precedence!

I held down two jobs in high school and enjoyed the experience and the money, yet I chose to be a stay-at-home wife and mom; to do without the clothes I would need at a job, the second car and gas to get there, the acceptance of peers and prestige afforded, the eating out and "extra" things, (and the babysitting costs); but mostly because I was a product of a working mom. Left sitting on the curb waiting to be picked up for a birthday party, or my Brownie Fly Up ceremony, or...; Mom's job took precedence even though she was the boss. **"...a child left will bring his mother to shame."** Proverbs 29:15 is true! I was left alone and brought shame to both myself and Mom. So, my choice was to never share the demands of my time and loyalty to another vocation; to be home when my husband was discouraged and confused with life and career changes – available to do and go at his good pleasure; to be present when babies' first words, steps, and life questions occurred. Money can't buy that. I tried some "at home" jobs now and then. I also taught phonics at my kids' school and I loved it. But observation of those around me repeatedly reminded me that woman's first priority must always be her husband. If you fail there, true success will elude you in all other areas of life. Marital failure caused by independent, working women is staggering.

Flip side: I have a friend who is indeed a working wife and an inspiration to all who know her. Sandra committed her life in marriage to a domineering man, and I say that with the utmost respect! After a failed marriage with two children, Brother George took his position as commander of their marriage as an assignment from God and exerted his control, not as a tyrant, but as ruler over his domain of influence. And an influence he was. I can't begin to list the boys and girls in whom he invested time, money and Solomon's proverbs according to George, including my own children. His heart was bigger than a billion dollar goldmine. And he was a giver! He never passed up someone in need, stranger, family, church... He borrowed money and made payments to give missionaries a van. Amid other jobs, his preference was truck driver which kept him on the road a lot. I say all that to set the stage for Sandra's willing submission.

Sandra exemplifies the Proverbs 31 wife! Bright, industrious, hard-working, compassionate... It's an understatement to say she was an excellent school teacher, educating not only her students' minds but also their moral character in the wisdom of God, investing love in each one with her mother's heart that had no other outlet. It's common for former students to come to her at a restaurant or shopping or..., 20/30 years later, and thank her for the difference she made in life. She hasn't taught for years. She has had numerous other jobs at her husband's urging. Never have I heard her complain! His decisions were not always right, but she always followed, being a good daughter of Sarah (1 Peter 3:5&6). He usually asked for her input on his newest venture, but they both knew George made the final decision. She submitted to her husband as unto the Lord and was blessed. From mobile homes to apartments, to the cab of an 18-wheeler, to a condominium (which included a pool for their guests) and then to a camper, Sandra was content with whatever home George provided for the moment. They never invested in houses or land, accumulated little for themselves and worked to bless others, storing treasures in heaven instead. Did she suffer for Christ? When she had time, she enjoyed the hot tub or massage recliner that George bought to benefit guests in their home, of which we were such to be blessed. He lavished her with his love and loyalty, gifts and cruises, which she worked out with her employers to get time off! Over the years he especially took delight in blessing his pastor and wife with gifts. He set homeless families up in apartments. I can't begin to explain Brother George to you; he had to be experienced. But, it was Sandra that earned most of the living and giving power, enduring change as the wind blew (and the Spirit led). She still has a super job because she is an excellent worker. George has gone on to his reward in Heaven. He did not take the best care of his own health, but he took care of his wife with a sizeable insurance policy and precious memories of a life well spent. They are the closest example I have experienced to abandonment of self and walking in the Spirit as a living testimony of God's love. Too much to be said about this couple …

My point in bringing up Sandra was to show you an example of a virtuous woman. She worked to perform a task God had entrusted to her: to be a glory to and please her husband in the Lord, and she did it well! That was her career. Not many women are called to work so their husbands can give their earnings away. Sandra is unique, fashioned especially for George and she is a total success in all areas of her life, particularly as a friend and an inspiration!

If God has gifted you to be a blessing to this world in whatever field you feel led, that's wonderful. But listen for the hissing of the serpent when your service to others leads to the neglect of your own family. Please go to Proverbs 31:10-31 for God's approval... These 22 verses are written in the form of an acrostic; the first word of each verse begins with a consecutive letter of the Hebrew alphabet. We might call it "the ideal wife from A to Z". It's a shame our alphabets don't match and the profoundness and easy teachability are lost in the translation. It is worthy of our study and incorporation into our lives! Read it with some definitions noted in parentheses. It sings the praises of a wise wife - the honor and dignity of a virtuous woman.

10 Who can find a virtuous woman? for her price is far above rubies. (Remember our definition of virtuous: a great force, valiant, full of virtue, strength, power, able, an army, a mighty host, wealth. That is exactly what you must be in your husband's life if you are to be a woman whose worth is priceless, far above rubies. God made you to be a valiant army, a mighty host, a great force, wealth!

11 The heart of her husband doth safely trust in her (attach self in confidence, feel safe to confide in, secure), so that he shall have no need of spoil (because she is his wealth!).

12 She will do him good and not evil all the days of her life. (respectful, doing what is in his best welfare, constant in love, faithful to death)

13 She seeks wool, and flax, and works willingly with her hands. (industrious, diligently seeking, willingly working)

14 She is like the merchants' ships; she brings her food from afar. (effective and thrifty in providing food for her family)

15 She rises also while it is yet night, and gives meat to her household, and a portion to her maidens. (self-starter, providing for those under her authority)

16 She considers a field, and buys it: with the fruit of her hands she plants a vineyard. (enterprising, sees potential in fallow ground, makes profitable decisions, laboring to bring fruit to her venture)

17 She girds her loins with strength, and strengthens her arms. (with bold confidence puts on a belt to protect the smallness of her back, alert physically and mentally courageous, willing to do hard work)

18 She perceives that her merchandise *is* good: her candle goeth not out by night. (confidently understanding the product of her labor is excellent, precious, morally good, willing to work long hours by the light she has even through dark, troublesome circumstances)

19 She lays her hands to the spindle, and her hands hold the distaff. (willing to do painful, monotonous work, resourceful in producing results)

20 She stretches out her hand to the poor; yea, she reaches forth her hands to the needy. (does what she has power to do in compassion for those depressed in mind or circumstances; feeding the destitute)

21 She is not afraid of the snow for her household: for all her household *are* clothed with scarlet. (no fear of adverse circumstances for she has doubly prepared her family physically and spiritually)

22 She makes herself coverings of tapestry; her clothing *is* silk and purple. (labors to clothe herself well knowing she represents her family and God)

23 Her husband is known in the gates, when he sits among the elders of the land. (not she, but her husband, is known and respected as a leader in judicial decisions)

24 She makes fine linen, and sells *it;* and delivers girdles unto the merchant. (prudently sells what she is talented in making and provides to the merchants what might be sold in the marketplace)

25 Strength and honor *are* her clothing; and she shall rejoice in time to come. (clothed in security, majesty and esteem, she confidently can rejoice in whatever the future holds)

26 She opens her mouth with wisdom; and in her tongue *is* the law of kindness. (known for positive words of knowledgeable experience, intelligence and insight; voicing kindness and mercy)

27 She looks well to the ways of her household, and eats not the bread of idleness. (dedicated to her family, peering into the distance to observe and guide the direction her family is going, never satisfied with laziness in herself, nor condoning it in others)

28 Her children arise up, and call her blessed; her husband *also,* and he praises her. (She is successful and prosperous in her children's eyes and her husband's; is the source of his boasting and celebrating)

29 Many daughters have done virtuously, but thou excel them all. (Wow! Many wives have been a great force, valiant, full of virtue, strength, power, able, an army, a mighty host, a wealth, but this woman has ascended higher than all, not satisfied with mediocrity)

30 Favor *is* deceitful, and beauty *is* vain: *but* a woman *that* fears the LORD, she shall be praised. (charm lies and beauty is empty and unsatisfying, but awe and reverence for her Creator who has made a covenant relationship with her is what clothes her with radiant glory)

31 Give her of the fruit of her hands; and let her own works praise her in the gates. (Let her enjoy the results of her labor and the reputation of honor that comes from her sustained mental, physical, and emotional efforts to achieve her assignment from God to fashion and produce a family fit to enter eternity)

Back to the Question: only you can answer it: where will you invest your heart, time, and energy? Work you must! but where? The home is what brings satisfaction – even when life goes haywire and the devil viciously pounces, making you think all is hopeless. You see, making a home = Work as a labor of love = a Paycheck of eternal rewards both here on earth and in heaven = perfect Pleasure = absolute Involvement = crucial Decision Making = effectual Usefulness = bountiful Excitement = abundant Adventure = ultimate Satisfaction.

The power God has given to the woman is incredible! The home should be a foretaste of heaven (no matter where you work), a living parable of our relationship to our Savior and overcoming the trials of life together! Look beyond what you can see with your eyes. Look to the spiritual world that you can only see with your heart and spirit. Woman has been given the most valuable job on earth! She has an enemy that wants to prevent her from doing it and will make the world's way (the forbidden fruit) look most attractive. Remember "... resist the devil, and he will flee from you." (James 4:7) and snuggle close to your hubby! You will quickly learn how it feels to rest in the arms of our Lord.

Our lives are not our own. Our time is limited, only on loan from God, and we will give an account to Him of how it was spent. We must labor hard to take every thought captive and make every work and act intentional for God's glory and honor. That is your purpose in being! Work wherever He has specifically assigned you, rejoicing.

Laboring in Love,
Your Titus 2 momma CK

Beauty from Ashes / Joy from Tears

My Beloved Susanna (& precious new Friend and Sister),

I'm through! All done! Finished, finally! This is a confessional letter. I almost felt hypocritical in some of what I had written; even knowing it is all true and proven in my own life! I learned much on this venture of letter writing - so much more than I ever did teaching this subject to a class of women. I suppose it's because I'm not quite as honest in public, not wanting to be vulnerable by exposing intimate details of my own journey. We always want to put our best foot forward, be admired by others, and all those other warped excuses for dishonesty. But these letters have forced me to be honest, with myself and with the Lord. I certainly want to be honest with you.

You have had your own share of trials in these first years of marriage. Wedded bliss wasn't as smooth sailing as hoped. Some of my advice wasn't too practical in your new world – dismissed as too old-school. Some things have been out of your control. Satan still has some of his demons assigned to you hoping for failure and destruction.

I have talked a lot about suffering and sacrifice. But let's be honest. Who wants to suffer? Who wants to sacrifice to one's own hurt? It troubled me to see you suffer so with the horrible sickness involved in those first few months of pregnancy - truly a curse! I am so sorry you had to endure that, twice. Pain is not an appealing lifestyle to choose. The pain may not necessarily be physical either. Emotional and spiritual pains are often even harder to bear. Pain deep in the heart is the worst. However, sometimes it is chosen for us for our own good and to reveal God's glory. Just remember, Jesus is the Alpha and Omega, the beginning and the end, the Script Writer for your life, knowing your character inside and out. What He has begun, He will bring to completion. You will not be left hanging. The plot of this story is clear and the climax, turning point, and conclusion are written in His own blood! You must trust Him completely with your life and all of your tomorrows.

Physician, heal thyself, you say? Ah, yes, I had my own struggles writing these last letters, searching for the answers to my whys. Words are so easy to say and difficult to live, aren't they? There were struggles for answers and solutions in my own marriage. Can you believe after all these years I haven't yet attained that state of perfection? Just about the time I think I have a good handle on the subject of marriage and oneness and submission and job descriptions – boom! Another lesson to learn is dropped on my desk. I'm still in school, though I would hope to call it graduate school at this stage of life. The tests keep coming. Some are passed. Some have to be retaken. Some of those inoculations are really painful and put one under the weather, fevered for a spell, while the Spirit is doing His work. Some make you downright sick and rendered helpless. But God is doing wonderful things through it all if we are looking with our spiritual eyes.

I am ashamed of my past grumbling. I have complained of the trials and tests that seem so hard to bear; of the attacks from the demons of defeat and despair, doubt and depression; of my own personal self-inflictions of rebellion and pride, self-pity as well as self-reproach. Life is hard and it is so easy to complain. I, too, have been "very afraid, camped at the mouth of the gorges, parked by the Read Sea of vulnerability and impossibility" so that God could prove Himself to be the trustworthy Covenant Keeper.

I can't explain what happened in my own marriage while working on these letters. Sleep apnea took over my beloved's life and a personality change so shadowed the man I loved that I began to question my vows unto death with this man I no longer knew. I attributed much to the devil, to willful rebellion and sin and neglect. I tried so hard to identify it, to find the source of the problem so I could alert my Killer Ts to action. I fervently sought the Father and earnestly gave the Spirit all the freedom that I knew how to give. I know the complement of the Savior's blood had been released to purify our marriage from the enemy. I sought most diligently not to be a source of allergy to my husband, nor an auto-immune disorder to our marriage. Yet it was like a cloud of slumber and apathy settled over us, choking the love, the unity, and the purpose for our existence – and I couldn't do anything to stop it. It wasn't a pretty sight. The devil's accusations had me believing I had no right to write you letters on how to have a good marriage. These letters were tossed to the wayside ...

Tears and confusion dominated my days. God knows... He always knows! I feared the ugliness of thoughts in my own heart that had never been experienced even in the worst of those early years of marriage. I could only rest knowing God knew my blindness and weakness. He intended this all for our good and His glory (John 9). Our good because we "two" were still "one" in His sight. Through it all I knew He was asking me, "Do you trust Me?" I finally heard Him speaking to me, "**...Rise up, my love, my fair one, and come away. For, lo, the winter is past, the rain is over and gone; the flowers appear on the earth; the time of the singing of birds is come... Arise, my love, my fair one, and come away.**" The winter is past? The rain is over? There are flowers and singing birds? No! but yes...! I believed Him even though I could not see any of those things yet – but if He said it, I believed it. I held on to those words from Solomon's Song.

"...weeping may endure for a night, but joy comes in the morning." (Psalm 30:5) It's in the midnight hour of those trials and afflictions, of failures and sin, of lostness and despair that the glorious light of our Savior shines brighter than the noonday sun – changing the heart and mind, even the very reason for living. The fear and doubt and confusion just drove me into His arms of love and protection, teaching me His grace is sufficient and all powerful. **"And he said unto me, My grace** (Divine influence) **is sufficient for thee, for My strength** (miraculous power) **is made perfect** (accomplished) **in weakness** (feebleness, frailty). **Therefore I take pleasure in infirmities** (frailty, sickness), **in reproaches** (insults, injury), **in necessities** (distresses, afflictions), **in persecutions** (unjust affliction of pain), **in distresses** (pressed in from the sides, calamities) **for Christ's sake: for when I am weak** (feeble), **then am I strong** (powerful, capable)." 2 Corinthians 12:9,10. I know I am repeating verses again, but truth is truth and worth repeating. I certainly have not suffered as did the Apostle Paul! however... The dark days and months were His reminder of my weakness, my feebleness in the flesh, and His omnipotent strength accomplishing miraculous things reserved only for Him. I am learning to glory in my infirmities that the power of Christ might rest upon me. This was, by far, my hardest and longest learning experience.

We are prone to wander, prone to leave the God we love, as the beautiful song "Come Thou Fount" so aptly reminds us. Those trials and afflictions that the all-knowing Father allows into our lives are there to teach us, strengthen our faith, or to bring us back into His arms. (Psalm 119:71,75) We just must trust Him.

I came out from under that cloud of confusion and accepted God's grace as sufficient for my circumstances. He spoke to me personally as Father to child, as Friend to friend. He made promises that I believed, even though they were for future days (which, by the way, soon came to pass). I know now how to better take pleasure in my feebleness, in insults and distresses, in afflictions of pain and ca-lamities because I know it only comes for my benefit – that I might know my God more fully, more intimately, more joyfully. When I understand my own weakness and insufficiency then I become powerful - capable. I am not sufficient to write to you about marriage, but He is, and He has chosen to allow me to be His handmaid to do His bidding. My inoculation took. It was the most painful and hardest to bear, but the beauty, joy, and trust that the Spirit brought were worth it all.

In His mercy, God teaches us the beauty of the trials and the joy of the suf-fering. Beauty? Joy? Oh, yes! My darling daughter, can you possibly grasp what God is doing through adversity in our lives? I am seeing it more clearly now than ever, and I so want you to see it, too. This "prosperity gospel" is out of the pit of hell. God has not saved us to pamper us. You will have to go through the struggle yourself, I know, but maybe you can learn some very valuable lessons of life by observation that will prepare and strengthen you for your journey. Our time here is so short with so much to learn, and eternity is forever...

God has a jealous love over us. He has called us to be the Bride of His Son. Jesus sacrificed Himself to purify us and make us His own. He wants to present us to His Father unblemished, **"... a chosen generation, a royal priesthood, an holy na-tion, a peculiar** (purchased possession) **people; that you should show forth the praises of Him who hath called you out of darkness into His marvelous light"**. You have to make up your mind that God has a right to do as He pleases with His own purchased possession. It is only when you submit that He wraps you up in His jealous love and you experience blessings which are reserved only for those who have had the secret revealed (Psalm 25:14). When you gain the attitude of accep-tance of God's dealings with us as good and not to be disputed or resisted, you be-come His own special treasure of great price. The Holy Spirit will rule your life with a personal, jealous guardianship. It will be okay if others receive your honor; you will learn humility. You will undoubtedly receive some persecution that you might be privileged to share in our Savior's sufferings. He gives you the true riches of eternity, seated in the heavenlies with Christ. If you choose to be this special treasure to Him, He will not allow you to take your life with Him frivolously, but will demand your faithfulness in every circumstance. He is growing a delicious fruit in your life that will bring Him pleasure and glory. Whatever He brings into your life, you can know that it is for His purpose and your good, that you may reflect the image of our dear Savior to a lost and doomed world, all the while you are being dressed in white to live in His Kingdom for eternity, His Bride matured into the Wife.

Do your best to draw from my life, amidst the successes and the failures, and see the glories God has bestowed upon me as I have followed His Word. I know no one more blessed than myself! What a fantastic husband and family I have! What a life! What a God and Savior! I pray God will take you even further into the beautiful, joyful life of fellowship with Him. Put your mind and heart and spirit upon Him, and serve Him with all your strength as the woman of God He created you to be. Trust Him! Whatever you are experiencing right now – trials, temptations, disasters – each one is an opportunity to know God in a way you would never know Him otherwise. Your heart is crying out for an intimacy with Jesus that can only be found in desperation for His tender touch. He created you for that intimate fellowship with Himself. He longs for it more than you could possibly imagine. He loves you more than you will ever understand until you experience His moving heaven and earth just for you. His power is yours for the asking. He delights in your presence before Him. He is longing for you to delight in His presence. "Come away with Me, My beloved, My fair one."

Joyfully yours through it all,
Mom (CK & 2nd momma)

POSTSCRIPT

Do you believe in miracles?

*I*f you are still reading, I have a story to tell you. Procrastination (disobedience disguised as good intentions "to do it later") is a cause of sin for me and great disappointment to the Lord. It took too long to get these letters to my own Susie, and tragically much too long to get them into book form for you. But I had found important jobs: secretary for our church, women's ministries, handbell director, Sunday School teacher, school teacher to my twin boys, and (after graduation) soaking up the last Mom days with my last babies before giving them up to their brides. They married and my Beloved husband reclaimed his wife, after being a full-time mom for 45 years! It was then harder than ever to concentrate on you and these letters. But that didn't lift the mandate from the Lord and He admonished me regularly.

Then, in 2013, on a Saturday night, Susie told us she was leaving David, had never loved him, and didn't want to hear any of that religious stuff. She "read" my letters as a courtesy to her mother, but she had seen words without seeing and heard without hearing. The letters were too contrary to her ideas of liberation from a childhood, and now a marriage, with too many boundaries. She was ready to be her own boss. This was the child for which I had prayed for ten years to conceive, the fulfillment of a mother's heart and answered prayers! I cried and agonized in prayer all night over her as my blood pressure climbed. By Monday Wayne knew he had to get me to the hospital, thinking I had had a stroke. It was a brain hemorrhage, but MRIs showed it had miraculously quit bleeding before the doctor opened my skull. As I lay in ICU for

10 days, drifting in and out of consciousness, I prayed, offering my death if it would bring Susie to Him. He gently reminded me He had already died for her! Her salvation was in His death, not mine! Duly corrected, I was left wondering what this was about.

The episode was devastating physically (disconnecting my brain from the left side of my body) and emotionally (revoking not only my secretarial skills but also my misplaced priorities and plans). What a joy that experience proved to be for me!!! Doctors didn't think I would walk again, much less care for myself, advising to have me put in a nursing home. No man on earth could have proved to be more like Jesus than my beloved Wayne! He took me home, waiting on me hand and foot, doing all the cooking, cleaning, shopping, laundry, bathing me physically with water and emotionally and spiritually with his love – all the while still preaching and ministering to his congregation. What I learned during those months as he nursed me back to health would fill another book. Our love had already grown beyond what most couples ever get to experience, matured and endured what Satan hurled at us. But I never dreamed I could love him so intensely, beyond my wildest expectations! Clearer than ever, I saw Jesus, my King, - through my husband - tending to His wounded bride and I was made well. And Wayne and Carolyn lived perfectly ever after...

No, we are both still living in fleshly bodies and susceptible to selfish desires. We seldom get cross with one another, but it does occasionally happen. (Can you believe it?!) I recovered and felt an urgency from God to complete this book and get it to you somehow. I tried teaching the principles once more at our church to a new group of women. It was a good experience but did not soothe my guilty conscience. I did "work" on these Letters for you but not with the diligence needed. Satan was still bullying me.

(By the way, Susie is still married, although in name only, living separately but civilly sharing their two beautiful, but confused, children. Still hoping and praying...)

Then, November 2016, I had a massive heart attack that knocked me for a loop and left only 38% usage of my heart. Again, Wayne took me home to pamper and encourage and remind me I was his reason to be and do. Still, the letters haunted me. Still, I procrastinated in finding a way to "finish" and "publish", hearing the hiss of "who do you think you are?"

April 29, 2017, I died! Really! I complained about having trouble breathing as we went to bed, but that was not unusual after the heart incident. Hubby awoke early in the night to check on me; I was lifeless, no breath, no pulse, eyes set. He immediately began CPR and called 911. Paramedics worked on me for another 30 minutes with no pulse, no blood pressure, no breath, using the paddles 3 times to shock life back into my heart, to no avail. They pronounced me dead, apologized to my husband, and Wayne began calling the children to tell them I was gone. They loaded me on the stretcher to take me away when one paramedic said: "I feel a pulse here!" They hooked me back up to the monitors and my pulse was 118 (making up for lost time?), blood pressure, 154/90 – no more flat line! Off to the hospital they swooped me, wanting to do all kinds of invasive surgery to look for a cause, to check on that stint, to insert a defibrillator in my chest, to observe me a while... No, no, and no again! It worried Wayne for a bit because I didn't know him or my children. Still, he thanked God for my life and vowed to care for me even brain damaged. My memory began to return; my Darling rescued me from the hospital the next day, took me home, and again my health was restored with his coddling and God's grace. The bruised muscles and ribs from intensive CPR were just a friendly reminder of the miracle of life God was extending to us. I am fully recovered with no ill effects... waiting for the final call home, "Come on, My Child, it's really time now."

I have all sorts of explanations for my health and the new lessons learned (enough for another book) – the first being, I believe in miracles! God is Lord of my life and has blessed me with some wake-up calls to put into practice Psalm 90. I must number my days, knowing they are limited (no more procrastination), and ask Him to establish the work of my hands (no longer will Satan shame me and make me feel unworthy to write about the mystery of marriage). God has made me glad in my afflictions; He has revealed His work in me and His glory to my children! I thank Him for restoring my mind, heart, and breath, that I might praise Him and complete the work He called me to do before I meet Him face to face. My husband needs me still. I pray you needed to read what you are reading, and that God will prolong your life that you might make your husband the ruling king he was created to be and you might receive your queenly crown! Who knows... maybe that book on motherhood will get finished as well... God bless!!!

Living day by day in His power & love,
CK

P.S. I would love to hear from you – know your name, where you are in your walk through life, something of your family, and especially your thoughts as you read these letters. I pray they give you a new perspective of your value as God's chosen vessel. Email me at Titus2mommaCK@gmail.com. If there is not a supplement at the end of this book with verses to answer the questions: Protect what? Protect from what? Protect how? then please email me and I will send it right to you!

The Mystery of Marriage through Adam's Prime Rib

POST POSTSCRIPT

To the Women of the Church

The information in these letters on the immune system, once understood in the analogy of marriage, can also be used in understanding the role of women in the Church. We are told in Ephesians 5 that the relationship between husband and wife is a picture of the union of Christ and His Church. With Christ as our Head and believers as the Body, the men are the first defense of that Body, (1) as the skin, being the outer covering protecting all that is within, (2) responsible for exercising the Body by faith, (3) feeding the Body nourishment from the Word, keeping it morally and doctrinally pure, and (4) resting in the confidence of God's promises. That then leaves the women of the Church to do what they have learned through their own marriages, to be the immune system of that Body, (1) covering a multitude of sin with love, (2) serving the Body silently behind the scenes, (3) recognizing the enemy, and (4) declaring war through prayer, the Sword of the Word, and dependence on the power of Christ's blood. When women don't know their responsibility, fail to understand their own value, and live in competition with the men, is it any wonder that the Church of today is so weak and sickly in carrying out the work of the Lord on earth? [When the Church is united and functioning as one body, the natural result is offspring being added to the Kingdom. It would make an interesting Bible study from that viewpoint... Are you up to the challenge?

SUPPLEMENT

SCRIPTURES TO ANSWER THE QUESTIONS...
Protect What? Protect From What?? Protect How???

*O*kay, so much information on the immune system and the job description of a help meet for your man...but just what does he need protected and from what does he need to be protected, and precisely how does a woman go about doing what is expected? This is the Bible study part. You must have your "Teacher" (Thymus) training if you are to recognize the enemy from which he needs protection as well as the self to be protected and strengthened. This will get you started...

The following A.B.C. 1,2,3, a-z outline has been limited almost entirely to the books of Psalms and Proverbs, merely by personal challenge to study those two books during my own Teacher training through a personal crisis. The New Testament is FULL of particular, direct instructions to women and their conduct, and the book of James is such a concise parallel to Proverbs, it was difficult to limit Scripture references to these two Old Testament books. This is not an exhaustive list, however "exhausting" it may be to complete, but rather an outline with which to start your own study, adding those particular needs of your husband and ways God leads you to meet those needs. Read from Genesis through Revelation and you will find God speaking to you from every page; write it down, add it to your list, and meet the challenge to be the wife God created you to be... **"Thy hands have made** (refined, fashioned) **me and fashioned me** (firmly es tablished, readied, prepared, brought into an indisputable existence); **give me understanding** (insight, superior knowledge, distinguishing between good and evil) **that I may learn** (be trained and educated in) **Thy commandments** (precepts, clear-cut directives, particular conditions of Your covenant). Psalm 119:73

Your Commitment to your Husband:

"A virtuous woman (a wife that is a force, valiant, full of virtue, a strength, an army, a great force, a mighty host) **is the crown** (a royal crown, from a root word meaning encircle, surround for protection) **of her husband, but she who causes shame** (disappointment of opinion, hope or expectation, causing public disgrace and confusion, humiliation and shattered emotions, utter defeat, disillusionment and broken spirit) **is like rottenness** (progressive decay) **in his bones** (strength, substance, life)." Proverbs 12:4

"**May the Lord answer you in the day of trouble** (a tight place, an opponent)...**may He send help** (aid, protection) **from the sanctuary** (sacred place or thing; a most holy consecrated, dedicated thing) **and strengthen** (support, comfort, establish, hold up, refresh, strengthen)..." Psalm 20:1, 2

Keep in mind Satan's purpose to kill, steal, and destroy, and remember well the wiles and methods of our enemy. Here are some particular areas in a man's life that need the protection of a virtuous wife:

A.   Protect his:

1. love / fear of the Lord -

- *Psalm 18:1*
- *Psalm 25:12-14*
- *Psalm 33:18, 19*
- *Psalm 34:7*
- *Psalm 81:8-16*
- *Psalm 90:11*
- *Psalm 103:11-13, 17*
- *Psalm 111:10*
- *Psalm 112:1*
- *Psalm 128:1*
- *Psalm 147:11*
- *Proverbs 3:7, 8*
- *Proverbs 9:10*
- *Proverbs 14:27*

love / reverence of holy things, the name of God, the Word of God

- *Psalm 5:7*
- *Psalm 19:7-11*
- *Psalm 26:8*
- *Psalm 29:1-2*
- *Psalm 46:10*
- *Psalm 86:11-12*
- *Psalm 93:5*
- *Psalm 99:1-3*
- *Psalm 119:161-16*
- *Proverbs 30:5-6*

2. time:

- *Psalm 90:12*

- *Psalm 39:4-5*

- *Psalm 32:6*

- *Ecclesiastes 3:1-8 (-17)*

a. personal:

- *Psalm 31:15*

- *Psalm 90:10*

b. family:

- *Psalm 127:3*

- *Deuteronomy 6:7*

c. prayer:

- *Psalm 55:17*

- *Psalm 69:13*

- *Psalm 116:1-2*

- *Psalm 51*

d. study:

- *Psalm 111:2*

- *Psalm 119:7*

- *2 Timothy 2:15*

e. service:

- *Psalm 51:13*

- *Psalm 100:2*

- *John 12:26*

3. reputation:

- *Proverbs 22:1*

- *Proverbs 27:21*

- *Proverbs 31:23*

4. **heritage (children, grandchildren)**

- *Psalm 71:18*
- *Psalm 102:18*
- *Psalm 112:1-3*
- *Psalm 127:3*
- *Proverbs 17:6*

5. **heart**

- *Proverbs 4:23*
- *Proverbs 14:30*
- *Proverbs 15:14*
- *Psalm 40:12*
- *Psalm 69:20*

6. **trust in me**

- *Proverbs 31:11 (safely confided in as to be secure and without fear)*
- *Proverbs 12:4*

7. **trust / confidence in the Lord / salvation**

- *Psalm 17:15*
- *Psalm 28:7*
- *Psalm 31:5*
- *Psalm 33:21*
- *Psalm 34:8*
- *Psalm 37:40*
- *Psalm 49:15*
- *Psalm 112:7*
- *Psalm 118:8, 9, 17*
- *Proverbs 20:22*
- *Psalm 91*

8. dreams / expectations / desires

- *Proverbs 10:24*
- *Proverbs 11:23*
- *Proverbs 13:12, 19*
- *Psalm 21:2*
- *Psalm 27:4*
- *Psalm 37:4*

9. vows

- *Proverbs 20:25*
- *Psalm 50:14*
- *Psalm 56:12*
- *Psalm 76:11*
- *Psalm 116:18*
- *Ecclesiastes 5:2-5*

10. honor

- *Psalm 8:4-6*
- *Psalm 21:5*
- *Psalm 112:9*
- *Proverbs 29:23*

11. humility / meekness

- *Proverbs 15:33*
- *Proverbs 16:19*
- *Proverbs 22:4*
- *Psalm 25:9*
- *Psalm 39:4-5*
- *Psalm 86:1*
- *Psalm 138:6*
- *Psalm 144:3-4*

The Mystery of Marriage through Adam's Prime Rib

12. integrity / innocence

- *Proverbs 20:7*
- *Proverbs 10:9*
- *Proverbs 11:3*
- *Psalm 7:8*
- *Psalm 25:21*
- *Psalm 41:12*

13. discretion / prudence

- *Proverbs 2:11*
- *Proverbs 14:15,18*
- *Proverbs 19:11*
- *Proverbs 22:3 (27:12)*
- *Psalm 112:5*

14. faithfulness

- *Proverbs 14:5*
- *Proverbs 20:6*
- *Proverbs 27:6*
- *Proverbs 11:13*
- *Psalm 101:6*

15. song / joy

- *Psalm 35:9*
- *Psalm 40:3*
- *Psalm 61:8*
- *Psalm 69:30*
- *Psalm 51:12*
- *Psalm 119:54*
- *Psalm 118:14, 24*
- *Psalm 137:4*

16. authority/submission to authority

- *Proverbs 28:1*
- *Proverbs 29:2*
- *Proverbs 20:2*
- *1 Corinthians 11:3 / Genesis 3:16*

17. home

- *Proverbs 15:6*
- *Proverbs 15:27*
- *Proverbs 17:1*
- *Proverbs 21:9*
- *Proverbs 31:21, 27*
- *Psalm 101:2*

18. foundation

- *Psalm 11:3*
- *Proverbs 10:25*
- *1 Corinthians 3:11*

19. diligence (eager, incisive) / determination

- *Proverbs 10:4*
- *Proverbs 12:24,27*
- *Proverbs 21:5*
- *Proverbs 22:29*

20. youthfulness / strength / masculinity

- *Psalm 103:5*
- *Psalm 92:13,14*
- *Proverbs 20:29*
- *Isaiah 40:30, 31*

21. love for me

- *Proverbs 5:18, 19*
- *Proverbs 15:17*
- *Proverbs 31:11, 12*

22. witness / testimony

- *Psalm 22:22*
- *Psalm 34:1-3*
- *Psalm 35:28*
- *Psalm 51:13, 15*
- *Psalm 119:111*

23. forgiveness

- *Psalm 32:1-5*
- *Psalm 34:22*
- *Psalm 130:3,4*

24. thankfulness / gratitude

- *Psalm 30:11, 12*
- *Psalm 75:1*
- *Psalm 92:1*
- *Psalm 116:17*

25. godly friendships

- *Psalm 119:63*
- *Proverbs 18:24*
- *Proverbs 27:6, 9, 10*
- *Proverbs 27:17*

26. protective nature for family, poor and defenseless / tenderness / generosity / kindness

- *Psalm 41:1*
- *Psalm 82:3,4*
- *Psalm 144:12*
- *Proverbs 21:13*
- *Proverbs 19:22*
- *Proverbs 22:9*
- *Proverbs 27:23*
- *Proverbs 31:8, 9*
- *Psalm 112:4, 5, 9*

27. life expectancy (long life) / hope for eternity

- *Proverbs 10:27*
- *Proverbs 9:11*
- *Psalm 17:15*
- *Psalm 73:24*

28. righteousness

- *Proverbs 11:4-6*
- *Proverbs 12:7*
- *Proverbs 16:8*
- *Proverbs 21:21*

29. labor / work / rest

- *Proverbs 14:23*
- *Psalm 128:2*
- *Proverbs 24:27*
- *Proverbs 27:23-27*
- *Psalm 55:6*
- *Psalm 127:2*

The Mystery of Marriage through Adam's Prime Rib

30. individuality / opinions / preferences / privacy / pocketbook

- *Psalm 139:14, 22*
- *Proverbs 22:16*
- *Proverbs 22:26, 27*
- *Proverbs 11:24, 25*
- *Psalm 112:3*
- *Proverbs 31:10-31*

B. Protect him from:

1. pride

- *Proverbs 11:2*
- *Proverbs 16:5, 18*
- *Proverbs 21:4*
- *Proverbs 26:12*
- *Proverbs 29:23*
- *Psalm 12:3, 4*
- *Psalm 138: 6*
- *Psalm 144:3, 4*

2. lust of eyes

- *Psalmalm101:3*
- *Proverbs 4:25*
- *Proverbs 7:10-27*
- *Proverbs 23:1-5*

3. lust of flesh / greed

- *Proverbs 1:19*
- *Proverbs 14:12*
- *Proverbs 15:27*
- *Proverbs 21:25-26*
- *Proverbs 25:16*
- *Psalm 106:14-15*
- *Romans 8:5*

4. jealousy / foolishness / silliness

- *Proverbs 27:4*
- *Proverbs 6:34*
- *Proverbs 19:3*
- *Proverbs 29:11*
- *Psalm 69:5-6*

5. envy / covetousness

- *Proverbs 3:31*
- *Proverbs 14:30*
- *Proverbs 24:1, 19-20*
- *Psalm 37:1*
- *Psalm 73:3-14*
- *James 3:14-16*

6. his own tongue / slandering others / lies / gossip

- *Proverbs 4:24*
- *Proverbs 10:18*
- *Proverbs 19:5*
- *Proverbs 29:20*
- *Psalm 34:13*
- *Proverbs 21:23*
- *Proverbs 24:28-29*
- *James 3:5, 6*

7. selfishness

- *Proverbs 18:1-2*
- *Proverbs 14:14*

8. anger / quick temper / vengeance / impulsiveness

- *Psalm 37:8*
- *Proverbs 14:17, 29*
- *Proverbs 15:18*
- *Proverbs 16:32*
- *Proverbs 25:28*
- *Psalm 18:47*
- *Psalm 59:8-10*
- *Psalm 94:1*
- *Proverbs 24:29*

9. stubbornness / rebellion

- *Proverbs 29:1*
- *Psalm 81:12*
- *Salaam 95:8, 11*
- *1 Samuel 15:23*

10. doubt

- *Psalm 78:19-22*
- *Psalm 78:32*
- *Psalm 73:21*
- *James 1:6, 7*

11. fret / worry

- *Psalm 37:1*
- *Psalm 94:19*
- *Proverbs 24:19*
- *Philippians 4:6*

12. fear

- *Proverbs 29:25*
- *Psalm 55:4-5*

13. depression / confusion / distress / fatigue

- *Psalm 143:4*
- *Psalm 42:11*
- *Proverbs 12:25*

14. disappointment / defeat / discouragement

- *Proverbs 15:22*
- *Proverbs 13:12*
- *Psalm 61:2*
- *Psalm 69:1- 3*
- *Psalm 118:18*

15. bitterness / hatred

- *Proverbs 14:10*
- *Proverbs 26:24*
- *Hebrews 12:15*

16. foolish friends / flattering lips

- *Proverbs 13:20*
- *Proverbs 14:7*
- *Proverbs 14:8*
- *Proverbs 14:9*
- *Proverbs 22:24-25*
- *Proverbs 23:20-21*

The Mystery of Marriage through Adam's Prime Rib

- *Proverbs 28:7*
- *Proverbs 29:9*
- *Ephesians 5:6-7*
- *Psalm 106:35-36*
- *Psalm 12:2*

17. seductress

- *Proverbs 2:16*
- *Proverbs 5:3-5*
- *Proverbs 6:24-26*
- *Proverbs 7:5*
- *1Corinthians 6:18*

18. opposition / enemies / wickedness / evil

- *Psalm 3:1-2*
- *Psalm 12:8*
- *Psalm 17:8-12*
- *Psalm 54:3*
- *Psalm 56:2*
- *Psalm 59:1-2*
- *Psalm 140:1-5*

19. reproach / lies / gossip

- *Psalm 31:13*
- *Psalm 41:5- 9*
- *Psalm 44:16*
- *Psalm 64:2-4*
- *Psalm 69:19-20*
- *Psalm 109:2-3*

20. presumptuous sin / grieving the Spirit

- *Psalm 19:12-13*
- *Psalm 106:24-25*
- *Numbers 15:30*
- *Ephesians 4:30*

21. alcohol / drugs / bad habits

- *Proverbs 20:1*
- *Proverbs 23:29-35*
- *Proverbs 31:4-5*
- *Ephesians 5:18*
- *1Corinthians 6:19-20*

22. ungodly counsel

- *Psalm1:1*
- *Proverbs 1:10-19*

23. temptation / judgment / wrath of God

- *Proverbs 4:14- 15*
- *Proverbs 6:16-19*
- *Psalm 6:1-2*
- *Psalm 11:6*
- *1Corinthians 7:5*

24. shame

- *Proverbs 12:4*
- *Proverbs 6:32-33*
- *Proverbs 9:7*
- *Psalm 25:2, 20*
- *Psalm 31:17*

The Mystery of Marriage through Adam's Prime Rib

25. hypocrisy / being a stumbling block

- *Proverbs 11:9*
- *Proverbs 28:13*
- *Psalm 32:3-4*
- *Proverbs 26:24-26*

26. frivolity / idleness / slothfulness / futility / apathy

- *Proverbs 12:27*
- *Proverbs 14:23*
- *Proverbs 15:19*
- *Proverbs 19:15*
- *Proverbs 20:13*
- *Proverbs 21:25*
- *Proverbs 24:30-34*
- *Psalm 127:1-2*
- *Proverbs 21:13*

27. rejecting godly rebuke / reproof

- *Proverbs 1:25, 26, 30*
- *Proverbs 9:8, 9*
- *Proverbs 15:31, 32*
- *Proverbs 27:5, 6*
- *Proverbs 28:9*
- *Proverbs 29:1*
- *Psalm 141:5*

28. contentious wife

- *Proverbs 19:13*
- *Proverbs 21:9, 19*
- *Proverbs 27:15, 16*

C. How?:

Memorize...

"He who finds a wife finds a good thing, and obtains favor from the Lord." Proverbs 18:22

"Houses and riches are an inheritance from fathers, but a prudent wife is from the Lord." Proverbs 19:14

"It is better to dwell in a corner of a housetop, than in a house shared with a contentious woman" Proverbs 21:9

"It is better to dwell in the wilderness than with a contentious and an angry woman." Proverbs 21:19

"A foolish woman is clamorous (noisy, much to do): she is simple (seducible), and knows (understands) nothing (failure)." Proverbs 9:13

1. **Be a help, aid, to my husband by preparing myself spiritually, morally, and physically:**

    a. fear nothing but the Lord...

    - *Proverbs 1:7*
    - *Proverbs 14:26-27*
    - *Proverbs 31:30*
    - *Psalm 27:1-3*
    - *Psalm 76:7*
    - *Psalm 130:4*

    ---

    b. learn the nature of God: merciful, gracious, slow to anger, forgiving; having experienced that mercy in salvation, I now must strive to reflect God's nature in my attitude/actions...

    - *Psalm 103:8-10*

c. understand the beauty & wonder of my creation and purpose...

Psalm 139

vs 1-6 God's omniscience - He knows everything about me and understands, my thoughts, my husband, my circumstances / I accept my frailty and His magnificence

vs 7-12 God's omnipresence - He is everywhere at all times, never leaving me, no matter how dark it may become / *I accept His presence and my circumstances*

vs 13-16 God's omnificence - His unlimited creative abilities are marvelous and awesome / *I accept myself*

vs 17-24 God's omnipotence - He is almighty with unlimited power and influence to make His precious thoughts of me come true in my life that I might bring glory to Him / *I completely yield to His power!*

---

d. seek wisdom and understanding, Proverbs 8

to find favor from the Lord, Proverbs 4:5-9

and knowledge to fill rooms, Proverbs 24:3,4

to be a source of wisdom and understanding to my husband, Proverbs 3:13-18

---

e. stay in the way of the Lord / trust Him to direct my way and reveal His secrets to me

- *Proverbs 10:29*
- *Psalm 139:23-24*
- *Psalm 37:5-6*
- *Psalm 25:14*

---

f. know that as one who protects and tends the fig tree eats of its fruit,

so one who waits (guards, protects, attends, hedges about) on his master is honored - God honors the wife that guards, protects, attends to, hedges about her husband, *Proverbs 27:18*

He is with me as I uphold him, *Psalm 54:4*

---

g. know the state of my flocks (family - my life work)

- *Proverbs 27:23*
- *Proverbs 31:21, 27*

---

h. give thanks and sing praises to God, declare His lovingkindness in the morning, faithfulness at night, for He has made me glad through His work; I will triumph in the works of His hands

- *Psalm 104:33-34*
- *Psalm 92:1- 4*

---

i. don't be lazy, slothful! it takes work, hard work to fulfill my vocation,

- *Proverbs 31:27*
- *Proverbs 6:6-11*
- *Proverbs 18:9*

---

j. learn to control my tongue,

- *Psalm 141:3*
- *Proverbs 15:1, 28*
- *Proverbs 29:20*

keep my mouth shut and trust God,

- *Proverbs 10:19, 20*
- *Proverbs 17:14*
- *Proverbs 26:20*
- *1 Peter 3:1*

The Mystery of Marriage through Adam's Prime Rib

know I hold the power of death and life in my tongue,

- *Proverbs 18:21*

- *Proverbs 15:4*

- *Proverbs 15:23b*

---

k. have a faithful spirit and keep private matters private!

- *Proverbs 11:13*

- *Proverbs 25:9-10*

---

l. be slow to get angry and overlook transgressions,

- *Proverbs 19:11*

let love cover all sin,

- *Proverbs 10:12; 17:9*

---

m. be a prayer warrior / make a list of scriptures to pray for him daily

- *Psalm 130:1-8*

- *Psalm 84:8*

- *Psalm 34:4*

- *Proverbs 15:8b*

- *James 5:16*

---

 n. understand submission, meekness and humility –

- *Ephesians 5:22-24; 1 Peter 3:4; Phil. 2:3-11*

reject "spoil" of feminism

- *Proverbs 16:18-19*

accept his authority, reproof, exhortation

- *Proverbs 25:12*

o. learn discretion (taste, perception, intelligence) rather than

  outer beauty,

• *Proverbs 11:22*

discretion will produce a lovely woman, inside and out,

• *Proverbs 31:22, 25-31*

---

p. keep myself pure, chaste, consecrated for God and my husband

• *Proverbs 31:11*

• *Psalm 51:7, 10*

• *Psalm 24:4-5*

• *Psalm 26:1-8*

• *1 Peter 3:2*

• *Philippians 4:8*

---

q. recognize worthless, perverse people and avoid

• *Proverbs 6:12-19*

• *Proverbs 16:27-30*

---

r. choose his loving favor over career, money, friends

• *Proverbs 22:1*

• *Proverbs 15:27*

dress for him, cook just for him, give myself to him, remember I was created for him! Be feminine so he wants to be masculine!

---

s. accept my position as the woman God created for my husband,

  believing the line fallen to me is pleasant, the inheritance good,

• *Psalm 16:5-6*

  that He will counsel me and I will not be moved, *Psalm 16:7-8*

  that He will show me the path of life, fullness of joy, pleasures forevermore, *Psalm 16:11*

  determine to turn wholly to the course of life God created for me as help meet for my husband, *Psalm 50:23*

The Mystery of Marriage through Adam's Prime Rib

t. know that my role as mother of his children means I am the "bond of the family" (Hebrew meaning of mother) and must bond my children's love and affection to other family members, but especially to Daddy, creating a bond that cannot be broken (same role as God's Spirit)

- *Proverbs 29:15, 17*
- *Proverbs 1:8*

---

u. live in the present and for the future, putting the past behind

- *Proverbs 31:10-31*
- *Psalm 25:7*

---

v. know where my help is from, Psalm 121

that I may perform my job as my husband's help,

- *Psalm 90:16-17*
- *Psalm 18:28-42*
- *Psalm 144:1-2*

cry out to God Most High who performs all things for me, Psalm 57:2

---

w. be strong in the Lord

- Proverbs 24:10
- Proverbs 31:25
- Psalm 29:11

know where my strength comes from / set my heart on pilgrimage, going from strength to strength, Psalm 84:5-7

---

x. rest in the knowledge that God knows my heart, my limitations, and understands my frailties, Psalm 103:14

- *Psalm 44:21*

2. As a "virtuous" wife (a force, an army, valor, strength, able, a band of soldiers, great forces, a mighty host) be the aid, the protection, the help, that fits my husband exactly, completing him:

   a. be his crown, Proverbs 12:4 - Ps 140:7

---

   b. encourage his reverence and fear of God,
   • *Psalm 119:120*
   • *Psalm 89:7*
   • *Psalm 147:11*
   that he might be wise, Proverbs 3:7-8
   that he might receive God's goodness and protection, *Psalm 31:19,20*
   • *Proverbs 14:26-27*
   that he might understand the secrets of the Lord, *Psalm 25:14*
   that he might be forgiven, *Psalm 130:3-4*
   that he might have his life extended, *Proverbs 9:10-11*
   • *Proverbs 4:10-11*
   • *Proverbs 3:2*
   that he might hate evil,
   • *Proverbs 8:13 -*
   that he might have his desires fulfilled, prayers answered,
   • *Psalm 145:19*
   • *Psalm 147:11*
   that his home might be established,
   • *Psalm 128:1-6*

---

   c. secure his "knowing" the Lord,
   • *Psalm 9:10*
   • *Psalm 91:14*
   (John 17:13)
   (I Peter 3:1-4)

d. keep him in church at all costs, Psalm 27:4

• *Psalm 26:8*

• *Psalm 84:4,10*

that he might understand! Psalm 73:13-17

---

e. keep him in the Word,

• *Psalm 119:9-11... 97-104...*

make time available for him to read,

• *Proverbs 22:17-21*

to study, seek out what God is doing,

• *Psalm 111:2*

to meditate,

• *Psalm 63:5,6; 119:15, 97, 99, 148*

...and to do God's Word, Psalm 119:57, 60, 112

• *Psalm 90:17*

as he rightly divides the Word of truth (2 Timothy 2:15), his priorities will find the path of life, fullness of joy in His presence, and pleasures forevermore,

• *Psalm 16:11*

from the Word he will find wisdom which reproves, brings safety/security from evil, *Proverbs 1:23,33*

armed with the Word he can execute vengeance, bind kings, demonstrate honor from God, *Psalm 149:6-9*

---

f. encourage him to seek wisdom and find knowledge & discretion & prudence, *Proverbs 9*

the principal thing, *Proverbs 4:5-9*

to use what he has found to curb anger & impulsive reactions, *Proverbs 19:11*

to be life to his soul, to walk in safety, to be confident in Lord,

• *Proverbs 3:21-26*

to control his mouth,

• *Psalm 19:14*

• *Psalm 39:1*

• *Psalm 141:3*

g. make his foundation sure, Psalm 11:3 - "If the foundations (a basis, purpose, moral support) be destroyed (pulled down in pieces, beaten down, overthrown, ruined utterly), what can the righteous do?"

• *Psalm 16:8*

• *Proverbs 12:3*

honor him as my spiritual and moral leader,

• *Psalm 8:4-5*

• *Proverbs 31:3*

• *Proverbs 27:18*

(I Corinthians 11:3)

(1 Peter 3:6)

(Ephesians 5:33)

follow him in worship,

• *Psalm 29:2*

---

h. do all I can to fulfill his hopes and desires (personal, vocational, spiritual),

• *Proverbs 13:12, 19*

• *Psalm 37:4*

• *Psalm 145:15-16*

---

i. express contentment and encouragement, especially while he must wait upon the Lord,

• *Psalm 27:14*

• *Psalm 33:20-22*

• *Psalm 37:7-11*

• *Psalm 69:3*

• *Psalm 147:6*

• *Proverbs 30:32 25*

j. build confidence in times of fear, distress, trouble,

• *Psalm 3:1-8*

• *Psalm 27:1-3*

• *Psalm 23:4*

• *Psalm 56:3-4-11*

• *Psalm 91:1-16*

remind him how God avenges His own,

• *Psalm 18:47-48*

encourage him to seek the Lord in prayer,

• *Psalm 119:169,170*

• *Psalm 5:2,3*

• *Psalm 142:1-7*

pray *Psalm 143:7-12* for him - "cause him to hear...cause him to know... deliver him...teach him...lead him ...revive him...cut off his enemies..."

---

k. direct him back to the faithfulness of God when men fail him,

• *Psalm 41:9-11*

• *Psalm 60:11-12*

• *Psalm 89:33-34*

• *Psalm 109:4-5, 26-27*

• *Psalm 27:10*

build his faith by remembering with him how God has worked in days gone by,

• *Psalm 66*

• *Psalm 77:11-14*

• *Psalm 119:52*

• *Psalm 78*

• *Psalm 143:5*

l. remind him that "success" only comes from God,

- *Proverbs 16:1, 9*
- *Psalm 44:3*
- *Psalm 138:8*
- *Psalm 113:7-8*
- *Daniel 6*

---

m. stick with him through the bad times, judgments, testings,

- *Psalm 38*
- *Psalm 30:5, 11-12*
- *Psalm 39:10-13*
- *Psalm 88:6-9*
- *Psalm 118:18*
- *Psalm 119:75*
- *Proverbs 3:11-12*
- *Psalm 11:5*
- *Psalm 66:10-12*
- *Psalm 80:5-6,12-13*

---

n.keep his heart merry, *Proverbs 15:13, 15, 30*

- *Proverbs 17:22*

keep his heart fixed on God,

- *Psalm 57:7-11*

praising God together, Psalm 34:3

- *Psalm 146:2*
- *Psalm 147:1*

keep him singing! Psalm 61:8

- *Ps 33:1-3*

• *Psalm 40:3*

• *Psalm 42:8*

• *Psalm 97:1-2*

• *Psalm 149:1,5*

(2 Chronicles 20:20-22!)

---

o. make the words of my mouth:

wise, *Proverbs 12:18;*   Proverbs 15:2, 7

soft, 15:1   timely, 15:23

sweet, 16:21   pleasant, 16:24

knowledgeable, 20:15   patient and gentle, 25:15

with the law of kindness, 31:26

no nagging, demanding, tantrums, spreading gossip

---

p. overcome his depression with good words, *Proverbs 12:25*

• *Proverbs 15:30*

• *Psalm 34:8-10*

---

q. protect his reputation: by my conduct, reputation of good

  works, household run well, respect to my husband; he will be

  respected and honored in community,

• *Proverbs 31:23*

• *Proverbs 27:21*

• *Proverbs 22:1*

defend him from criticism, reproach, gossip / be on his side /

be a faithful ambassador

• *Proverbs 13:17*   *Psalm 101:7b*

r. praise him daily!

• *Proverbs 25:27; 27:2, 21*

give him a reputation he wants to live up to; the more I brag on him, the less he has to; the more I build him up, boast, pat his back, the more humble he becomes, *Psalm 131:1*

humility will keep him from shame and bring him salvation and honor, • • • • *Psalm 149:4*

• *Proverbs 11:2*

• *Psalm 147:6*

• *Proverbs 22:4*

• *Proverbs 30:32*

---

s. pray for boldness & encourage him to witness, give testimony of God's goodness,

• *Psalm 22:22*

• *Psalm 51:12-13*

• *Psalm 109:30*

• *Psalm 66:16*

• *Psalm 126:5-6*

• *Psalm 119:136*

• *Proverbs 11:30*

---

t. guard him from wrong "friends", *Proverb 4:14; 14:7*

• *Psalm 1*

• *Psalm 26:4-5*

be a source of counsel and encourage him to seek godly counsel,

• *Proverbs 15:22*

• *Proverbs 11:14*

• *Proverbs 24:6*

help him accept godly reproof from real friends,

• *Proverbs 15:31-32*

• *Proverbs 27:6*

• *Psalm 141:5*

u. encourage him to be active, busy diligent,

• *Proverbs 13:4*

give no room for slothfulness, *Proverb 15:19*

• *Proverbs 6:6-11*

• *Psalm 128:2*

see that he gets the rest he deserves, *(Exodus 20:9-11)*

• *Psalm 127:2*

• *Psalm 116:7*

• *Proverbs 3:24-26*

---

v. encourage his kindness, truthfulness, generosity - the more he gives the more God blesses & the less he desires selfishly,

• *Psalm 15:2-5*

• *Psalm 41:1-2*

• *Proverbs 3:9-10, 27-28*

• *Proverbs 11:25*

• *Proverbs 19:17*

• *Proverbs 21:26*

• *Proverbs 22:9*

---

w. understand him, *Proverbs 13:15*

see him as God does, through the righteousness of Jesus & encourage him to walk in that favor for that is where his strength & joy come from - the light of His countenance,

• *Psalm 89:14-17*

• *Psalm 80:3,7,19*

• *Psalm 4:6*

---

x. be vocal & physical in expressions of love,

• *Song of Solomon 1:2-4,13-14; 2:2-6,10-14,16; 4:16; 5:10-16; 8:6-7*

keep him enraptured (intoxicated) with my love,

Proverbs 5:18-19

give my body freely to him; it is his,

• 1 Corinthians 7:3-5

y. keep him from the evil woman by keeping him in God's

commandments & law, *Proverbs 6:23-35*

• *Proverbs 7:1-5-27*

• *Proverbs 2:10-11, 16-19*

and by keeping him thoroughly happy with me,

• *Proverbs 5:15-23*

only God's law in his heart will make him moral and keep him loyal!

---

z. work together in the discipline of children, supporting his

decisions for the sake of unity,

• *Proverbs 29:17*

• *Psalm 133:1*

Conclusion:
MAKE HIM HAPPY; LET GOD MAKE HIM HOLY!
PRAY FOR HIM:

• *Psalm 39:4-6*

• *Psalm 25:1-22*

• *Psalm 51:10-15*

• *Colossians 1:9-14*

• *Philippians 1:3-6*

• *Ephesians 1:15-21; 3:14-21*

• *Romans 12:1-2*

• *Joshua 1:8*

3. Be a help, aid, to my husband through our heritage (children, grandchildren):

a. promised blessing

(1) Psalm 127:3-5 - "Behold, children are a heritage (inheritance, heirlooms) from the Lord...His reward (payment of contract, compensation, worth, benefit)

(2) Psalm 128:3-6 - blessing of God come by children and grandchildren

(3) Proverbs 17:6 - grandchildren are a crown / the father is the glory of children

(4) Proverbs 20:7 - the righteous walk in integrity, his children are blessed after him

---

b. responsibility to train / results

(1) Proverbs 22:6 - train (discipline, dedicate, narrow) up a child...he will not depart (rebel)

(2) Proverbs 1:8; 23:22 - teach them to respect what parents have to say (30:17, mocks & scorns; 28:24, robs)

(3) Proverbs 13:24 - he that withholds rod, hates his son; he that loves, chastens him early

(4) Proverbs 19:18 - chasten while there is hope (attachment, expectancy), despite his crying

(5) Proverbs 22:15 – rod (branch) of correction to remove foolishness

(6) Proverbs 23:13-14 - don't withhold correction...deliver him from hell (death, grave)

(7) Proverbs 29:15 - the rod & reproof give wisdom; a child left to self brings mother shame

(8) Proverbs 10:1 - a wise son makes a glad father; a foolish son is grief to mother

(9)   Proverbs 15:20 - a foolish son despises mother

(10)   Proverbs 17:13 - a foolish son is ruin to father

(11)   Proverbs 29:17 - correct child & get rest; delight to your soul!

(12)   Proverbs 23:15-16, 24-25 - rejoicing, delighting, gladness of parents of righteous children

---

c. teach by example and utterance

(1)   Proverbs 23:26 - be the examples they can observe and follow

(2)   Proverbs 7:1 - teach children commandments, wisdom, understanding

(3)   Proverbs 31:1 - teach children by utterance of mother (bond of family)

(4)   Proverbs 3:11-12 - teach children to accept and love chastening and correction of the Lord

(5)   Proverbs 6:20-22 - make sure commands and laws are of God

(6)   Deuteronomy 6:6-11 - every opportunity throughout day & night should be used to direct to God

---

d. influence of testimony and prayer

(1)   Psalm 44:1 - be a witness / testimony to children of what God has done in our lives

(2)   Psalm 7:17-18 - declare Your strength to this generation

(3)   Psalm 145:4 - one generation shall praise Your works to another

(4)   Psalm 78:4-7 - telling generations to come...make known to children...that they declare to their children

(5)   Psalm 22:30-31 - they will come and declare His righteousness to those who will be born

(6)   Psalm 102:18 - that a people yet to be created may praise the Lord

(7)   Psalm 144:11-15 - deliver from foreigners that sons may be plants grown, daughters/pillars

4. Be a help, aid, to him through our home:

a.   Proverbs 14:1 - The wise woman builds her house, but the foolish pulls it down to utter desolation with the power of her hands (the woman does rule the house, wisely or foolishly).

b.   Proverbs 15:17 - "Better is a dinner of herbs where love is, than a fatted calf with hatred."

c.   Proverbs 17:1- "Better is a dry morsel with quietness, than a house full of feasting with strife"

d.   Proverbs 31:21, 27 - family well taken care of; keep watch over present/future needs of household

e.   Proverbs 24:30-34 - be diligent, active, busy / observe & learn well that laziness brings poverty

f.   Psalm 101:2-7 - behave wisely (act intelligently, prudently, in truth, undefiled)...walk (behave, exercise self) within my house (in my home and among my family) with a perfect (innocent) heart.

g.   Psalm 127:1-2 - "Unless the Lord builds the house...vain to rise early, sit up late, sorrow..."

h.   Titus 2:5 - keep at home - guardian of the home, including good housekeeping

i.   1 Timothy 5:14 - take charge of home, guide, manage, rule it well so the adversary is silenced

j.   Isaiah 32:18 - God wants our dwelling place to be one of peace, full of assurance, safe, quiet, comfortable

k.   Proverbs 24:3-4 - "Through wisdom (skillfulness, wit) a house (home, family) is built (obtained children, made, repaired, set up); by understanding (intelligence) it is established (set erect): by knowledge (cunning, cleverness) the chambers are filled with precious (valuable) and pleasant (delightful) riches (wealth enough!)."

Promise of Victory!

Genesis 2:18;   Psalm 18:28-40;   Psalm 118:15;   Philippians 4:17

What every Christian woman wants in her husband, what every marriage must have to be successful in God's eyes, is: (1) a man humbled before God because of his iniquity (Psalm 38); (2) a man searching for salvation with a broken, contrite spirit, understanding he has no power to save himself (Psalm 39); (3) a man lifted up (Psalm 40): rejoicing in his answered prayer, salvation from a horrible pit to a solid rock; singing a new song; spreading the gospel through his testimony of God's goodness; secure in his salvation; delighting to do God's will, God's law now written in his heart; unrestrained lips of what God has done for him; trusting God when the battles of the warfare ensue; seeking deliverance from evil, temptations, false doctrine; praying for others; praising the Lord; humbly trusting the Lord in faith.

God has ordained man to be the head of woman, her covering (1 Corinthians 11:3-15). God ordained woman to be man's aid, corresponding to his need in every area of their marriage (Genesis 2:18). How beautifully the human body and its internal immune system illustrate the protective outer covering of man over his own fragile but powerful protection. How sadly we view man's destruction in the Garden of Eden as his own help was overcome by the spirit of deception, a vivid picture of AIDS - man's very help attacked, succumbing to the enemy, providing access into his life and bringing certain death.

Stay faithful and believe! As a woman's life of godliness (not perfection) is lived out in meekness and quietness of spirit, ministering to her husband's physical, mental, social, emotional, and spiritual needs, being the help God created her to be, then she can lay hold of the 1 Peter 3:1 promise. God is faithful and all the promises of God in Him are Yes, and Amen, to the glory of God through us (2 Corinthians 1:20).

Made in the USA
Columbia, SC
20 January 2019